MEDIEVAL MYSTERIES

MEDIEVAL MYSTERIES

A GUIDE TO HISTORY, LORE, PLACES, AND SYMBOLISM

Karen Ralls, Ph.D.

IBIS PRESS
Lake Worth, FL

Published in 2014 by Ibis Press
An imprint of Nicolas-Hays, Inc.
P. O. Box 540206
Lake Worth, FL 33454-0206
www.ibispress.net

Distributed to the trade by
Red Wheel/Weiser, LLC
65 Parker St. • Ste. 7
Newburyport, MA 01950
www.redwheelweiser.com

ISBN: 978-089254-172-0
Ebook ISBN: 978-0-89254-592-6

Library of Congress Cataloging-in-Publication Data
Available upon request.

Book design and production by Studio 31.
www.studio31.com

Printed in China

TABLE OF CONTENTS

Preface   6

Chapter 1: The Knights Templar   8

Chapter 2: Mary Magdalene   26

Chapter 3: The Black Madonna   50

Chapter 4: The Grail   67

Chapter 5: Cathars   91

Chapter 6: Medieval Guilds   110

Chapter 7: Heretics and Heresy   129

Chapter 8: The Troubadours   150

Chapter 9: The Arthurian Mysteries

          King Arthur   185

          Merlin   192

          Glastonbury   198

Chapter 10: Rosslyn Chapel   226

Appendix 1: Additional European Sites for Mary Magdalene   253

Appendix 2: Additional European Sites for Black Madonnas   255

Endnotes   258

Bibliography and Recommended Reading   272

Photo Acknowledgments   293

Index   294

PREFACE

Why are many of us so intrigued by the High Middle Ages? What is the allure beckoning us into its world, like a mysterious shaft of crystalline light from a bejewelled stained glass window? Umberto Eco, in a famous 1986 essay, commented that ever since medieval times, Western culture has been "dreaming" the Middle Ages. That our never-ending fascination with all things medieval—the Grail, the Knights Templar, Arthurian legends, Gothic architecture, esoteric symbolism, and so on—is part of a modern-day quest for our Western roots.

Indeed it is. From the 12th to the 21st centuries, the well-worn path of the spiritual pilgrim continues unabated, its essence reverberating on, cajoling us to join the quest. We still ponder today: for whom does the Grail serve? And will we—can we—"restore the Wasteland"?

While often misunderstood as a mere feudal outgrowth of the earlier deeply repressive "Dark Ages," in fact, the High Middle Ages (11th–late 13th centuries) was not all "monks, serfs and Black Death," as the old stereotype implies. In a myriad of ways it was one of the most creative eras of Western European history.

It may surprise us to recall that in the midst of a time of other powerful changes, the High Middle Ages brought Western Europe a number of practical inventions, new concepts and creations that are key parts of our lives today—the rise of towns, eyeglasses, new printing methods, windmills, the concept of a university, Bachelor's, Master's, and Doctorate degrees, a great increase in trade, new perfumes, spices, and exotic teas, the rise of merchant guilds, the return of the astrolabe via Islamic Spain, and the rediscovery of the works of Aristotle.

But this period also spawned a cultural "peak" all its own—witnessing the rise and fall of the famed Knights Templar Order; the Grail manuscripts; the building of the Gothic cathedrals; a dramatic increase in pilgrimage; a renewed appreciation for the sacred Feminine, Black Madonnas, Mary Magdalene and other female saints; the time of the troubadours and the Courts of Love; international trade; new ideas and interfaith exchanges; and the pre-Renaissance early rise of certain hermetic and alchemical themes after a period of relative dormancy. Along with increased travel and the growth of towns, heresy and new ideas were also on the rise during this time, partly due to the overall climate of increased intellectual excitement—a creative stimulation and flow of ideas that was occurring during the 12th–13th centuries. This cluster of cultural phenomena, expressing the spirit of the age, existed alongside the growth of the universities of Paris, Oxford, and Bologna; the signing of the Magna Carta; and the reigns of Eleanor of Aquitaine, Henry II, and other famed rulers.

In the midst of our rapid scientific and technological development today and the growth of a digital age of social networking and electronic gadgetry, we witness the modern-day Western near-obsession, at times, with many medieval-themed phenomena: musicals, computer games, products, books, and films like *Excalibur* and *The Name of the Rose*. We also see the popularity of medieval chants, vampires, and a steadily growing surge of visitors to European medieval sites. In what pundits have described as an increase of an "age of Light" amidst our times of great social changes and stressors, the darker medieval ages seem to enthrall us all the more—with a mobile phone in one hand and a proverbial pilgrim's staff in the other—as we "quest on" with our lives. But what are the various "strands" of the tapestry of this period?

I am an medieval historian, art, film, and historical sites consultant, and the former Deputy Director and Curator of the Rosslyn Chapel museum exhibition (1995–2001). Following the publication of my books *The Templars and the Grail* in 2003 (released prior to *The Da Vinci Code*), and *The Knights Templar Encyclopedia* (released in 2007), readers have been consistently asking me for a guide to some of their more favorite medieval topics—one that offers solid factual history along with some of the more intriguing and lesser-known aspects as well. A number of my students, heritage and travel organizations (US and UK), charities, and various contacts in the film/media world have made similar requests.

To help meet this growing demand, I have chosen twelve "doorways" for the most-requested, popular medieval topics (organized in ten chapters). Each of the topic discussions includes a factual *Historical Overview* for those who may be relatively new to these topics (or only somewhat familiar with them), and I have added two smaller sections in each chapter illustrating the most interesting and visitor-friendly *places* associated with each topic, along with its relevant lore/legends and symbolism. We cover here the **Knights Templar, Mary Magdalene, the Black Madonna, the Grail, the Cathars, the Medieval Guilds, Heresy and Heretics, the Troubadours, King Arthur, Merlin, and Glastonbury, and Rosslyn Chapel**.

In an effort to help you continue your studies, I have listed some of the best books and resources in each area of inquiry, as well as providing a full Bibliography at the end. While the Historical Overview section attempts to provide a general survey of the topic in question, it is, of course, not comprehensive. But it is hoped that by providing a relatively solid introductory guide to each "doorway" regarding its History, Places, Lore/Legends, and Symbolism the reader will be well on the way to learning more about these fascinating medieval subjects.

May each topic covered here become a doorway, a portal, into a new Quest for all readers to explore, deepen, and enrich their lives. It starts with a single step.... Enjoy the journey...

Dr Karen Ralls
Oxford, England

Chapter One

THE KNIGHTS TEMPLAR

The time of the Crusades identified the figure of the "holy warrior" with a concept of "spiritual warfare."

Historical Overview

The medieval Knights Templar (1119–1312) famed monastic warriors of the Crusades, were the most powerful military religious order of the High Middle Ages. Long shrouded in mystery, the knights of the Order of the Temple of Solomon were believed by some to conduct special rites, guard relics, possess the lost treasures of Jerusalem—and much more. A colossal force with an empire spanning many countries and consisting of thousands of commandaries, the Templars were major landowners and managers, bankers to kings and nobles, industrialists, trusted diplomats, guardians and transporters of pilgrims to and from the Holy Land, navigators, and exponents of spiritual wisdom.

The Order initially emerged in the twelfth century (1119) and was officially recognized by the Roman Catholic Church at the Council of Troyes (1129). Its ending began with dramatic dawn arrests in France by King Philip IV's forces in 1307. Its final suppression occurred in 1312, when Pope Clement V disbanded it. This famous medieval Order of the Temple thus officially lasted for nearly two hundred years.

Initially conceived as a holy militia, the Templars were not an ordinary monastic order. They combined the roles of *both* knight and monk—a totally new concept.[1] The highly influential Cistercian abbot, the persuasive Bernard of Clairvaux, was one of the Order's earliest and most enthusiastic advocates. He was instrumental in helping the tiny, fledgling group of only nine knights obtain prestigious official Church recognition at the Council of Troyes in 1128–9. Bernard wrote to his colleague Hugh de Payns in a widely-circulated public letter, *In Praise of the New Knighthood,* where he exalted the Templars above all the other Orders of the day—a strategic move which popularized the now-famous image of the Templars as fierce fighting warrior-monks. Bernard's idea was that the Templars "were religious people who followed a religious Rule of life and wore a distinctive habit, but who, unlike monks, did not live in an enclosed house."[2]

The ideal Templar knight was robed in the simplicity of his calling. (Eran Bauer)

After Bernard wrote his groundbreaking letter, controversy erupted not only in the Western church, but also in the East, with the Byzantine church observing that they were "deeply shocked to see in the Crusader armies so many priests who bore arms."[3] To Bernard, however, the Templars provided the best of both the practical and the spiritual—"lions in war, lambs in the house."[4]

ORIGINS

According to 12th century chronicler Guillaume de Tyre, the Order of the Temple began when two French knights, Hugh de Payns and Godfroi de St. Omer, led seven others to the Patriarch of Jerusalem, Warmund of Picquigny, to take their vows. Initially referred to as *Milites Templi Salomonis,* or Knights of the Temple of Solomon, and later dubbed "Templars," their presence in the area was well-known. However, not all medieval chronicles agree with each other about the earliest years of the Order.[5]

The first Templar Grand Master was Hugh de Payns, a vassal of Hughes I, Count of Champagne. Others among the initial nine were André de Montbard (the uncle of Bernard of Clairvaux),

Godfroi de St. Omer, Payen de Montdidier and Achambaud de St.-Amand, of Flanders. The other four knights were listed simply as Godfroi, Geoffroi Bisol, Gondemar, and Rossal.

Troyes in Champagne (old Burgundy) was a primary focus of this early group of interrelated families. In the treasury of the Cathedral of St. Peter and St. Paul at Troyes, the bones of St. Bernard of Clairvaux, along with other relics including an important portrait, are still venerated. "Troyes was also the birthplace of one of the most brilliant Jewish intellectuals in Western European history—Rabbi Solomon ben Isaac, affectionately known as Rabbi Rashi. He was a frequently honored guest at the court of Hughes I—a court known to have been a haven for Jews and other prominent non-Catholics who fled persecution."[6] Rabbi Rashi started his famed kabbalistic school, with its renowned Hebrew, biblical (and other language) translators at Troyes, in 1070.

Like other monks who took stringent vows of poverty, chastity and obedience, Templars were required to live by very strict standards with no ostentatious displays or luxuries allowed. Bernard and others felt a strong need to react to the rapidly increasing numbers of Christians being attacked on their way to the Holy Land—especially following a tragic incident on Easter Sunday (1119) when three hundred Christian pilgrims were massacred. This served as the "final straw" crisis for the Church. In response, Bernard put forth his new solution—the fighting warrior-monk.

Previously, Christian pilgrimages to Jerusalem had come under Islamic rule, and "for the most part the Islamic rulers, in accordance with the Prophet's instructions, were happy to allow their subject races to practice their religion without interference."[7]

While it seems obvious that pilgrim routes desperately needed guarding and that the Templars definitely did play some role in providing security, how only nine knights could have possibly policed nearly all of the dangerous highways and byways to and from Jerusalem, even in a limited capacity, remains quite unclear. The first nine Templars were strongly encouraged and assisted by both King Baldwin II, the Christian ruler of Jerusalem, and Patriarch Warmund. They were given prime accommodation in King Baldwin's palace. Overall, the numbers of Templars in the Holy Land did not begin to increase until after 1129. By the 1170s we know there were about three hundred knights in Jerusa-

Medieval enigmatic panel painting, identity of subject unknown for certain at present. This was found in 1945 at Templecombe, (Somerset), an area that once included a medieval Templar preceptory, and was later, occupied by the Knights Hospitaller. (Simon Brighton)

lem. Regarding questions of the extent of the full range of specific activities of these first nine knights during their first nine years, unfortunately there is not enough surviving manuscript evidence or eyewitness testimony to draw any conclusions; future discoveries may shed further light on the situation.

Organization

The Templar Order was a vast enterprise much like a large modern-day multinational corporation. Administration was hierarchical, with the Grand Master and key officers of the Order based at the headquarters in the Holy Land. In the West, territories were divided into provinces, each managed by a local Commander. As Crusades were very expensive, the primary function of the Western houses was to provide men, funding, and supplies for their brothers fighting in the East. The Templar Grand Master was elected for life. Travelling with his huge entourage was at least one Saracen interpreter ("Saracen" was the generic medieval term for Muslim), a chaplain, a clerk, a sergeant, etc. The Seneschal was the Grand Master's deputy, responsible for ceremonially carrying the famed *beauseant,* the Templars' black-and-white banner; the Marshal was the chief military officer; the Commander of the Kingdom of Jerusalem was the treasurer of the Order; and the Draper issued the famed white mantles and other clothing to the knights.

Major meetings of the Order were called "general chapters" in the East, with periodic chapter meetings also held in Western provinces. Officials called *bailies* were in charge of day-to-day running operations. The entire Order consisted not only of the prestigious white-mantled full-fledged knights we know of today, but also, a great variety of officers, sergeants, lay consultants, and other supportive staff, all of whom played much-needed roles to ensure the order's overall efficiency and success. The knights themselves made up some ten percent of the Order's total membership.

THE RULE

The Templars developed a detailed set of strict regulations in French called *The Rule,* which included a translation of the original Latin Rule that described how members of the Order were to live their daily lives. The Rule's seven subdivisions include the Primitive Rule, Hierarchical Statutes, Penances, Conventual Life, the Holding of Ordinary Chapters, Further Details on Penances, and Reception into the Order. Penalties were harsh for any violations. Scholars believe the original manuscripts of the Latin Templar Rules were probably destroyed at the time of the arrests in France in 1307.[8] Sadly, no copies have survived or yet been discovered, so experts must work from the later French translations.

WOMEN

Rule 306 states that "the hours of Our Lady should always be said first in this house." Clearly, the Templars very highly revered Mary, the patroness of their Order, giving her first priority. At their reception into the Order, Templar novices were required to make their solemn pledge to the Blessed Mary as well as to God.[9] In section 75.17 of the Rule, there is a list of the specific saint's days that the Order was to officially honor—revealing that the Templars highly revered female saints and honored their feast days—specifically listing Mary Magdalene and Catherine of Alexandria, for example, by name. In some areas, particularly in the Languedoc region of France, Black Madonnas, and shrines, basilicas, and churches dedicated to Mary Magdalene are prolific, with some near Templar-related sites. Templars imprisoned and awaiting death in the dungeons of Chinon after their sudden arrests

A foggy morning, west view, at St Catherine's church at Temple, Cornwall. (Karen Ralls)

in 1307 specifically composed a prayer dedicated to Our Lady, acknowledging St. Bernard as the founder of the religion of the Blessed Virgin Mary.

Although reception of full sisters as members was prohibited by the Templar Rule, in certain locales scholars acknowledge that the Order did have active women members, classified as associates, somewhat like our modern-day concept of a "Friend" of a charitable organization. While not full members, such associates (men and women) often provided the Order with a wide range of assistance. For example, in some areas, records show that wealthy women contibuted large amounts of money and other gifts, in addition to influential family connections. Many of the women on record as sisters *(soror)* or associates *(donata)* of the Order are listed in the cartularies from Catalonia in Spain where more records survived.[10]

EMPIRE AND BANKING

The wealth of the Templar empire was massive and due to the great variety of their activities, was spread widely across numerous commercial subsidiaries. The Templars held stores of gold, money, and other valuables in their treasuries, and kings, nobles, Popes, and merchants were known to borrow large amounts of money from them. Some of their methods were an early prototype for modern-day banking practices, i.e., the concept of a letter of credit with a security code cipher, and the safe deposit

Approaching the tower
of Temple Bruer,
part of the medieval
preceptory's round church
(Lincolnshire). (Eran
Bauer)

box.[11] Essentially what had started out as basic financial services
for pilgrims from all levels of society, ended up developing into
a massive full-scale financial empire with many diversified operations. In some countries, the Order became a virtual branch of the
royal government with Templars serving as powerful diplomats
and judges. Ever-resourceful with property, they were renowned
for working arid lands donated to them and re-working them to
achieve renewed agricultural productivity. Wool, lumber mills,
animal husbandry and produce, as well as the transport by ship
of pilgrims, produce, and wines to and from the Holy Land were
examples of activities that helped raise money for their brothers in
the East.[12] As to what a given preceptory or commandery would
specifically do, it largely depended on where they were based.

CENTRAL ARCHIVE

The central archive of the Order was originally held in Jerusalem, then at Acre, and, following the devastating fall of Acre for
Christendom in 1291, the archive and any remaining relics were
transferred to Cyprus. After their suppression in 1312, any official
remaining archives were ordered to be turned over to the Templars'
rival order, the Hospitallers. Scholars believe the main archive in
the East was most likely destroyed when the Turks finally captured
Cyprus in 1571. Perhaps much of it was, but there may also have
been archives and relics in other locations that history and archae-

ology may yet discover in the future. Unquestionably, the tragic loss of the central archive in the Holy Land makes it difficult to determine exactly what property and privileges the Templars held in the East and on Cyprus, a topic that has generated much speculation. There have been various Templar archives found in other countries, but they are spread out over many areas in Europe and many still await translation. Inevitably, in time, more information will come to light about these matters as more documents are translated and/or discovered.

CULTURAL CONTACTS

The Templars' main adversaries in the Crusades were the Saracens, expertly trained warriors and martyrs. It is widely acknowledged that the leadership of both the Templars and the Saracens regarded each other with a surprising "interfaith" diplomacy. They were known to have shown a careful respect for each other on a number of occasions during the Crusades. As much of Western Europe had been in cultural decline during the so-called Dark Ages, when coming into contact with the East, Europeans would undoubtedly have been exposed to new information about architecture, mathematics, geometry, and other arts and sciences that were flourishing among the Muslims in those territories. Such contact would later result in the Templars being directly accused of "fraternizing with the enemy" by the Inquisition. Western researchers have sometimes overlooked or downplayed Templar contacts with medieval Jewish, Islamic, gnostic and other groups in the East, including eastern Christians, Druses, and others.

Design, number, and proportion were important to the Templars. None other than St. Bernard of Clairvaux had famously defined God as "length, width, height, and depth,"[13] giving a nod to the idea of the "New Jerusalem" as having a cubic geometric component. Some believe Templars returning from the Holy Land (post–1127) may have had a more influential role than previously supposed in encouraging the development of High Gothic architectural style in twelfth-century France; and that they, in conjunction with other monastic Orders of the day like the Cistercians, may have helped spearhead this extraordinary change in ecclesiastical architecture. As we know from Templar Rule 325, the Order had its own mason brothers. Some of the Templars' own castles

Visitor's guide floor plan of Temple Church (London), the headquarters of the medieval Knights Templar in England, then called New Temple. (Eran Bauer)

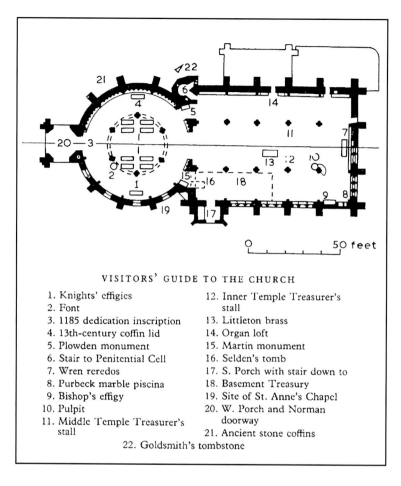

VISITORS' GUIDE TO THE CHURCH

1. Knights' effigies
2. Font
3. 1185 dedication inscription
4. 13th-century coffin lid
5. Plowden monument
6. Stair to Penitential Cell
7. Wren reredos
8. Purbeck marble piscina
9. Bishop's effigy
10. Pulpit
11. Middle Temple Treasurer's stall
12. Inner Temple Treasurer's stall
13. Littleton brass
14. Organ loft
15. Martin monument
16. Selden's tomb
17. S. Porch with stair down to
18. Basement Treasury
19. Site of St. Anne's Chapel
20. W. Porch and Norman doorway
21. Ancient stone coffins
22. Goldsmith's tombstone

and buildings had interesting architectural designs and innovations; in fact, the Templars were regarded as expert builders. Atlit (Castle Pilgrim), their most famous fortress of the Crusades, was built in 1218 at the direction of Templar Grand Master William of Chartres. It featured superb architectural protection against Saracen siege practices. In 1139, Pope Innocent II granted the Order the right to build its own churches. Some Templar churches had circular naves, after the Church of the Holy Sepulcher in Jerusalem, while others featured designs like the octagon. Perhaps not surprisingly, the Templars were especially interested in the design of the Temple of Solomon.

Scholars believe there were also some medieval Templar links with certain Muslim groups, especially the Nizari Ismailis, an Islamic group that still flourishes under the leadership of the Aga Khan. The Nizari Ismailis,—known in medieval times as "the Assassins," were trained as holy warriors, similar to the Templars.

Christian crusaders had some contact with the Assassins at the beginning of the twelfth century, even prior to the official founding of the Templar order in 1119, as James Wasserman observes:

> [Assassin founder] Hasan-i-Sabah's mission to the Ismailis of Syria resulted in the early European contact with the Assassins during the Crusades. The mythical Old Man of the Mountain ... was the Syrian chief of the Order ... The first documented contact between the Assassins and the Crusaders took place in September 1106. Tancred, prince of Antioch, attacked the newly acquired Nizari castle of Apace outside of Aleppo. The Christians defeated the Nizaris and leveled a tribute against the sect. Tancred captured the new Syrian chief *dai,* Abu Tahir, "the Goldsmith," and forced him to ransom himself. In 1110, the Nizaris lost a second piece of territory to Tancred.[14]

Idealized portrait of Assassin founder Hasan-i-Sabah. (18th century, from *An Illustrated History of the Knights Templar*)

World explorer Marco Polo enthralled 14th century Europe about the Assassins, compiling and embellishing many legends about them into a major collection.[15] His writings feature exotic tales of "a magnificent enclosed garden hidden at Alamut in which all details corresponded to Muhammad's description of Paradise."[16] Since then, legends about both the Templars and the Assassins have continued to generate their own mystique.

Arrests, Charges and Trial

At dawn on that fateful day—Friday, 13 October 1307—every French member of the Order was suddenly arrested by agents of King Philip IV of France in collusion with Pope Clement V. By then the Order had grown so rich and powerful, and, at best, answerable to no one but the papacy, that they had their inevitable political enemies; but, on the whole, the Templars were still highly regarded. News of abominable "heresies" and heinous crimes by which these famed white knights of the Crusades were slandered astounded much of the populace and many other kings of Europe. Although both pope and king had discussed arresting the French Templars, the pope himself was apparently not informed about the specific date of the arrests. Three days later, Philip IV informed the other kings of Europe about the Templar

The charges leveled against the Templars included blasphemy and trampling on the Crucifix. (*An Illustrated History of the Knights Templar*)

arrests in France, encouraging them to do likewise. At first, many simply did not believe him; nearly all rebuffed him, and others simply refused to arrest the Templars. James II of Aragon and Edward II of England lobbied the other European kings and the pope in defense of the Templars, writing letters on the Order's behalf. Concurrently, brutal interrogations and torture began of the imprisoned Templars in France. Increasingly, the pope put great pressure on the other kings—and their souls—in all of Europe, so arrests and trials began to occur in other countries.

The charges were many and varied—that the Templars denied Christ and/or spit on the cross; alleged worship of a cat and/or a powerful, mysterious idol called Baphomet; obscene kisses at reception meetings of novices held at night; Templar lay commanders rather than priests accepting confessions, and so on. The 19th century work of historian Charles Lea went some distance to illustrate the knights' innocence, showing how many of the 1307 charges themselves stemmed from popular myths and

superstitions about so-called heretics and magicians from earlier times.[17]

It is important to note that there was not "one" Templar trial. In fact, the entire process was complex and took place over a long, drawn-out period of seven agonizing years, with trials in various countries and by various ecclesiastical and political bodies. Finally, after the initial 1307 arrests and the ensuring 'tabloid scandal' environment and wild rumors that continued to swirl all over Europe about the Templars. Pope Clement V decided to simply formally dissolve the Order with his bull *Vox in excelso* in March 1312. He felt the Templars had been so badly defamed they could no longer properly defend Christendom. Yet, in the same bull, he stated that the charges leveled against the Order itself were "not proven." On 3 April 1312, he solemnly read out the bull in public and the suppression of the Templars was officially complete.

Interrogation of last Templar Grand Master Jacques de Molay. (*The Scarlet Book of Freemasonry*)

AFTER THE SUPPRESSION

The papal bull *Ad providam Christi Vicarii* of 2 May 1312 declared that all Templar property and assets were to be transferred to their rivals, the Hospitallers.[18] The only exceptions were the Templar properties in Portugal, Castille, and Majorca, which were to be transferred to existing local orders. In some countries the entire transfer process took years to finalize. Contrary to popular belief, not all Templars were tortured in prison or burned at the stake. In fact, it is likely that thousands survived in various parts of Europe. As historian Edward Burman points out in *Supremely Abominable Crimes,* it seems the majority of Templars were freed after 1312.[19] On the whole, after 1312, Templars in custody were to be allowed to live on at previous Templar properties, and those who had been reconciled to the Church were to be given pensions. Many ex-Templars ended up joining other monastic communities, such as the Order of Christ, the Order of Montesa, and the Cistercians.

The suppression did vary, with some countries having a less severe policy towards the Order, while in others, especially France, Templars continued to languish in prisons. The courageous last Templar Grand Master, Jacques de Molay and his loyal Treasurer, Geoffrey de Charney, were burned at the stake in Paris in March of 1314.[20]

Ever since, the powerful legacy of the Templars has lived on, extolling the extraordinary courage of the Templars in facing a brutal Inquisition after having fought for Christendom. Yet, for many, questions still remain; future historical and archaeological finds await discovery and clarification. Immortalized in church and spiritual histories, and in story, song, and film ever since, the extraordinary memory of the medieval Knights Templar still reverberates through time, some nine centuries after their founding.

Places to Visit:

All over Europe are places to visit with a medieval Templar connection. Such sites may once have been a Templar commandery or preceptory, a chapel, barn, farm, or port. There are other books that focus more specifically on various regions or specific countries in Europe. In my (2007) Templar reference book for the general reader, *The Knights Templar Encyclopedia*, there are A-Z entries about some of the key sites in the British Isles and a Templar Sites Appendix.

While there are thousands of Templar-related sites all over Europe—many of them are not on public property, nor accessible to the public, nor necessarily in good condition. It is most important when visiting any Templar (or historical) site that you can access, that you take utmost care when on the premises. Try to support the local church, charity, or organization that is responsible for its upkeep in whatever way you can. Indeed, after the harrowing trials of the medieval Inquisition, we must all be genuinely thankful that any of these sites are still with us today. So, do "handle with care" and respect and enjoy your visit!

Here a few key examples of the most easily-accessible and visitor-friendly sites that you may wish to consider on a journey to Britain or Western Europe. It is by no means a comprehensive list, but a great way to get started. At each site, you should ask yourself: What does it all mean in the context of the medieval Templar Order? Often, there are fascinating architectural features, unique carvings, and intriguing symbols. If the site includes a church that is still in use, there may also be shrines, gravestones, or a Templar-related museum nearby.

A few examples of favorite sites in **England** include Temple Church (New Temple) in London; All Hallows-by-the-Tower in London; Temple Garway (Herefordshire); Temple Bruer (Lincolnshire); Templecombe (Somerset) with its enigmatic painting of a head; St. Catherine's Temple church in Cornwall; and Cressing Temple (Essex) for its remarkably well-restored wooden Templar wheat and barley barns.

In **Scotland**'s Midlothian region just south of Edinburgh, there is Temple (Balandradoch), the church and ruins of the medi-

One of the many hundreds of Green Man carvings at Rosslyn Chapel, near Edinburgh, here as a youthful portrayal. (J. F. Ralls)

View of the church ruins and graveyard of Balantradoch, the medieval headquarters of the Scottish Knights Templar. Today, the village is called "Temple," in their honor. (Simon Brighton)

eval Scottish Templar headquarters; and, nearby, is Rosslyn Chapel, a site not to be missed for any visitor to Scotland.

On **Cyprus**, visit Famagusta, Kolossi and Kyrenia castles.

In **France**: a few key sites include Notre Dame cathedral; Gisors in Normandy; Laon in Picardy, with its beautiful cathedral, Black Madonna, and Templar museum; Metz in Lorraine; Domme in the Dordogne; Cahors (Lot); Arville, with its Templar commandary and museum located between Le Mans and Chartres; La Courvertoirade at Aveyron; and a vast number of other sites in regional areas such as Lyons, Provence, and the stunning Languedoc—including the enigmatic Rennes-le-Chateau and its extensive landscape and fascinating environs.

If you are planning to visit **Italy**: when in Tuscany do not miss the Templar church in Siena, with its interesting carvings and unique paintings in fresco; or the Templar churches in Perugia (San Bevignate) or Ormelle.

In **Slovenia**, there is the Templar church at Dora.

In **Poland**, visit the commandary of Quartschen and its chapel.

Spain has sites in Barcelona, Granyena, Pensicola, Ponferrada, Tarragona, and the Templar fortress of Xiert.

In neighboring **Portugal**, there are Templar-related sites relatively easy to visit at Almurol, Pombal, and Tomar that are among the better-preserved today.

The Garway horned green man, situated on the north capital of the interior arch. He may represent a varied depiction of Cernunnos, an ancient horned deity also associated with many woodland settings, forests, and their lore. (Simon Brighton)

In the **Middle East**, the Crypt of St John at Acre has a few subterranean remains left; and, in Jerusalem, of course, one can visit the Temple Mount area, the Church of the Holy Sepulcher, and many other sites that remain places of pilgrimage.

Key Symbols, Seals and Relics

While there are many symbols associated with the two centuries of the Templar Order, we present below a series of the more well-known symbols you may encounter at various Templar sites in European territories.

The most recognized Templar symbol today is the *red cross* of the Order, a privilege the Templars obtained from Pope Eugenius in 1147 to add to their white mantles. But there was no "one symbol" of the Order per se, nor only one red cross design in use during the time of the Order (1119–1312). The *official seal* of the Grand Master of the Order featured the round dome of the Al Aqsa Mosque on one side, and the well-known symbol of two knights on one horse on the other.[21] Regional Templar Masters also had their own seals, each with its own unique focus. For example, the *Agnus Dei* (Lamb of God) was mainly used in England and Provence; an eagle or an image of the head of Christ in Germany; or the image of the dome of the Church of the Holy Sepulcher, often preferred in southern France. Provincial Templar

Stained glass window of Knight Templar at Temple Rothley. (Karen Ralls)

Templar Cross awarded the Order by the Pope in 1147

Templar Seal obverse shows two knights riding one horse illustrating the Vow of Poverty. (Antiqua, Inc.)

Reverse of Templar seal showing al-Aqsa Mosque that the Templars believed was the Temple of Solomon. (Antiqua, Inc.)

seals would sometimes include other motifs ranging from various types of crosses, the fleur-de-lis, doves, stars, a lion, a crescent moon, a tower with a pointed roof and a cross, or a castle tower. St. George appears on some Templar seals, and there was a statue of him in the Order's castle at Safed in the Holy Land.[22]

Templar graves were often depicted with only a simple sword. In some locations, such as the Templar church of Santa Maria do Olival in Tomar, Portugal, a five-pointed star window is featured high above its altar; and at Atlit (Castle Pilgrim) in the East, the *eight-sided Templar cross* ("Maltese cross") was portrayed at the center of the Templar's high altar. It was brought back to London by Templars and is currently on display in the undercroft museum of All Hallows by the Tower, near the Tower of London.[23]

Although the Inquisition never accused the Templars of being gnostics, among their most interesting symbols is a gnostic seal called *Templi Secretum.* It features an image of Abraxas and is portrayed on a Templar Grand Master's seal in the *Archives Nationales* in Paris. It was used in a French charter dated 1214.[24] Experts maintain that Abraxas—whose seven letters equal a numerical value of 365—was a common form of the Jewish Jehovah, often referred to as "Our Father" and "Lord of Hosts" in some gnostic writings. Abraxas gemstones were often used as magical protection devices in the Roman period.

Other symbols such as geometric grid patterns, the six-pointed star, the Calvary step cross, and a hand with a heart on its palm are found on the walls of Chinon Castle, where imprisoned Templars, including some officers, languished for a time in the dungeons.[25] At some Templar sites, the number eight features in some way—as an octagon, eight-pointed cross, "figure 8," or "infinity symbol."

Relics

Like many orders of the day, the medieval Templars were certain that they had a cherished piece of the True Cross in their possession. We note this from section 122 of the Hierarchical Statutes of the Rule, where it specifically outlines precisely how this precious relic is to be transported under very heavy guard in the Holy Land. Other relics the Order openly claimed to possess include the Crown of Thorns; the heads of at least two female saints; the head of St. Polycarp; a vial of the Precious Blood; and, in southern Spain, the precious Cross of Caravaca. The mysterious "Head no. 58," revealed via French trial records, is believed by some scholars to have been the head of one of St Ursula's maidens—as her cult was particularly strong in Europe at the time.[26]

Ever since their suppression in 1312, speculation has continued to mount as to precisely "where" any other Templar relics or assets may have been located. However, until they are discovered and/or surface in the public domain and are verified by experts, existing manuscripts, documents, objects and artifacts are all that historians and archaeologists may rely on. Legends and lore continue to celebrate the memory of the Templars in many different ways. It has proven itself to be an enduring mythos, the Dream That Refuses To Die. What will the future reveal?

Mysterious Templi Secretum seal displays the Gnostic deity Abraxas. (Simon Brighton)

CHAPTER 2

ON THE ROAD TO… MARY MAGDALENE

Vesica Piscis geometry and details on pillar, Basilica of Vezelay. (Jane May)

Overview: The shifting image of Mary Magdalene

Mary Magdalene … gifted mystic, charismatic teacher, illuminatrix, loving partner and confidante of Jesus, "apostle of apostles," the first witness, reformed penitent. Her constantly shifting image in the eyes of both Church and society through the centuries has been an interesting phenomenon to behold in and of itself, a reflection of the historical era in question. Like a universal Mirror of All Mirrors, Mary Magdalene has served as an inspiring and challenging archetypal lens about the Feminine for much of Western society—in the past and into our own time.

In the past, the Church as well as academic theologians had the exclusive power to shape or alter her image in the eyes of the public; today, we are witnessing the increasing influence of the arts, media, and social networking sites that are bringing in new angles, neglected ideas, and fresh concepts to her story. As many now note, Mary Magdalene continues to enlighten, bless, cajole, or shock—jolting many in the process into a new spiritual awareness, up another rung of the ladder to greater understanding and wisdom. From disparaged so-called "bad girl," to enlightening "beacon of hope," Mary Magdalene is back. And in full color. And this time, it seems, she is here to stay.

As important new questions, historical issues, and ever-evolving concepts are discussed about her in Christian and other circles, Mary Magdalene is still very much the "star of the show." She remains a favorite topic at conferences across the ideological spectrum, featured in books, articles, blogs, artworks, musicals, and music albums. Controversial as ever, many feel she symbolically prods us on culturally—yet again—demanding nothing less than total honesty, relentless perseverance, a love of truth, justice, the desire for a greater balance between the feminine and the masculine, new ways of relating for both men and women, and a deeper wisdom or faith from *all* parties concerned, regardless of one's particular views about her.

The much-talked-about, transformative cyclic return of the divine Feminine in our contemporary time is illustrated by an increasing worldwide interest in Mary Magdalene. It is only one example of the classic "sand-in-the-oyster irritant" that simply will not go away—at least for the more orthodox. More importantly, she brings forth important issues that deeply challenge organizations and individuals. Beyond providing a deepening spiritual focus on the divine Feminine, at the very least this phenomenon may be viewed as a symbolic impetus to encourage everyone to more discussion and open debate. Mary acts as a stimulating leaven in the bread of genuine spiritual and cultural evolution, shaping a new pearl to come.

Long disparaged, neglected, despised or feared, Mary Magdalene is now being deeply reassessed in the West by scholars, individuals, and spiritual organizations alike, viewed as an inspiring-but-challenging lodestar. Many have heard of interesting new research and interpretations following fresh scholarly analyses of biblical texts, new discoveries, and a plethora of interesting theories about Mary Magdalene. A recent example was in September of 2012, when Harvard Divinity School Professor Karen King announced to the 10th International Congress of Coptic Studies Conference, held in Rome, that an ancient Coptic fragment had four words that could be translated as "Jesus said to them, my wife." The usual scholarly controversy erupted shortly thereafter. The debate continues about who exactly Mary Magdalene was, if she may have actually been married to Jesus. (Weren't rabbis usually married?) Regardless of one's views on this topic, nearly everyone agrees that her power and intrigue remain, as strong as they always have. Textual scholars and other experts continue to debate such discoveries, while the general public seeks more clarity as well.

As a medievalist, I feel that new manuscript discoveries and genuine archaeological finds are welcome developments in any field, stimulating questions that further serve to spur everyone on to a path of greater enquiry. I believe the new emerging openness about Mary Magdalene can be very positive in the long run. More information about her is certainly needed.

Until recently, the usual biblical portrayal of her as a passive reformed penitent has remained the most familiar. This image is currently shifting. Scholars, mystics, and lay people continue to

Mary Magdalene statue at the Church of St Mary Magdalene, Oxford [wooden carving by Sr. Angela Solling, osc.] (Karen Ralls)

ask: Just who was this extraordinary woman—really? Why does it matter so much to us—still—centuries later? Why was celibacy only made official church policy as late as the Lateran Council of 1123? Yes, biblical and textual scholars will undoubtedly be busy for some time to come!

During the High Middle Ages (1100–1300), Mary Magdalene was one of the most popular saints of all. Far from a mere "Dark Age," the High Middle Ages brought medieval Europe from a stagnant, intellectually, culturally and economically-deprived backwater to the peak of achievement in major areas. And Mary Magdalene played a central role. She was acknowledged and/or venerated by several contemporary groups at the time—certain guilds, local city corporations, the Knights Templar, the Cathars, the Waldensians, the Knights Hospitaller, troubadours, and others. Mary Magdalene was also a clear favorite of medieval pilgrims and her popularity at certain sites remains uneclipsed.

To begin to understand the importance of Mary Magdalene in the High Middle Ages, let us remember that in the feudal era, life was very difficult—especially for women. Some medieval accounts of her role allow us to see occasional "glimpses" of the attempted reintegration of previously excluded and denigrated aspects of early views of Mary. This cultural embrace of the divine Feminine may have been as much a "miracle" as any medieval wonder. Here follows an account of some of the most important stories of Mary.

The Golden Legend

Jacob de Voragine's 13th century bestseller, *The Golden Legend,* was one of the key sources about the lives of the saints in the High Middle Ages. Here the medieval pilgrims, the clergy, and the public could learn about their favorite saints. It has been said that the only book that was more widely read at the time was the Bible itself—quite a feat for the 13th century!

Written in 1260 by the monastic scholar who later became Archbishop of Genoa, the book was initially published in Latin and French. It was immediately popular and even more so after 1450, when printing presses ensured it was available in almost every European language. *The Golden Legend* is a compilation of the major sources about the lives of the various saints—ranging

Mary Magdalene as the Madonna of the Sacred Coat, painting by C. B. Chambers *(The Mystery Traditions: Secret Symbols and Sacred Art)*

from the second to the thirteenth centuries—taken from the writings of both Western and Eastern church sources. It is still studied by contemporary experts and art historians.[1]

As many critics agree (religious or not), simply from the literary standpoint, this work is an engaging example of great medieval storytelling, vividly bringing alive stories, deeds, and wonders from the saints' lives and providing new details about their activities. Some of the tales are solemn in character; others are peppered with hilarious, unpredictable, even shocking episodes. Long commemorated in paintings, stained glass windows, sculptures, and assorted folklore and legendary accounts, the stories from *The Golden Legend* greatly fired the imagination of people in the High Middle Ages. They were a welcome beacon to pilgrims in a challenging era. For medieval Christian pilgrims from all walks of life, *The Golden Legend* was one of the few sources that included easy-to-understand and lesser-known information about their favorite saints, beyond what they knew from the usual biblical portrayals or heard from the pulpit. A fascinating, entertaining mixture of both fiction and fact, it provided a goldmine of anecdotes, often using humor as an effective teaching device to illustrate a far more serious point. As we know, esteemed literary works like Chaucer's *Canterbury Tales* include truly unforgettable humorous anecdotes about medieval pilgrimage, saints or relics, as do more modern popular productions like *Monty Python and the Holy Grail.*

The modern reader may be surprised to see the re-emergence of Mary Magdalene as a charismatic preacher and especially gifted mystic in her own right in such a work as *The Golden Legend.* Yet, here we find portrayals of her in a manner reminiscent of the more gnostic view from centuries before. (Of course, as with all such writings, monastic politics and patrons had a role in how a particular saint would be portrayed, and major orders often became serious rivals over such issues.) *The Golden Legend* was a creative amalgamation of several different eastern and western stories of a particular saint, all rolled into one account. In its portrayal of Mary we can experience the glimmering flickers of light from long ago emerging off the page after centuries of repression.

MARY MAGDALENE AS "LIGHT-BRINGER"

While the church had long felt the need to denigrate or marginalize Mary Magdalene for various reasons, some of the monastic scholars in medieval times—such as the Italian writer de Voragine (*The Golden Legend*) or the French author Rabanus Maurus—tried to portray her in a different and more positive light.

JÉSU.MEDÉLA.VULNÉRUM ÷ SPES.UNA.PŒNITENTIUM.

Centerpiece altar featuring Mary is the altar in the church) Magdalene, with landscape and other iconography, in the church at Rennes-le-Chateau. Said to be one of the few items in the church designed by Fr. Berenger Sauniere (1852–1917). (Simon Brighton)

Rarely in the traditional ecclesiastical accounts do we encounter Mary Magdalene as an active preacher and teacher of the public, or as a serious mystic in her own right. But *The Golden Legend* goes so far as to directly refer to her as an enlightened one, and as *Illuminatrix* , i.e, one who bestows enlightenment, a "light-bringer"—a title that earlier female deities had often been given in ancient times. (In one of the major early gnostic texts, as leading textual scholars today inform us, Mary Magdalene was referred to as "The Woman Who Knew the All.")

The higher octave, Gnostic vision of Mary was culturally acceptable in early Provence, for example, as it was known to have had an earlier spiritual tradition involving women leaders, priestesses, or female speakers. Mysteries of Isis, Cybele, Artemis, et al, had been brought there by travelers from distant lands. The author of the medieval *Legend* may have felt that the populace in Provence would easily accept a portrayal of a Christian Mary Magdalene as an active female preacher and/or enlightened mystic. After all, the "dreaded" Cathars in that area had long had active women 'perfects' (priests) as did other heretical groups. There were lingering pockets of Cathars in the Languedoc for some years after the fall of Montsegur in 1244. (See Chapter 5.)

French church, Leicester square, London. Part of the crucifixion scene painted by Jean Cocteau. Depicting the three Marys, John the Baptist, and more. (Simon Brighton)

Soon after, by as early as 1260, *The Golden Legend* arrived on the scene.[2] While the *Legend* gives a conventional account much of the time, the image of Mary as preacher and mystic accords with earlier gnostic perspectives and the lay preaching movements that were active at the time it was written.

On the whole, the Magdalene of many of the gnostic texts is the opposite of the distorted penitent prostitute image of traditional Church hagiography, and the *Legend* appears to lean more in the gnostic direction. This work also informs the reader that Mary Magdalene and her circle at Bethany funded Jesus' ministry—thus introducing her role as a wealthy patron.

Art historians acknowledge that many of the most enduring popular images we have of saints today stem from the vivid portrayals of their lives in the medieval *Golden Legend*.

A few medieval Mary Magdalene pilgrimage sites and their associated legends and relics:

There are a vast number of traditions regarding Mary Magdalene. These include early oral and folklore accounts, and manuscript fragments about historical sites and pilgrimage legends during the

St. Mary Magdalene, here depicted as a penitent whore, lies resting beside her jar in the Church of Mary Magdalene, Launceston, Cornwall. A tradition is attached to this figure that if a coin is thrown up onto her back and remains there—an offering to the Goddess which is accepted—a wish will be granted. (Simon Brighton)

High Middle Ages. So where can a modern-day visitor go to see some of the major medieval Mary Magdalene pilgrimage sites? What follows is a brief synopses of four of the major places in France that a traveller can still see. We focus on the easy-to-visit sites and those places that would have been familiar to a medieval pilgrim. For now, let us imagine that we are going on a medieval pilgrimage ... a journey of exploration.*

Mary Magdalene and the Marseilles area
Saintes-Marie-de-la-Mer

A number of medieval legends—some earlier, but many written down in the 11th–12th centuries—have maintained that Mary Magdalene and her early entourage arrived by sea from the Holy Land after the traumatic time of the crucifixion. Having fled great persecution, they landed on the shores of Provence, where they have left a powerful and enduring legacy in their wake.

As to precisely who accompanied her from the Holy Land, accounts vary widely. But most include Mary Magdalene; Martha; Lazarus; Mary Jacobe, the mother of James; Mary Salome, the mother of the apostles James Major and John; Marcella, the maidservant of Martha; and a young girl named Sarah. After they

---

* For other books and recommended reading about Mary Magdalene, please consult the Selected Bibliography at the back of the book. In Appendix 1, there is a short list of pilgrimage places to visit in Belgium, Italy, and elsewhere. For information about Mary and the Cathars, please see Chapter 5.

St. Sara the Egyptian statue (Ste-Maries-de-la-Mer), revered by pilgrims, as part of the colorful annual May 23–25 festival held in her honor. She is also called "Sara Kali, the Black Queen." by Romany gypsies. (Jane May)

arrived on the shores of Provence at Saintes-Marie-de-la-Mer, near Marseilles, legend says they first dedicated a small church before going on their separate ways to preach. Martha went to Tarascon; Mary Magdalene to nearby St-Maximin and St-Baume; and Mary Salome, Mary Jacobe, and Sarah remained at Ste-Marie-de-la-Mer.

Mary Jacobe and Mary Salome, it is said, were later buried in the church. The ultimate fate of Sarah remains unclear, but every May 23–25, at -St-Maries-de-la-Mer, a major festival is held in special honor of St. Sarah the Egyptian, called by the Romany gypsies "Sara Kali," the Black Queen.[3] Other festivities in the area include veneration of St. Mary Magdalene and the Blessed Virgin Mary.

St-Maries-de-la-Mer, the mythic landing location, is an ancient Provencal site situated at the end of an area of marshes and flats called the Carmargue. Its first historical record is generally thought to be from as early as the fourth century BC. The ancient port had been used by Phoenicians, Egyptians, and other earlier travelers who had long been arriving in the area. For many years before and after the first century, historians know that Jewish migrations had been arriving in the Marseilles and Languedoc as well. Historians believe some of the early visitors to Provence included Christians fleeing the Holy Land after the crucifixion. The tiny church at St-Maries-de-le-Mer was eventually dedicated to Santa Maria-de-Ratis (St. Mary of the Little Isle) in the fifth century.

Legends say that the people of Marseilles were initially so impressed by the dynamism, courage and dedication of the early group of mysterious arrivals from the Holy Land that they elected Lazarus as bishop of the city. St. Maximin was ordained bishop of Aix. Mary Magdalene is portrayed as an especially inspiring and charismatic teacher. Some of these events were commemorated in the beautiful St. Mary Magdalene stained glass windows in cathedrals, such as those at Chartres (1200) and Auxerre (1230).[4] Through the centuries, a number of additional legends grew and developed around the initial story of the early arrival in France of this mysterious entourage from a distant land.

OPPOSITE: Exterior of The Church of Ste-Maries-de-le-Mer. (Jane May)

Magdalene relic, La Sainte Baume. (Jane May)

St-Baume grotto, Mary Magdalene, and St. Maximin

There were Magdalene-related pilgrimage sites all over medieval Europe and France, including Vezelay. But due to the politics of the time, after 1279 in particular, the heavily promoted shrine of St-Maximin and the grotto at St-Baume in Provence became among the most popular. The official burial site of Mary Magdalene at the Abbey of St Maximin at nearby Sainte-Baume was initially guarded by dedicated Cassianite monks, who carefully constructed a footpath with steps to ensure that pilgrims could more easily make the long steep trek to see her tomb.[4]

After spending years of active teaching in the Marseilles area, legends maintain that in her advancing years, Mary voluntarily decided to go into retirement—to the hilltop cave at Sainte-Baume, a beautiful local area of peace and quiet. Sainte-Baume means "Holy Balm," a healing ointment of special herbs and spices named after Mary Magdalene's famed alabaster jar. At this secluded cave, Mary lived a private life of especially great spiritual awareness, knowledge, and prayer, sustained by angels. She spent her last thirty years in deep mystical contemplation.

Historically, until 1170, the patron of the grotto at Sainte-Baume had been the Blessed Virgin Mary and not St. Mary Magdalene. Eventually, however, although her relics were long believed to be at nearby St-Maximin, the grotto of St-Baume would also become a major pilgrimage site of Mary Magdalene. A steady succession of royalty, nobles, churchmen, members of the populace, and prominent medieval ladies periodically endured the steep climb up to her cave to pay homage to their beloved Mary Magdalene.

Legends about her death at St-Baume recount that a priest in the area managed to coax her out of the cave and speak with the mysterious woman hermit. To his utter shock, while listening to her talk about her life, she quietly admitted that yes, she was Mary, the friend of Jesus. She added that, after preaching for years in the Marseilles area, she chose to withdraw and retire at the grotto. When he heard this, the priest ran and told St. Maximin, who is said to have met her at his church and, after speaking with her, to be greatly impressed with her profound spiritual presence and radiance. St. Maximin accepted that she was indeed the elderly Mary Magdalene. The story continues that shortly after this epic meeting, "her time had come" and she died peacefully in the church. St. Maximin embalmed her body with precious oils, gave her an honorable burial, and issued orders that after his own death he was to be buried next to her.[6] The reader is assured that her tomb and relics were located at the church of St Maximin, close to her nearby St-Baume hilltop cave.

The church at St-Maximin thus had a strong tradition of venerating the body and relics of St. Mary Magdalene—a tradition it claimed for centuries. But in the eighth century, during the difficult times of the Saracen invasions, monks of St-Maximin covered the opening to their crypt and safely moved Mary's remains to the nearby sarcophagus of Saint Sidoine in the same crypt.

However, around this time, the increasingly envious Benedictine brethren at Vezelay, further up to the north, declared that they possessed the genuine relics of St. Mary Magdalene, and that her remains were not housed at St-Maximin in Provence. This created a serious monastic showdown that would not be clarified by the church until as late as 1295 (see below).

Mary Magdalene and Vezelay

The magnificent basilica of Vezelay, among the finest examples of the Romanesque style in France today, is dedicated to Mary Magdalene. Founded by Count Girart de Roussillon and his wife Berthe in 860, it was originally quite a modest church; three years later, they gifted it to Rome.

Regarding the relics of Mary Magdalene, accounts vary. According to the Vezelay version, when the Saracens threatened southern France, a monk from their community was sent down to St-Maximin to obtain Mary's relics for safekeeping. This is quite a different position from what the monks of St-Maximin have long maintained, i.e, that they retained the saint's relics. Vezelay was directly challenging this. The duel-to-end-all duels had just begun.

Ironically, at first Vezelay did not have any particular direct historical association with St. Mary Magdalene. Its original patrons were the Virgin Mary, St. Peter, St. Paul, and the martyrs Andeux and Pontian. As far as historical documentation regarding the claims of Vezelay and Mary Magdalene, it was not until the

Front view, Basilica of St
Marie Madeleine, Vezelay.
(Jane May)

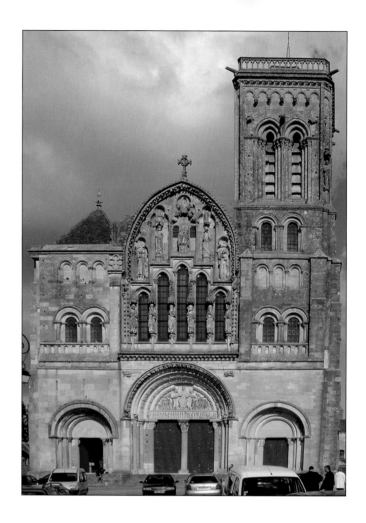

rather late papal bull of 1050 that she was declared to be one of
its major patrons. In 1058, the pope declared that Vezelay had the
only official relics of Mary Magdalene and that she now had the
distinct privilege of being their one and only patron.

From that point on, the rivalry between the two sides helped
to popularize the Magdalene cult in a major way. Pilgrims at all
levels of society were not happy that Vezelay's relics were not
openly displayed. The relics were stowed away, out of sight, under
the altar. Yet over time, an enormous number of pilgrims came to
Vezelay. By the early 12th century, the originally humble church
was a stunning, wealthy Romanesque basilica, with prominent
visitors—including kings, nobles, and abbots. It enjoyed the additional distinction of being one of the four major starting points
for pilgrims on the famed road to Santiago de Compostela. But,
even so, there were nagging doubts as to whether or not Vezelay's
relics of Mary Magdalene were genuine.

OPPOSITE: Interior view,
Basilica of Vezelay.
(Chris May)

In 1267, the crypt at Vezelay was opened and only a few bones were found—but not a body—a disappointment to many at the time. In December of 1279, at the insistence of Charles II of Anjou, the sarcophagus in the crypt of St-Maximin in Provence was similarly excavated.[7] It was alleged that a nearly complete skeleton was found. While as questionable as any relics claim often is, this new discovery at St-Maximin was hailed. In 1295, Charles II obtained official papal recognition for the St-Maximin discovery over the claims of Vezelay. From that date on, and according to present Catholic church policy, the official site for the relics of St. Mary Magdalene is St-Maximin in Provence.

Today, the alleged skull reliquary of Mary at St-Maximin—in its crowned golden container—is a special focus of her colorful July 22nd feast day celebrations.[8] At Vezelay, her reputed relics are also on display in the crypt for several months of the year—from Easter to All Saints' Day.[9] Both sites celebrate her feast day as do many other communities throughout the world.

The Abbey of St. Victor and the Church of St. Lazarus

The monks of the Abbey of St. Victor and the church of St. Lazarus in the Marseilles area also claimed relics of St. Mary Magdalene. The church of St. Victor and its crypt were where she had lived and prayed during her earlier days of preaching in Southern France. The church of St Lazarus maintained that it still had the first altar upon which she preached.

Even today, the ancient feast of Candlemas is celebrated by the devout in the Abbey of St. Victor with special green candles on February 2nd every year. The abbey is also known for baking its famed, boat-shaped, orange-flavored pastries called *navettes*, representing the "boat with no oars" that legends say guided Mary Magdalene and her entourage to the shores of Provence millennia ago.

Rennes-le-Chateau

The Languedoc is ground zero for myth, legend, and speculation about Mary Magdalene and the early founding survivors of Christianity. Nowhere is this more apparent than in the fascinating perennial mystery of Rennes-le-Chateau, an important ancient

Tour Magdala, Rennes-le-Chateau. (Simon Brighton)

and historical medieval site that remains, a tangled web—beckoning one and all from a tantalizing, elusive distance.

People throughout the world from all walks of life, those of different religious beliefs, and members of the media are clamoring for more definitive answers about Mary Magdalene. Modern interest in Mary and medieval Rennes-le-Chateau has been fueled by the release of bestselling-but-controversial books like *Holy Blood, Holy Grail* and *The Da Vinci Code*. People want more historical answers about this intriguing saint and inspiring woman, and the interconnected speculations that have been raised about her.

Biblical scholars have more sources of information today than in earlier centuries. People are asking carefully thought-out questions about many of the topics related to Rennes-le-Chateau and the surrounding area(s). Inquirers tell me they are weary of what appears to be centuries of uncertainty, confusion, and misunderstanding about Mary Magdalene.

Asmodeus, Rennes-
le-Chateau. (Simon
Brighton)

It is interesting to note, and not often always fully appreciated, that the church of Rennes-le-Chateau was not only dedicated to St. Mary Magdalene centuries ago, but that its environs and surrounding landscape are an important area for the study of symbolism, the arts, medieval pilgrimage, saints, and so on. At the church at Rennes-le-Chateau, for example, you will see its famous altarpiece featuring Mary Magdalene, the St. Marie Madeleine statue, the Tour Magdala, the Villa Bethania, Rennes-le-Bains, and, in nearby Limoux, a beautiful and fascinating stained glass window featuring Mary Magdalene and a beautiful Black Madonna.

Sincere seekers say they wish to get to the core of the matter of the meaning of the mysterious and enigmatic symbols and legends that surround Rennes-le-Chateau in order to better examine and explore their faith, philosophy, and belief(s). Yet, until the Church and other experts on this region are willing or able to share their more recent research and help clarify the situation, little can be said for certain. Sadly, as with sacred sites around the world, some people have resorted to coming merely to seek or dig for "lost treasure"—often damaging the environment in the process.

However, it seems the overall situation is very complex, inevitably involving many individuals, churches, and various vested interests over the centuries. The net result being that, at the present time, the average seeker has had little solid information to go on about the more modern-day mysteries discussed about this site. So a genuine spiritual hunger tends to remain about Rennes-le-Chateau. Hopefully, further information will come to light in the future from archaeologists about medieval-related ruins or artifacts that may be found in the area.

Biblical scholars and various textual experts have been further exploring various interpretations about the life of Mary Magdalene for years, as well as examining those questions that relate to modern concerns about this locale and its mysteries. A vexing question for many is this: "Were Mary Magdalene and Jesus married, and, if so, did they have a family?" We hope that more information will come to light in the future.

Yet, elusive as ever, questions remain and the perennial Quest continues. Indeed, that is the best pilgrimage of all—the process of making the spiritual Quest itself, the *real* treasure.

OTHER SITES ASSOCIATED WITH MARY MAGDALENE

If you have never been to the Languedoc and are planning a visit to southern France, do at least try to explore the area and incorporate these entrancing sites into your itinerary. The medieval town of Carcassone is another one of the easier-to-visit sites that should be part of your larger journey to the region. As many travelers have noted, the stunning views alone are worth the trip!

Equally so, when in northern Spain, try to visit Girona, not far from Barcelona. Girona was an important early medieval city—with its stunning cathedral for Christians, and "the Call," its vibrant Jewish quarter. Girona has become of more interest in recent years because of the mystery put forth by author Patrice Chaplin—that Girona may have a key connection to the enduring mystery of Rennes-le-Chateau. Her interesting novels outline what, for her, has been a lifetime of questing and searching about this fascinating city. This area is part of beautiful Catalonia, a fascinating region that also includes Salvador Dali's birthplace in Figueres.

Indeed, throughout history, it seems that for nearly everyone who visits the Languedoc, Provence, the Pyrenees and neighboring regions, whether spiritually inclined or not, comes back in some way transformed—the very goal of the medieval pilgrimage—to "return anew."

A key symbol: the Alabaster Jar

Certain symbols have long been associated with the Magdalene. Familiar artistic depictions portraying her in red (or in red and green), with long hair, at times next to a skull and/or a book are well-known. But it is the ***alabaster jar*** that is considered to be the trademark symbol identifying Mary Magdalene in works of art.

In ancient times, this alabaster jar was a special container that held rare, expensive perfumed oils or ointments. Often, such sealed vessels held especially precious perfumes like spikenard, the oil that was used to anoint Jesus in the New Testament.[10] Sometimes a spice box, an *alabastron*, would be used instead for important rituals involving luxurious perfumes or ointments; so some images of Mary Magdalene show her with a rectangular spice box rather than an upright jar. Similar containers were used to hold the special oils used in burial and funerary rites as well.[11] Myrrh oil was often used for healing, while spikenard oil was generally reserved for anointing a king, high priest, or other prominent person, in addition to healing. It is interesting that James, the brother of Jesus, was known to refuse the use of oil,[12] while other early Christians did use it for special occasions.

A medieval variation of the ancient traditional alabaster jar or spice box was the ***chrism***—a small vessel, gold in color, shown in many medieval and some Renaissance portrayals of Mary Magdalene.[13] It, too, was designed to hold special aromatic spices and luxurious perfumed oils or ointments to be used for special religious occasions. Today, in many Christian denominations, the term "chrism" refers to the anointing oil itself, not to its container as it did in medieval times. In modern times, the anointing oil is often a mixture of olive and balsam and is used in church rites and special ceremonies. Other world religions and spiritual organizations have their own special oils, ointments, and perfumes used for their rites, a practice that is centuries old. In the ancient world, Egypt was especially known for its use of oils in anointing and burial procedures, in which priestesses were also involved.

THE KNIGHTS HOSPITALLER RELIC OF MARY MAGDALENE

Both the medieval Knights Templar and their rivals, the Knights Hospitaller (later dubbed the "Knights of St John") had relics and precious objects in their treasuries. The Hospitallers, like many other orders at the time, highly venerated St. Mary Magdalene. Established in Jerusalem, the Hospitallers were ministering to pilgrims even before the Crusades began. They built the church of St. John the Baptist and had a hospital in full operation as early as 1080.[14] The official Rule of the Hospitallers claimed the Order possessed a precious relic of the Magdalene—a finger bone kept in a special silver reliquary.[15] In 1286, this relic was donated to the Hospitaller church in Aix-en-Provence by brother William of Villaret, then Prior of Saint-Gilles. who later became Master of the Order. By contrast, the Templars never directly claimed a relic of Mary.

ORTHODOX CHURCH RELICS OF ST. MARY MAGDALENE

According to Eastern Orthodox beliefs, Mary Magdalene is viewed as "Equal-to-the-Apostles." She is especially honored as the leader of the holy *myrrophores*, the loyal group of grieving myrrh-bearing women who arrived very early at the tomb of Christ on Easter morning. Mary Magdalene was never regarded as merely a penitent in the Byzantine Church. Unlike the Roman Catholic tradition, the Byzantine Church has always seen her as a distinctly different person from either Mary of Bethany or the "sinful woman" in the gospels. Each of the three Marys has her own feast day in the Eastern calendar.[16] While the Western Church, since 1969, no longer maintains that Mary was a prostitute, the Byzantine Church never claimed that about her in the first place. Eastern Orthodox tradition holds that Mary Magdalene died in Ephesus (Turkey), was buried in a cave in 886, and that her relics were taken to Constantinople (Istanbul) where they can be seen in the Church of St. Lazarus' monastery today. Other branches of the Orthodox church also claim to possess her relics. The St. Mary Magdalene Russian Orthodox Church in Jerusalem claims to possess a special icon and a relic of a bone.

FEAST DAY OF MARY MAGDALENE

July 22nd is celebrated worldwide as the official feast day of St. Mary Magdalene in the Roman Catholic, Anglican, Eastern Orthodox and Lutheran churches. Her memory is also celebrated

Mary Magdalene holding a red egg. (Blue and gold encaustic painting by American artist Dawn Gaskill.)

on this day, and at other times throughout the year by gnostics, some guilds, and by members of the Ba'hai faith.

In addition to July 22nd, the Eastern Orthodox church commemorates Mary on its own special *Sunday of the Myrrh-bearing Women*, held on the second Sunday after Pascha (Easter). This occasion features beautiful Orthodox icons of Mary holding a red egg in honor of the story of her lively preaching to the Roman Emperor Tiberius. One popular Eastern Orthodox version of the miraculous red egg story is that, following the death and resurrection of Jesus, Mary Magdalene used her position to get invited to a huge banquet hosted by Tiberius. She arrived at the banquet, and began to speak very eloquently about Jesus and his life, all the while holding an egg in her hand. She ended with the proclamation "Christ is risen!" As might be expected, Tiberius laughed, commenting that Christ rising from the dead was as likely as the egg in her hand turning red while she held it. At that moment, in front of all present, the egg in her hand mysteriously turned a bright red, after which she continued to proclaim the Gospel to the entire imperial assembly. To this day, on Easter, in many Orthodox traditions, eggs are painted red to commemorate her and celebrate Easter Sunday.

In medieval times, towns all over Europe held not only major church services on her feast day, but also, colorful July fairs, pageants, and plays—all in her honor. These fairs were often sponsored by guilds and wealthier members of the community. People honored her by attending church services; going on pilgrimage to one of her shrines, if they could; as well as coming to the local fairs and plays. For example, on every July 22nd in Fife, Scotland, a major annual St. Mary Magdalene's Day fair was held, often drawing huge numbers from other neighboring provinces.[17] As leading British historian Professor Ronald Hutton states, the corporation of the city of Grimsby in England specifically chose to celebrate her day with a town feast.[18]

History has shown Mary Magdalene to be one of the most popular female saints in all the High Middle Ages. Today, modern travelers incorporate a journey to St-Maximin, St-Baume, Marseilles, Rennes-le-Chateau, Vezelay and other key Magdalene sites as part of an annual holiday, to celebrate her feast day. Both Christians and non-Christian devotees of Mary seek to more deeply reconnect with the exiled Feminine—a principle still largely excluded from much of Christianity and a number of other institutional religions. The legacy of centuries of patriarchal domination and administration is loosening its hold on modern Western culture. What, then, will the future hold?

The wisdom of Mary Magdalene

Beckoning us from long ago, the universal figure of Wisdom, a key aspect of the divine Feminine, calls to us today from her depths. Many of the early gnostic and biblical texts portray the universal Feminine and its spiritual wisdom as an "outsider," calling one from the street corners. Indeed, as one American scholar put it, "Magdalene Christianity offers an alternative and a challenge to Petrine Christianity, which has never been able to silence it. It might move us towards a religion of Outsiders."[19]

A number of biblical and related texts—such as the Song of Songs, Proverbs, Wisdom of Solomon, Ecclesiastes, Psalms, Sirach, and other near eastern literature—are evidence of the ancient regard for the universal Feminine. One example is *Thunder, Perfect Mind,* one of the great Gnostic texts that was found as part of the Nag Hammadi Library. The primary female figure of Wisdom is the narrator and spiritual teacher in the text. Here, Wisdom declares:

> I am the first and the last
>
> I am the honored one and the scorned one
>
> I am the whore and the holy one
>
> I am the wife and the virgin.[20]

Such polarities within an overall unity have encouraged one Jungian analyst to comment, "paradoxically, there seems to be a link between the two opposing forces in the image of Mary Magdalene."[21]

The overall theme of the exiled Feminine has been addressed by many writers, including leading theological scholars such as the late renowned professor, Marvin Meyer.[22]

The ever-evolving image of Mary Magdalene down through the centuries includes the archetype of sacred sexuality. Ever since Eve and that wily serpent in the Garden of Eden, the classic "madonna-whore" psychological split in Western consciousness has remained. Psychologists and sociologists have continually noted that it is still projected onto society today, affecting men as well as women. Regarding loving sexuality, and healing, since the 1960s in particular, experts note that a growing number in the West today, are exploring tantra and other ways of incorporating these themes into their spiritual lives.

In the biblical apocryphal book of Sirach 24:32:33, the figure of Wisdom declares:

> I will again make instruction shine forth
> Like the dawn, and I will make it shine afar;
> I will again pour out teaching like prophecy,
> And leave it to all future generations.[23]

Perhaps Mary Magdalene may be likened to a "new Elixir" for our time—akin to an alchemical jewel in the crown, whose wisdom will ultimately reward those who choose to include her in a larger way in their spirituality of choice.

Today's great resurgence of interest in the Feminine in general, and with Mary Magdalene in particular, is a phenomenon not seen on anything like this scale since the High Middle Ages. Perhaps Wisdom, too, is returning to inspire and challenge us in the West and in the wider global community. The neglected Feminine returns again, propelling us toward a new, more balanced Vision for future generations.

As of this writing, little is still known for certain, about the actual life of Mary Magdalene. Her ultimate mystery remains.

As always, Her memory lives on, ever-evolving and shifting, and, as ever, unrevealed in its totality.

CHAPTER 3

THE BLACK MADONNA

Historical Overview

Modern head sculpture of St. Sara, carved in jet, from Santiago de Compostella, Spain. (The Brydon Collection)

Among the most widely venerated shrines in all of Western Europe are those that feature a Black Madonna. Through the centuries, pilgrims claimed these unique shrines possessed special healing powers for certain ailments and concerns. Just what is it about these enigmatic images that continue to evoke such interest and fervor in people from all walks of life?

In the High Middle Ages, Gothic cathedrals were dedicated to *Notre Dame* (Our Lady), as were the medieval Knights Templar, the Cistercians, key medieval guilds, and other monastic and chivalric orders. Interest in *Notre Dame* and chivalric values greatly increased among the troubadours, and many of the Grail stories were written during this period. The popularity of the Black Madonnas was another factor in this cultural "renaissance before the Renaissance."

Black Madonna shrines are found worldwide, but those that date from the High Middle Ages (1100–1300) are located especially in France and northern Spain. Royals, nobles, guild members, ordinary members of society, and pilgrims from afar regularly visited these shrines. Certain cathedrals became especially popular during this era, their shrines becoming renowned far and wide—Chartres, Montserrat, and Rocamadour, among them.

A 17th century verse has been found that lists some of the then contemporary key national shrines in Europe. It illustrates the continuing traditions of devotion and veneration of the Black Madonnas from much earlier times.[1] While the role of the Black Madonna is a longstanding tradition, ironically, few people outside of traditional religious circles are fully aware of their importance.

Appearance and symbolism: In the Dark Places of Wisdom

Many Black Madonna statues exist today having survived the ravages of time, wars, thefts, attempts to destroy them or alter their design, or just plain neglect over the years. Some are in large cathedrals or churches, others remain in smaller chapels, museums or private collections.[2]

The imagery of Black Madonnas varies widely, as each has its own unique story and historical tradition. They have been found in forests, caves, a hedge, in a boat that mysteriously arrives on shore, or in or near trees in unusual circumstances. Strangely enough—as priests and witnesses at the time could attest—some Black Madonna statues were known to have become immutably heavy, as if utterly refusing to move from the locale in which they were found or from one they seemed to prefer, resisting all human efforts to lift or transport them. At Montserrat, for example, the bishop himself and his assistants tried to move the Black Madonna to his cathedral to no avail. Inevitably, in such circumstances, a grotto, shrine, or church would grow up around the original site.

Experts estimate that there are at least 300 Black Madonnas in Europe alone, exhibiting varying iconography. Some statues are standing images with a mother holding a child; others portray her sitting; some show her crowned and/or holding a sceptor or orb; while others still are quite simple and have little or no ornate features at all. From archaic, earthy aspects to ornately crowned Queens of Heaven, all of these images are black or dark brown in color. Many statues of Black Madonnas are painted on wood, such as pear, oak or walnut; others are carved from stone. Some images are found on murals, textiles or tapestries, or are featured subjects in paintings. Historians, curators, theologians and others have attempted to learn more about these images on-site, and from churches, documents, archives, and libraries.

Black Madonnas exist in nearly every western European country. Some of the better-known today are at Chartres, Le Puy, Rocamadour, Vezelay, Orleans, Einsiedeln, Oropa, and Montserrat. (Please see Appendix 3.) They are also found in Mexico (Guadalupe), and at other sites outside of Europe.

Wisdom and the Song of Songs

So why are the Black Madonnas black? Some priests claim these statues are black in color from centuries of candle smoke or soot; frankly, a rather hollow explanation. Others say that such representations are allegorical and meant to be symbolic—perhaps recalling the beautiful dark lady (the "Shulamite") described in the Old Testament book of Song of Songs (Song of Solomon). Still others maintain that they were intended to be black in color from the beginning, painted or carved black simply because the Virgin Mary may have been non-Caucasian. Other experts have surmised that these statues are a Christianized version of the ancient Egyptian mother goddess Isis holding her divine child Horus. Opinions vary widely, but nearly everyone agrees that there is a longstanding history and early tradition of some Madonnas being intentionally portrayed as black or dark in color, and that some of these shrines have been among the most popular through time.

As one historian puts it, "the Church often explains their blackness in allegorical terms from the Song of Songs: 'I am black, but comely, O ye daughters of Jerusalem' (Song of Songs 1:5)"[3] This tradition comes from what is called the Biblical Wisdom tradition, which has been an inspiration to Jews, Christians, kabbalists and others. The powerfully persuasive 12th century Cistercian Abbot and churchman Bernard of Clairvaux, a key advocate for the fledging Templar Order, wrote an extraordinary number of sermons and writings about the Song of Songs in particular. His lifelong veneration of the Blessed Virgin Mary in general was noted by his contemporaries, and, in particular, his high regard for the Black Madonna of Chatillon, near Dijon, where he grew up. Tradition says that as a boy, while praying, he received three symbolic initiatory drops of milk from her, a spiritual event that inspired him for the rest of his life.

One of Bernard's most beautiful quotes comes from his letter 106: "You will find more things in forests than in books; the trees, the stones will teach you what the masters cannot … do the mountains not distill sweetness? Are the hills not flowing with milk and honey? There is so much I could tell you…." Bernard challenged his community to have a deeper and broader perspective. The obvious connection of some of the Black Madonnas with natural themes is often reflected in where and how they were found—such as in a tree, by a hedge, or a grotto.

The association of darkness and blackness with wisdom is also found in other writings; for instance, the Sufi mystic Rumi refers at various points to radiant black being the color of Divine Light. The 13th century theologian Meister Eckhart wrote commentaries on the Gospel of John verse 5 (i.e., "The Light shines in the darkness"). Darkness has, in many esoteric traditions, been equated with a deeper wisdom and greater knowledge. And indigenous peoples have ancient traditions honoring the darkness and appreciating its inherent wisdom as well as that of the light. Indeed, it is interesting to note that the Latin phrase, *Lux Lucet In Tenebris,* is generally translated as "Light shines in Darkness."

Like the portrayals of the figure of Wisdom from the biblical and apocryphal writings (which were, at times, neglected or strongly discouraged), the Black Madonnas have often been exiled, excluded, or disparaged by religious authorities. But the Black Madonna archetype is experiencing a revival of interest in modern-day culture. Yet, even so, as Jungian analyst Ean Begg points out, Black Madonna statues are still in danger of theft, possible "whitewashing" or alteration, or being moved to private areas off limits to the public.

Replica of the Black Madonna at Montserrat. (Alan Glassman)

The spiritual import of the color black embodied by the Black Madonnas, implies a connection to the higher (and earlier) wisdom of Our Lady. Her universality includes the concept of the darkness as an ultimately *positive* characteristic—rather than darkness being ignored or perceived as negative, as is rather common in the West. The Black Madonnas also imply a connection to the groundedness of the wisdom of the dark earth below, and a greater appreciation of the spiritual "dark night of the soul." Indeed, many were, and are, located in crypts or found in caves or trees. The inspiring effects of the Black Madonnas on pilgrims from all walks of life is evidence enough of their great importance, let alone the miracles associated with cures—for infertility, grave illness, blindness, and so on.

Origin theories about the Black Madonna

Historians acknowledge that the Romans brought early images of the goddess Cybele from Phrygia in the third century to the hills of Rome and other areas. Early seafaring peoples such as the Phoenicians and Egyptians also brought statues of early deities with them to some European ports. It is known that crusaders, kings, and nobles returning from the Holy Land in medieval times would often bring back religious statues, art or relics in their caravans— some of which were Black Madonnas. Ancient images of Diana at Ephesus and other female deities in Asia Minor and the Middle

East were often carved from large black stones or meteoric fragments (ebony or jet). So some of these early images of a black goddess were very likely later Christianized as Black Madonnas in honor of the Christian mother of God, the Blessed Virgin Mary. Most medieval Black Madonnas are carved of wood.

Black is the one color that represents an absence of color in the entire spectrum. The words *matter, matrix,* and *mother* all derive from the Latin *materia,* meaning "substance."[4] And, of course, there is the *prima materia* in alchemical tradition, the initial black material needed for the first stage of a series of further transformations, the dark potentiality out of which everything will eventually emerge.

There is a connection with the universal relevance of the Great Mother archetype in nearly all cultures. One of the more poignant comments about our world today was that of University of Warsaw anthropologist Prof. Andrzej Wiercinski to author China Galland when she interviewed him about Black Madonnas: "We live under the spell of the Great Mother. The material world is the female side of God, *mater.* The problem is that we don't recognize it, so we are consumed by it rather than nourished. We are under the spell of *mater*-iality; if we don't recognize this, we will be devoured."[5]

Some Black Madonnas became greatly feared by certain clergy as a result of their miracles, and/or the fact that their shrine or church may have been built directly over a previously ancient or powerful pagan site.

Yet, as any parent knows, a "taboo factor" for anything often merely further enhances any existing interest and beliefs in the alleged powers of the so-called tabooed subject. Censored topics seem all the more intriguing. One scholar points out that "in Catholic countries, where blackness is the climate of the devils, not the angels, and is associated almost exclusively with magic and the occult, Black Madonnas are considered especially wonder-working, as the possessors of hermetic knowledge and power."[6] The "taboo factor" of the Black Madonnas was further enhanced by the fact that many of the most extraordinary miracles were often reported by those on the so-called margins of society—prisoners being freed, criminals chastised and then helped in some way, single mothers assisted, and so on. Healings or miracles, however, were also reported by certain royals,

Black Madonna, Lluc.
(Mallorca). (Karen Ralls)

nobles, merchants, and warriors—Joan of Arc is an example. So over time, the fame of certain Black Madonna shrines for assistance or blessings grew far and wide, fueled by reports from those in all walks of life.

Due to increasing worldwide interest, new research is being done about the Black Madonnas by scholars in religious studies, art history, and wisdom literature, as well as by archaeologists, gender studies specialists, theologians, psychologists, and others. It will be interesting to see what more emerges.

Examples of Black Madonna shrines

Visiting pilgrimage sites and sacred places in person can provide not only an artistic experience of beauty, but a genuine nourishment of the spirit. Each visitor experiences a site in his or her own way. This is as true now as it was in the High Middle Ages. No two Black Madonnas are alike, and no two have the same history or story; neither are any two pilgrims alike.

Modern encaustic painting of the image of Our Lady of Guadalupe (Mexico). (Dawn Gaskill)

There are hundreds of Black Madonnas that one could visit today. To best share some of the historical aspects and lore about them, what follows are four key examples of popular Black Madonna shrines that are easy to find. Each has its own unique, story … its "whispers of Wisdom."

ROCAMADOUR (FRANCE)

The Black Madonna of Rocamadour is one of the oldest and most famous Black Madonnas in France. A 12th century carved walnut image, blackened and then partially covered in silver plate, it sits in a reliquary, which was one of the important stages on the famed road to Santiago de Compostela in the Middle Ages. Crowned and seated on a throne, she and the Christ child together symbolically embody the wisdom of God. Such images are called a *Sedes*

Sapientiae, a "Throne of Wisdom"—like the figures at Aurillac, Le Puy and Meymac, descended from Roman Cybele, originally from Asia Minor.[7] Rocamadour was where Cathars were sent in penance, and also where Henry II went to publicly atone for the murder of archbishop Thomas a Becket at Canterbury.

The historical origins of the cherished Black Madonna of Rocamadour are lost in antiquity. But early traditions claim that Zacchaeus (of biblical fame re: the sycamore tree) and his wife Veronica brought a statue of a Black Madonna that had been carved by St. Luke to Soulac, and then on to Rocamadour. Dr Jean Markale informs us about its history, saying that the origins of the sanctuary here began in 1166, when a:

> … perfectly preserved body was found at the entrance of a chapel dedicated to the Virgin Mary. For fairly obscure reasons, the people there regarded this body as the remains of a mysterious Saint Amadour, for whom this place is named. The 'saint' was buried in front of the altar to the Virgin and another legend spread, according to which Amadour was the husband of Saint Veronica, the one who wiped Christ's face when he was climbing Golgotha. But during the fifteenth century, Amadour was incorporated into the publican Zaccheus, which was a convenient way to get the two traditions to coincide. Amadour does not appear in the official Roman calendar, nor does Veronica or Zaccheus.[8]

Markale states that recent research indicates that the hermitage of Rocamadour existed long before the discovery of the saint's body. After all, the Black Madonna tradition here is reputed to be at least a thousand years old. Such was the repute of this shrine and its Black Madonna in the High Middle Ages that Royal pilgrims such as Henry II, Louis XI, and Eleanor of Aquitaine visited this site, as did a steady stream of saints, nobles, and others.

Some scholars believe that there may have been sound reasons for stressing Rocamadour's close relationship with Mary. Rocamadour scholar Dr. Marcus Bull comments that, "in the first place, Rocamadour was not a Marian shrine in the strict sense in that it did not claim possession of relics linked to the Virgin. In this it differed from a number of other Marian centers such as Chartres, Laon, and Soissons."[9] So by stressing the early

Black Madonna (le Puy).
(Karen Ralls)

connections with Mary, and its Black Madonna becoming a major shrine, Rocamadour was better able to compete for pilgrims with other abbeys and much larger monasteries and churches. Although Rocamadour's Black Madonna has long been famed for its great miraculous healing powers, it is also the place where the sword of Roland—called Durandal—is still venerated, in the cloven rock above the chapel of the Black Madonna, "though now out of reach of all the brides who sought fertility by its touch."[10]

Although there is no specific Mary Magdalene connection, per se, legend states that the Holy Chalice brought from Caesarea by Joseph of Arimathea landed in Marseilles and was taken from there to what was then called Gallia Narbonensis (the Narbonne region). It was kept at Rocamadour until the eighth century.[11] Perched on the top of a gorge with stunning views above the River Dordogne, maintaining its popularity as a pilgrimage site is a testament to its magnetism and the enduring memory of the Black Madonna tradition here.

EINSIEDELN (SWITZERLAND)

The greatest Black Madonna pilgrimage shrine in all of Switzerland is Einsiedeln, a stunningly beautiful locale long associated with hermits and hermitage; in German, *einsiedler* means hermit. Known as one of the best places in Europe for winter sports, as well for its longstanding traditions of horse breeding and racing, Einsiedeln is centrally situated not far from the scenic Sihlsee reservoir. Its unique Gingerbread Museum, the Mouta valley "Holloch" cave system, and the Jakobsweg (St James Path) also runs near the area. The birthplace of Paracelsus, Einsiedeln is also famous for its massive Benedictine Einsiedeln Abbey, the chapel of which houses its revered Black Madonna.

The story of this Black Madonna begins with the eighth century hermit St. Meinrad. Born in the family castle near Sulchen, Meinrad had taken his Benedictine vows as a young man in his twenties. He became a monk at the renowned monastery of Reichenau. Around the age of forty, Meinrad desired a more reclusive setting for his religious life. He decided to enter the dark, powerful and foreboding Finsterwald—the Dark Forest—of northern Switzerland. Here he lived as a devout hermit—bringing with him a Black Madonna statue.

Having rescued two young ravens from predatory hawks, Meinrad lived alone in the forest in his simple sanctuary for many years, with the loyal ravens as his companions. Legends tell us he was suddenly murdered in 861 by two bandits. (This was too often the fate of lone hermits.) However, it is said that he had spiritually foreseen his own death while saying Mass earlier that day. The two ravens screamed and screeched very loudly during his murder. They also aided and guided the villagers during the search by flying directly to identify the culprits. Even today, the monastery flag at Einsiedeln bears the symbol of these two ravens.

After Meinrad's murder, other priests and monks came to Einsiedeln to live around his original chapel in the forest. St. Eberhard, a French nobleman, arrived in 934 and became the first Abbot of the Benedictine Abbey on this site, placing his monks under the direct protection of Our Lady of the Hermits. The Black Madonna of Einsiedeln was officially consecrated on 14 September, 948 by Konrad, bishop of Constance. On this day each year since, and on all Sundays, the Feast of the Miraculous

The Black Madonna, in the church at Saulieu, southeast of Paris, in the Burgundy region. (Jane May)

Consecration takes place. Four-part *Salve Regina* chants are sung by the monks and pilgrims around the beautifully candlelit illuminated abbey square.[12]

The present-day Black Madonna chapel reportedly sits atop Meinrad's original hermitage site.[13] The current Black Madonna is believed to date from the 15th century. It was restored in the 18th century.

Chartres (France)

Chartres Cathedral has always been recognised as a powerful, sacred place, one of the wonders of the High Middle Ages. It is a site of ancient roots with a long history of devotion and appreciation of the Feminine. In the mid–7th century, St. Bethaire prostrated himself "before the altar of the very glorious virgin Mary."[14] The first Christian relic was given to Chartres by Charlemagne's grandson Charles the Bald in 876. It was the *chainze* (veil) on which the Virgin Mary was said to have given birth to Christ, This important gift bestowed a unique prestige on the already-popular pilgrimage site.

Today, Chartres is especially known for its tribute to Mary, the Queen of Heaven. There are currently two Black Madonna statues at Chartres. One is the officially recognized, more recent *Notre Dame du Pilier* ("Our Lady of the Pillar") which sits upstairs in the nave. The second is in the crypt, *Notre Dame Sous Terre* ("Our-Lady-Under-The-Earth"), a 19th century replacement of an ancient pre-Christian statue with much earlier origins.

Black Madonnas and the natural environment

Pilgrims made the trek to Chartres for centuries before the cathedral was established in 1194. It was a pilgrimage site even before the coming of Christianity. The veneration of the dark *Notre Dame Sous Terre* has ancient associations with the archetype of the Virgin who will bring forth a child, as does the well at the entrance to the subterranean chapel. Pliny and Caesar make reference to Chartres as a place of druidic sacred assemblies. Examples abound of Celtic or druidic-sounding names for other early Black Madonnas in certain areas of France as well, "Our Lady of the Hollies at Arfeuilles, an old druidic centre, is also noted as black, ancient…"[15]

Earliest black virgin veneration at Chartres: Virgo Paritura

The earliest black virgin venerations at Chartres are known to have occurred in the area where the underground crypt is today. Princeton scholar Irene Forsyth relates that the earliest statue in the crypt was originally known as *Virgo Paritura*, the Virgin-about-to-give-Birth, even though, paradoxically, she held a child in her arms.[16] The ancient statue was placed in its own shrine in the cave-like grotto which had its own well, *Puits des Saints Forts* (Well of the Strong Saints), and was the very origin of Chartres cathedral.[17] Many today believe that this much earlier Our-Lady-Under-The-Earth Black Virgin tradition at Chartres may have been a primary factor that influenced the continuing devotion to Mary and female saints in medieval times. Chartres seems to have always been a place where the sacred Feminine has been honored and venerated.

The 12th century French statue of the Black Virgin of Meymac (Notre Dame Meymac), who, rather uniquely, is also depicted with very large hands, wearing a turban or toque, and a green dress and red cloak. Also of interest in the village are the Chapel of St Roch and the Chapel of Mary Magdalene nearby. (Karen Ralls)

THE LABYRINTH AT CHARTRES

The beautiful, winding 11-circuit labyrinth at Chartres is one of the very few medieval cathedral labyrinths that have survived the fate of the many that have been destroyed. In general, medieval pilgrims believed that the labyrinth was symbolic of the sacred, initiatory walk towards the center of Jerusalem—a purification of the spirit and heart, offering great spiritual insights and inspiration. Today, the labyrinth has retained its ancient power and beauty for spiritual pilgrims and visitors from all over the world. As a meditative symbol of meandering towards a unified Center, and providing a focal point of one's spiritual or archetypal journey, walking the labyrinth at Chartres remains a serious contemplative activity. In fact, for many it is a highlight of their visit to Chartres. Some say they will "never be the same again"—the very goal of many a medieval pilgrimage—to return spiritually anew.

British author Philip Carr-Gomm comments that, "the 'rich stone forest' of Chartres is powerful because it seems to combine in one majestic structure elements that nourish and inspire mind, body, and spirit. The heart is opened in walking the labyrinth—taking the long journey closer and closer to the center of being."[18] Another writer notes that "the beauty and mystery of Chartres is realized in the notion that the cathedral itself is the cavern of the

Diagram of the labyrinth at Chartres. (Karen Ralls)

OPPOSITE: Close-up view of the Black Virgin shrine, carved in wood (1848), in the Cathedral of Our Lady of Laon (Aisne). Laon was the Carolingian capital of France and a former Merovingian fortress. It is also a town with an interesting Templar chapel and museum nearby. (Jen Kershaw)

Virgin Wisdom, decorated profusely with images and symbols of her teachings."[19]

I would add that the darkness of the crypt itself—the "home" of the early well and the site of the original Black Virgin and pilgrimages at Chartres—still seems to provide a clear "anchoring effect," a real grounding. Visitors to the cathedral have just seen and experienced its soaring nave, stunning Rose-stained glass windows, sacred geometry, and the shafts of light coming in—while they were upstairs. Next, they proceed down into the crypt with its Black Madonna, making the entire site a metaphoric, resonant, unified chamber of Wisdom—from the depths of the earth below to the unlimited light above. It is as if the dark crypt itself provides the spiritual "roots" of a proverbial tree of Wisdom. That tree ascends from the fertile darkness of the crypt below to the heights of the nave above. As one recent pilgrim describes his experience of Chartres, it "totally re-charges me spiritually every time I go."

THE ORIGINAL BLACK VIRGIN STATUE AT CHARTRES

Only one major description of the ancient original statue of Our Lady in the crypt at Chartres has survived. The statue of the Black Virgin was famously described in 1681 by the celebrated art historian Pintard:

> The Virgin sits on a chair, her Son sits on her knees and he gives the sign of blessing with his right hand. In his left hand he holds an orb.... His face, hands and feet are bare and they are of a shining grey-ebony colour. The Virgin is dressed in an antique mantle ... Her face is oval, of perfect construction, and of the same shining black colour. Her crown is very plain, only the top being decorated with flowers and small leaves. Her chair is one foot wide with four parts hallowed out at the back and carved. The statue is twenty-nine inches tall.[20]

Chartres, a site of many wonders, has been dubbed an *omphalos,* a navel of the world.

Oropa (Piedmont, Italy)

On top of a mountain above Biella, in the Piedmont area of Italy, home of the House of Savoy, is the beautiful sanctuary of the Black Madonna of Oropa. This shrine is part of a much larger complex of buildings. *La Madonna di Oropa* is a black virgin statue about 132 cm high, carved from what is possibly cedar wood. It is housed in a 13th century Basilica on the High Altar. Her child, held in her left arm, is holding a dove in his left hand, evoking what Ean Begg describes as the ceremony of the Purification and Presentation (Candlemas).

This is an ancient statue with a long history. Strangely enough, it still shows no real signs of aging even though it has been kept in a relatively damp place for many hundreds of years.[21] Tradition states that it was originally a Lucan wooden statue (in honor of St. Luke), brought from Jerusalem by St. Eusebius. He also brought two other Black Madonnas with him: one for the Sanctuary of Crea near Monferrato, and the other for his birthplace at Cagliari in Sardinia.[22] The March 24, 1957 papal bull of Pius XII confirms that all three statues brought back by St. Eusebius in 345 were, according to tradition, black.

The Black Madonna of Oropa in Biella is part of a complex of some nineteen chapels. The Cappella del Sasso or del Roc, the oldest extant building, is near a stone bridge built by the inhabitants of Fontanamora in the early 8th century. Inscribed on the rock which forms the chapel's foundation is the date of 369 AD. Begg contends that at that time, "Eusebius would have placed the statue there to counter the pagan traditions of the site—the woods were sacred to Apollo and the waters and rocks to the Celtic mothers."[23]

Scholar Lucia Birnbaum informs us that this Black Madonna shrine's location was once a "Waldensian sanctuary for the poor; later it became a place where heretics were persecuted in a region where women were burned as witches."[24] The Waldensians were respected for their ideals of poverty and simplicity. They held to their idea that *no* oaths were to be made to anyone but God (thus, excluding church authorities). They believed that lay men and women held the same right to preach (and refused to stop preaching despite being told to do so). They met secretly and went from town to town to spread their teaching. They also believed that one could pray outside of the church. None of these concepts sat well with the Church. By 1215, the Waldensians were officially declared heretics and persecuted—often violently. But a remnant survived and today, in Italy the Waldenses are one of the major Protestant sects.[25] Since St. Eusebius was credited by folklore with founding the shelter for the poor at Oropa, the Waldensians were most likely building on an earlier tradition about this site when conducting their dynamic ministry.

The Black Madonna of Oropa has long been called upon for spiritual help—specifically against pestilence and drought. Perhaps it was another miracle that Biella and its surrounding districts suffered no damage during World War II. Oropa features a beautiful stained glass window of St. Mary Magdalene and St. Michael; there are galleries of St. Anne, St. Mary Magdalene and St. Joachim; and a fountain sits in the center of the square.

A crowned Blessed Virgin Mary statue, with red dress and blue robe, at Saulieu, in the Burgundy region of France. (Jane May).

St. Victor's and St-Marie-de-la-Mer (Provence)

In chapter two, we discovered the legend of St. Sara the Egyptian, patron saint of the gypsies in St-Marie-de-la-Mer. She, too, is depicted as black, and honored at the annual gypsy festivals on May 23–25. Not far from St. Sara's home is a famous Black Madonna shrine at St. Victor's (Marseilles). Both sites are visited today, often incorporated into the same journey by travelers.

A Sacred Trust

At Manosque in Provence, ecclesiastical historian Marie Durand-Lefebvre in *Etude sur l'origine des Vierges Noires* informs us that, the Black Madonna known as Our-Lady-of-the-Brambles had been hidden away and the church closed for repairs since 1937. No one could tell her if or when it might be open again.[26]

Such is the fate of a number of Black Madonna statues. Many were also destroyed at the time of the French Revolution (1789). Others have been stolen by thieves and never recovered. Some churches have opted to hide or lock their Black Madonnas away for safekeeping. Such was the case with the rather druidic-sounding Our Lady of the Oak Tree on the Col d'Ares near Prats-de-Mollo, where it was reported that she "has been removed

Early depiction of a Carnute druid grotto in Gaul. The area of, and around, Chartres in earlier times was a major assembly meeting place for Druids; the town of Chartres derives its name from the Carnutes, an important Celtic tribe.

from public veneration to the safekeeping of the presbytery."[27] No one seems to know what has happened to others. This makes those that are still available to be seen all the more special in our own era. Preservation and conservation of surviving statues and artefacts for posterity is imperative.

Whispers of Wisdom…

Black Madonna shrines have long been special places of pilgrimage. While medieval sites have always been part of European travel itineraries, modern travelers seem to be expressing increasing interest in visiting the major Black Madonna shrines.

This is a hopeful sign to me. Long may her Wisdom enrich us all.

Chapter 4

The Grail

The Grail has intrigued the Western imagination possibly more than any other tradition. From ancient tales to medieval romances to modern-day interest in the perennial quest for the Grail, it "is the embodiment of a dream, an idea of such universal application that it appears in a hundred different places ... Yet, although its history, both inner and outer, can for the most part be traced, it remains elusive, a spark of light glimpsed at the end of a tunnel, or a reflection half-seen in a swiftly-passed mirror."[1] Though perceived primarily as a medieval theme, fascination with the Grail is both ancient and very much alive today.

Gundestrup cauldron, 130 BC to 50 AD, the largest known example of European Iron Age silverwork. It was found in a peat-bog in Himmerland, Denmark, 1891. (Simon Brighton)

The Grail is almost always portrayed in medieval sources as profoundly mysterious. "It can be dangerous, even deadly, to certain people—with good reason, tradition says. Some people see the Grail, but others don't. To those who do, it often appears surrounded by brilliant light, sometimes carried by a beautiful maiden, in other accounts, moving by itself in midair."[2] Some of the stories imply that it may not be a material object at all. In the end, the ultimate Grail quest often involves something far more priceless—a spiritual treasure.

The Grail romances

Despite the antiquity of the Grail stories, they did not appear in literary form until the twelfth and thirteenth centuries, many written down by Cistercian or Benedictine monks. Given the complexities of the medieval calendar, we cannot always determine the precise dating for a manuscript, but most of the Grail romances come between 1190 and 1240.

There is no such thing as a single, unified Grail story. The Grail romances are many and varied, and often do not agree with each other. One could say there is a general, prototypical Grail story, but it usually involves a combination of themes, people, and places from different sources.

Grail chalice carving, St. Martin's church, Ancaster, Lincolnshire. (Simon Brighton)

CHRÉTIEN DE TROYES AND ROBERT DE BORON

So, who wrote the first Grail romance? One of the earliest known instances of the Grail theme in writing is *Le Conte du Graal,* written by Chrétien de Troyes in 1190. Chrétien's main character, Perceval, is a guileless knight, the archetypal Fool, whose primary trait is innocence. He sees the Grail during a feast at "a mysterious castle presided over by a lame man called the Fisher King ... Chrétien calls the object simply *un graal* and its appearance is just one of the unusual events which take place during the feast ... at this time, Perceval is also shown a broken sword which must be mended. The two objects together, sword and grail, are symbols of Perceval's development as a true knight."[3]

Unfortunately, Chrétien died before he could finish his story, so other writers attempted to complete it. These versions, called the *Continuations,* embellish the tale and bring in other Grail themes.[4] As more were written, other details were added, and Perceval undergoes more challenging adventures.

Robert de Boron wrote two Grail romances, *Joseph d'Ari-mathie* and *Merlin*—his most famous works—sometime between 1191 and 1200. De Boron gives a definitive Christian emphasis to his Grail stories, presenting the knights' quest as a spiritual search rather than the usual courtly adventures undertaken for a lady's heart or the king's honor. Early-thirteenth-century versions of Robert de Boron's works link the Grail story more closely with Arthurian legends.[5] *Diu Krone* presents Sir Gawain as the hero, while *Queste del Saint Graal* features Sir Galahad and the search for a mystical union with God.

Sir Thomas Malory's famous late-fifteenth-century work *Le Morte d'Arthur* became the major source for much of the film *Excalibur* and the musical *Camelot.* Broadway also produced a new rendition of the famed British comedy hit *Monty Python and the Holy Grail* and a spoof on "Camelot" ("*Spamelot*"). Mod-ern-day quantum physicists have metaphorically described a new discovery as a "Holy Grail of science," implying something of extraordinary value. As we can see, the Grail mythos is very much alive in contemporary culture.

Wolfram von Eschenbach

Wolfram von Eschenbach, a gifted Bavarian poet, is especially known for his famous poem *Parzival,* composed around 1205. Here, he retells the tale of the quest of the hero brought to light by Chrétien de Troyes. But in Wolfram's work, the Grail *is a stone*—a luminous stone fallen from Heaven—not a cup, as is common in other versions—and it is guarded by knights that he calls the *Templeisen.* Sound familiar? Obviously, he was referring to the Knights Templar who would have been well known to his medi-eval audience.

The young hero of Wolfram's story, Parzival, heads for the Grail Castle on Munsalvaesche (Mount of Salvation) encounter-ing many adventures on the way. Here he meets Anfortas, the Wounded King, and sees the Grail. Parzival fails to ask the question that must be asked in order for Anfortas to be healed of his wound. After a troubled night, Parzival awakes alone in the castle. A squire informs him of his error.

At the Fountain of Salvation he meets a wise old hermit, Trevrizent, who turns out to be his uncle. For fifteen days Parzival stays with him to hear the Grail teachings. He tells Parzival that the Grail story came to him from one Kyot of Provence, a very wise man. Most scholars suppose Kyot was a troubadour from Provence—or from Provins, in Champagne. According to historical record, one Guiot de Provins, a troubadour, was present at the knighting of Frederick Barbarossa's sons, including the future emperor Henry VI, at Mainz on Whitsun in 1184, before the writing of *Parzival*.[6] However, this Guiot did not write a Grail romance. According to another theory, Kyot was from Provence on Lake Neuchâtel, in present-day Switzerland, an interesting idea since some consider the nearby town of Sion to be Parzival's home. The Merovingians, important early kings of France, are associated with Jerusalem or Sion as well as a number of the Grail legends.

But the mystery of Kyot's identity remains. Trevrizent says Kyot had found the Grail story in a book in a "heathen" language—most likely he is referring to Arabic—in Toledo, Spain, and that it was originally written in the "wisdom of the stars." This special book, Trevrizent tells young Parzival, was written by Flegetanis, a wise adept born of a Jewish mother of the line of Solomon, and a "heathen" father, who was an expert astrologer with extraordinary knowledge of the wisdom of the heavens and much more. Trevrizent explains to Parzival that God gives a young person, like himself, the spiritual freedom to choose between wisdom and foolishness, purity or corruption. But, he says, only God can judge whether someone is fit to achieve the Grail, and success in finding the Grail is not guaranteed. No one achieves the Grail alone. In other words, *you don't seek the Grail; it summons you.*

Parzival leaves his uncle and returns to the Grail Castle for a second time and again encounters the mysterious the Fisher King. He is asked an enigmatic question, and, thankfully, gives the right answer. The king is then healed and Parzival becomes the Grail king. There are many versions of the Grail romances from the High Middle Ages, but these are among the best-known and most familiar sources today.

Angel emerging from Grail-like chalice, 16th century wooden bench end, carved by Robert Daye, from Altarnun church, Cornwall. (Simon Brighton)

Templar-related themes in the Grail romances

Although there is no historical evidence that a Templar, per se, ever wrote a Grail romance, some of the tales do have Templar-related themes and details, as discussed at length in my previous books. Templar and Grail themes occur in *Parzival*. Wolfram is the only Grail writer to imply that the guardians of the Grail were prototypical Templar knights. The medieval German word for "Templars" was *Tempelherren,* but scholars generally acknowledge

Wolfram intended his *Templeisen* to be viewed as Templars. *Parzival*'s unique focus on the Templars may be partly because both Wolfram and his patron, Hermann I of Thuringia, were known to be drawn to the East. Hermann I, a promoter of the knightly ideal, went on crusade. He was also fascinated by astrology—which was gaining popularity in twelfth-century European courts following the influx from Spain of Arabic texts in Latin translation.[7]

Wolfram describes Parzival as being related to the Arthurian line through his father and to the Grail family through his mother. "Wolfram's Grail family is not the courtly society of Arthurian legend but is portrayed as a divinely chosen vehicle in world affairs, comprising those whom God, through the Grail, silently selects to carry on its tradition. Women are also included in this Grail family."[8]

The early-thirteenth-century Old French Arthurian romance *Perlesvaus* (Perceval) was written by a Benedictine cleric. Here, the Grail castle sits in both the earthly and the heavenly Jerusalem. The *Queste del Saint Graal*, written by a Cistercian monk in 1215, has numerous Templar allusions. The hero of this romance is Galahad, portrayed as a descendant of Solomon, devout, chaste, and destined from birth to achieve the Grail. Galahad is not called a Templar outright—he is a secular knight—but at the mysterious monastery of the white brothers he receives a white shield with a red cross on it that once belonged to Joseph of Arimathea, most likely because he is portrayed as a direct descendant of Joseph through his mother. While in *Perlesvaus* the Grail castle *is* Jerusalem, in the *Queste* the Grail knights go to Jerusalem with the Grail after they complete their quest.[9] All twelve knights then celebrate communion with Christ as the priest, in a reenactment of the Last Supper. Galahad, after eating the consecrated host

RIGHT: Knight as waterbearer holding Grail-like vessel, from early 12th century round Church of the Holy Sepulchre, Northampton. (Simon Brighton)

administered by Christ, has a vision of himself as Christ crucified and dies in ecstasy before the altar.

Symbolism, meaning and places: the many forms of the Grail

First and foremost, we note that however it is portrayed, the Grail is mysterious—often revealing itself differently to each seeker. In some of the stories it is an earthly object, but in others it may be portrayed as the end of a long, discerning spiritual search. Ultimately, however, the Grail remains a mystery. The various medieval Grail romances describe the Grail in different forms: as a cup or chalice, a relic of the Precious Blood of Christ, a cauldron of plenty, a silver platter, a stone from Heaven, a dish, a sword, a spear, a fish, a dove with a communion Host in its beak, a bleeding white lance, a secret Book or Gospel, manna from Heaven, a blinding light, a severed head, a table, and more. The many forms of the Grail depend on the tradition, scribe, patrons, and context. The Grail is not merely "one artifact" and there is no penultimate "single Grail story." The Grail is transcendent. It is a spiritual journey

THE GRAIL AS A CUP, DISH, CAULDRON, CORNUCOPIA, OR WELL

A common Christian interpretation of the Grail is as the cup Christ used at the Last Supper, an image many still have today. A close variant is the cup or vial with which Joseph of Arimathea collected Christ's blood while preparing his body for burial. Legends dating as early as the third century say Joseph eventually brought the Grail to Britain via Gaul. The Grail has also been interpreted as a dish for the consecrated communion Hosts.

Earlier accounts have wondrous descriptions of the Grail as a cauldron, a magical horn of plenty, or a cornucopia, most notably in Celtic lore. Other early portrayals simply call it the *Graal,* but say very little else specifically about it.[10] The ancient Celtic cauldron was certainly symbolic of an early Grail, e.g., the magical cauldron of Cerridwen; the Welsh cauldron of Annwn, which could magically revive the dead; or the healing cauldron of regeneration of the Dagda, the mythical god and chief of the ancient tribe of the Tuatha de Danaan in the Old Irish sagas. The

Mid-13th century medieval graffiti carving of Chalice at Husborne Crawley church, Bedfordshire. (Simon Brighton)

theme of a magical Grail-like vessel or cauldron occurs in other world folklore as well.

Early pagan cup or magical vessel imagery was later Christianized in forms such as the cup associated with the supernatural blood of Christ. Since the Grail could take many forms in medieval sources, there are a number of worldwide contenders for what may be "the" original Grail chalice: the Valencia chalice in Spain; the emerald Genoa cup; the Antioch chalice; and, in Britain, a couple examples are the Nanteos cup, the dish kept at Chalice Well in Glastonbury, or the bronze "Glastonbury Bowl" in the Taunton Museum.

Grail as modern-day harvest cornucopia. (Simon Brighton)

The Rosslyn Chapel

The 15th-century Rosslyn Chapel, near Edinburgh, Scotland, with its intricate stone carvings has long been considered a "chapel of the Grail." (See Chapter 10.) Rosslyn has a carving of Melchizedek holding a cup. It is located near the stained glass window up to the right as one enters the crypt, the oldest part of the chapel.[11] There is a similar sculpture of Melchizedek on the north porch of Chartres cathedral, where he is portrayed holding a chalice with a cubic stone. Another site that feature Grail-as-stone imagery is the ancient Men-on-Tol quoit in Cornwall.

Mary of Guise—Queen Regent of Scotland and mother of Mary, Queen of Scots—wrote a rather enigmatic letter to Lord William St. Clair of Rosslyn in 1546. She referred to being shown "a great secret at Rosslyn." Some maintain that the underground crypt at Rosslyn—which has not yet been officially excavated—may include not only the expected knights in effigy of the noble St. Clair family, but possibly other artifacts or relics. Rosslyn has long been imagined to be a home to a Grail.[12] The two heart stone carvings, unexpectedly discovered on the roof during a major restoration in 2012 after being hidden for centuries, may be seen as a timely, symbolic "return of the Grail" as heart and spirit for our modern-day era. But unless and until an official excavation is done and the results verified by experts and the family, speculation will continue regarding this interesting Scottish site.

Traditional Grail Qualities

In the medieval Grail stories, the Grail cup has special powers and is often surrounded by a blindingly brilliant *light*. It can summon worthy seekers into its presence, bestow on certain individuals immortality, protection from evil, and healing and restorative gifts. The light of the Grail has been displayed in paintings and other works of visual art. One example is the beautiful Aragon Pyrenees frescoes of Taull, now housed in the National Art Museum of Catalonia. Here Mary holds up a Grail-like bowl from which shine many supernatural, brilliant rays of light—similar to descriptions of the Ark of the Covenant and the extraordinary spiritual light it emits.

Men-an-Tol quoit, Cornwall. (Simon Brighton)

In earlier pagan times, the cauldron or vessel of nourishment was viewed as representative of the living energy of the Goddess and the feminine—a celebration of life itself and its myriad transformations. Still other accounts in folklore around the world envision the Grail as a sacred well, lake, or spring. The Grail has been associated with the mystical Lady of the Lake, custodian of Excalibur and Grail teachings, and her maidens in the Arthurian tales. The search for spiritual and material transformation was a theme for medieval alchemists. The iconography of alchemical laboratories featured various vessels and equipment, including what is today known as the *bain-marie,* a water vessel used in cooking

As we can see, a great number of legends, pagan and Christian, describe the Grail as a cup, vessel, or cauldron. Drinking from the cauldron or chalice in the Grail legends often creates great changes in the character of the seeker—and this after he or she has already been 'tested' with trials and tribulations for some time before finally arriving at the Grail chapel for the final test.

Linga-yoni in the shape of the Grail on the floor of the inner shrine of the Candi Sukuh Temple in Indonesia. *(Tantric Temples: Eros and Magic in Java)*

The Precious Blood

Relics of the Grail described as Precious Blood come from several sources in medieval manuscripts, legends, saint's lives, and older oral traditions. The best known of the Holy Blood memes associated with the Grail is the blood said to have been collected at the Crucifixion by Joseph of Arimathea, Nicodemus, Mary Magdalene, or Longinus, depending on which version you read.

Another school of thought connects the Grail with the bloodline of Jesus. Here he is said to have married and had children with Mary Magdalene. The Precious Blood and the Grail are seen to be the descendants of a Grail family. The womb of Mary Magdalene is thus the vessel of the Grail and the Precious Blood. Some have interpreted the Grail as "the vine," linking the bloodline of Jesus to the early medieval Merovingian kings of France—an idea further popularized in the late 20th century.

OPPOSITE: Corbel featuring a toasting couple with two Grails, Basilica of St Marie Madeleine, Vezeley. (Jane May)

Another medieval portrayal of the Grail as Precious Blood occurs in descriptions of some pilgrimage centers, where the bread and wine of the Eucharist are said to have spontaneously turned into the literal body and blood of Christ. One of the most

The Roman baths steaming pool at Bath, England (Aquae Sulis), originally built by the Romans in honor of the goddess Minerva. (Simon Brighton)

Joseph of Arimathea holding chalice, stained glass window panel, far left, at the Church of St John, Glastonbury

fascinating medieval pilgrimage sites is the beautiful basilica of Bruges in Belgium, where there is a reliquary of the Holy Blood as well as a number of other most interesting stone carvings relating to the Grail.

The Precious Blood has also been said to be a mysterious "blood of unknown provenance"—supernatural, with miracles involving drops of blood suddenly appearing on the statues of saints. The Precious Blood cult was very popular in the early Middle Ages. Cathedrals and chapels that claimed to have a vial of the Precious Blood were and are popular places of pilgrimage. Even today, scientific research and debate continues about dating blood particles believed to be found on the famous Shroud of Turin and similar relics.

What is also becoming much more widely acknowledged is that the modern increase in pilgrimages to Black Madonna shrines also occurred during the High Middle Ages. And some of these Black Madonna sites included shrines of Precious Blood relics. St. Bernard of Clairvaux was greatly devoted to the Virgin Mary. (Chapter 1 describes his key role in helping the Knights Templar Order gain the necessary official papal credibility in 1128.) Bernard preached the Second Crusade from the magnificent Basilica of Vezelay, long revered as a key center for Mary Magdalene. Vezelay also features Grail-related carvings.

The Sword, Lance, and Spear of Destiny

Accounts of the power of, and quest for, a magical sword, lance or spear go far back in human history. Ancient Celtic myth describes the magical spear of Lugh, for example, and legends abound even today about the alleged historical "Spear of Destiny."[13] In some medieval Arthurian Grail sources, a bleeding white lance or spear is described as accompanying the Grail procession, the weapon that deeply wounded the Fisher King, resulting in a tragic Wasteland for the kingdom. And who can forget the scene where the gallant Sir Gawain encountered the mysterious broken sword in the Chapel of the Black Hand?[14]

In other accounts of the Grail, the sword relic is identified with the spear of Longinus—the Roman centurion, who pierced the side of Christ on the cross. This spear, the "Spear of Destiny," is a relic which various rulers in history have claimed to possess or seek—for good or ill. The spear of Longinus was made by "Phineas, grandson of Aaron, according to a legend, admittedly transmitted by the Gnostic Ephrem the Syrian. Saul, in his madness, hurled it at David, and it was later used by Longinus to pierce the side of Christ and release blood and water into the Grail."[15]

The cult of the spear took especial hold during the High Middle Ages. Relics attached to the Grail stories are often credited with unique powers that call for unique discernment.[16] The spear of Longinus was believed to have been discovered at Antioch during the First Crusade. A monk named Bartholomew had a vision in 1098 as to its whereabouts. Thereafter:

> It passed for a time into the hands of the Count of Toulouse. This was presumably the relic discovered by St. Helena, mother of the Emperor Constantine, along with the True Cross and other instruments of the Passion. The Lance was for a time in the possession of the Emperor of the East in Constantinople, who pawned the head, later redeemed it and sent it to St. Louis IX of France. The rest of the Lance remained in Constantinople until the fall of the city in 1453, when it passed to Sultan Mohammed II. His son, Bajazet, gave it to the Grand Master of the Knights of St. John of Jerusalem in exchange for certain favours. The Grand Master, in turn, gave it to the Pope. It was received with rejoicing in Rome, in 1492 and placed in St. Peter's. [17]

Melchizedek holding Grail chalice, with cubic stone in center, at Chartres. (Karen Ralls)

Yet another "spear of destiny" is the one that had belonged to St. Maurice, the leader of the Theban legion in the third century. The legion consisted primarily of Egyptian Gnostic Christians stationed in what is now Switzerland. When they refused to follow Roman emperor Maximian's dictates, which included orders to kill all Celtic Christians on the site, they were ruthlessly slain to a man. Emperor Maximian himself is said to have taken the spear from the dying Maurice. It has remained a relic of interest ever since.[18]

The theme of a sword associated with the Grail is also seen in the sword of Parzival, which had a sparkling ruby hilt; in Tristan's sacred sword; and, most famously, with Excalibur, the sword of King Arthur.

OPPOSITE: Shield depicting Chalice, sword, and axe, at the early 12th century round Church of the Holy Sepulchre, Northampton. (Simon Brighton)

But the Grail cup—and a sword or a spear—were often used together in ancient times—the chalice *and* the blade. It is no wonder that many tales speak of both potent magical icons in the same story.

The Grail as a stone

Wolfram identifies the Grail in *Parzival* as a luminous stone. "A stone of the purest kind ... called *lapsit exillas* ... There never was human so ill that if he one day sees the stone, he cannot die within the week that follows ... and though he should see the stone for two hundred years [his appearance] will never change, save that perhaps his hair might turn grey."[19] The term *lapsit exillas* can be translated as either "stone from Heaven" or as a "stone from exile," probably a meteorite. Later, Wolfram says the Grail stone is an emerald that fell from the crown of Lucifer during the war in Heaven, i.e., a gemstone that continued to emanate power and wisdom on the earth.

Trevrizent, the hermit, tells Parzival that the special Grail guardians, the *Templeisen,* live at the Grail castle and *exist by this stone alone.* The Grail knights are not only nourished by this brilliant stone source, but it sustains them and bestows upon them perpetual youth and the power of healing. Wolfram's tale was written about 1205 during the height of the Templar Order's power and influence. (It was also the time of the troubadours.) But Wolfram's Templars are portrayed as having a turtle dove as the symbol on their shields, i.e., they were depicted as peaceful knights rather than warlike crusaders.[20]

When Parzival comes to the hermit's house, he seems totally unfamiliar with Christian customs. Trevrizent shows him the Grail chapel and says that he happened to arrive on a special day—Good Friday—when, each year, a dove descends from Heaven and puts a wafer on the *lapsit exillas.* This annual miracle empowers the sacred stone.

Various writers have suggested that the Grail as a stone refers to the famed philosopher's stone, *lapis elixir,* mentioned in alchemical writings. Wolfram's stone could also have a "phoenix" connotation, i.e., deriving from the legendary *lapis exilii,* the alchemical Stone of Death and Rebirth. He tells us that a phoenix bird sits on the luminous stone and is burned to ashes and reborn

At Launceston, Cornwall, in the Church of St. Thomas—a geometric baptismal font with various geometric carvings on it, including a labyrinth with a cross in the center and a pentagram. (Simon Brighton)

there—again symbolizing the profound inner transformation of the Grail seeker.

The quest for the mysterious eastern king Prester John

Letters about a fascinating-but-elusive king, "Prester John," circulated around Europe from the 12th through the 17th centuries, resulting in a lingering myth of epic proportions. The first letter, in 1165, was addressed to none other than the Byzantine emperor. The enthusiasm it created was extraordinary.

Legends claimed that this mysterious Christian king would assist the West against the infidels in their midst, offering help at a difficult time. The search for Prester John's realm was taken seriously by kings and nobles, becoming a near obsession for years. He was described as a descendant of the ancient Magi, and a most generous and wise ruler. He was said to possess Grail-like relics and treasures such as gems, jewels, the fountain of youth, and the Gates of Alexander. Prester John's magnificent kingdom was said to border on earth's paradise itself.[21] His famed magic scrying mirror—through which every province in his kingdom could be seen—was the fabled original from which later medieval and Renaissance "speculum literature" was derived.

But where, exactly, was his extraordinary kingdom? Everyone wanted to know. Feverish efforts by the rulers of Western

Europe to find it were undertaken and even the Pope made inquiries. At first, Prester John's kingdom was imagined to reside in India, Ethiopia, or somewhere in central Asia.[22] As the legend grew after the Mongol invasions of the West, the story placed Prester John mostly in the Orient.

Today, the only memorial to this powerful mythical king exists in Port Elizabeth, South Africa, in the eastern Cape province, with a commemorative statue in his honor.

Prester John's kingdom is symbolic of the penultimate mythical Quest, spurring the imaginations and dreams of generations of explorers. Yet it is as elusive as ever, which only adds to its enduring allure.

Prester John memorial, close-up view, Port Elizabeth, South Africa. (Phil Rademan)

The Grail as sacred Geometry

In some traditions, visual art, and modern-day interpretations, the "Grail" is understood as relating to sacred geometry, i.e. with comparisons made to proportion, number, geometric shape and form. While many books and articles have been written about sacred geometry from a number of perspectives, for our purposes, here are a few examples of Grail and geometry-related themes.

We have mentioned the Grail as a symbol of the universal Divine Feminine, a celebration of the Goddess. The iconographic representation of the Grail as the Goddess is discussed by British author Gareth Knight. He writes that in the Rosicrucian alchemical manuscript *The Chymical Wedding of Christian Rosencreutz,* "The Feminine Principle appears in an underground tomb, as the sleeping form of … Venus … the Isis of Nature, or God-head as expressed in manifestation as a power center of cosmic feminine force …"[23]

One of the major medieval Grail legends with feminine personages features the enigmatic Melusine, the powerful "Lady of Light," married to Count Raymond of Poitou. She who shape-shifts back into a mermaid one day a week—half-serpent, half-human, a medieval example of a fish-tailed Aphrodite. Her ancient shrine is at Lusignan, France.

Medieval visual depictions of the Grail and feminine symbolism would include envisioning the Grail as a rose, a downward-pointing triangle, the almond-shaped geometric Vesica Pisces design, or as found embedded in various designs in cathe-

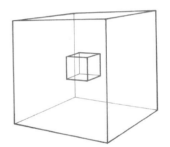

The Grail as a cubic Jerusalem.

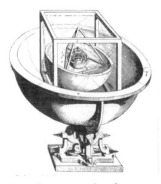

Another example of a geometric depiction of a Grail as cubic in form.

85

A series of Platonic Solids. (James Wasserman, from *Pythagoras: His Life and Teachings*)

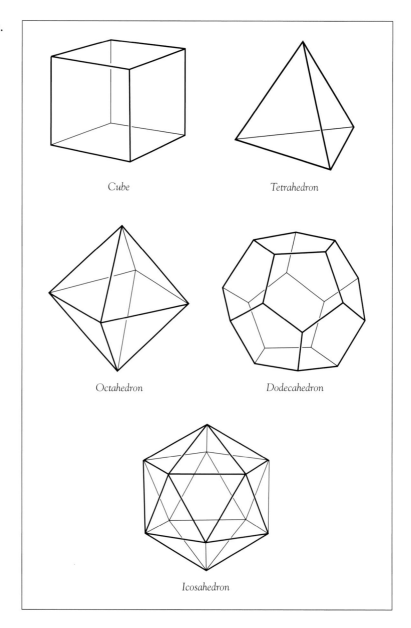

Cube

Tetrahedron

Octahedron

Dodecahedron

Icosahedron

dral stained glass windows and wooden misericord carvings in ancient buildings. The variations are endless.

Grail as relating to the constellations and stars

In *Parzival*, Wolfram von Eschenbach said that the source for his Grail story was a mysterious adept in Spain named Flegetanis, who said that the Grail was in the stars. Some of the greatest of Grail heros, such as Sir Gawain, whose energies wax and peak at noon, also have connections with the sun or stars.[24] For many,

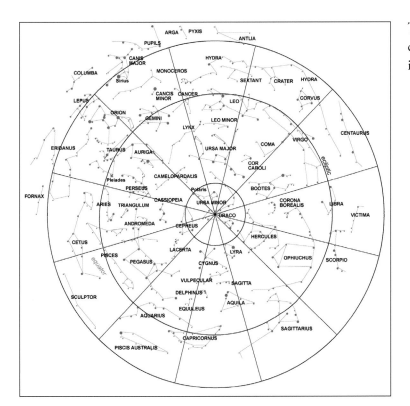

This map of the constellations is a Grail all its own. (Peter Dawkins)

such starry wisdom means introducing topics like the precession of the Equinoxes, planets, stars, and other celestial phenomena in relation to the overall theme of the Grail. For others, it implies an inner dimension of discovering the interior heavens though meditation and spiritual practices. The ancients had a much greater appreciation and awareness of the universe and night sky—its wisdom and mysteries—than we do today.

The Grail and severed head imagery

The severed head theme is fairly common in early Celtic portrayals, as well as in the famous Arthurian Grail romances where the procession at the Grail chapel includes a maiden carrying a severed head on a platter. Christian examples of the severed head motif would include the Veil of Veronica and the Mandylion relics. (The Mandylion relic is believed to be a cloth from the tomb of Jesus with an image of a head. There are several contenders today claiming to be the cloth, a Grail-related relic. This cloth differs from a shroud, such as the Shroud of Turin, a full-length cloth depicting both the head and body of Christ. As an aside, some traditions equate the Shroud of Turin and the Mandylion cloth.)

The Land as the Grail

Another symbolic understanding of the Grail is that it represents the land itself. The sovereignty of the land—its history, lore, and encoded memories of the past remind us of a central Grail teaching: "the King and the Land are one." In ancient tales, the sacred marriage of a male ruler or king could only take place with the blessing of Sovereignty, the Feminine. Their divine unity produced the flowering of society.[25]

Words alone can never convey the mysterious spiritual power and beauty of the land itself and certain sacred sites within it. People believe such terrene energy centers serve as gateways to a higher consciousness.

At the same time that modern-day civilization is more removed from the earth than ever before, a greater appreciation of the land is emerging in many quarters. The Earth itself is perceived by many modern seekers as a healing "Grail" through which humanity may be redeemed. As the medieval Grail romances and others today might inquire: can we restore the "Wasteland"? Are we truly ready to take responsibility?

Books, films, Byrne-Jones tapestries, and Broadway shows have continued to immortalize the Grail in popular formats in modern times. Many poets

Bridge over the river Tamar, Cornwall.
Photo by Simon Brighton

and famous writers of literature have written about the Grail, including Tennyson and T.S. Eliot.

Perennial interest in the Grail is here to stay; its history and myth continuing to evolve and inspire. The current interest in the Grail is no random occurrence: "it is the acknowledgement of a deep desire to find meaning in our existence … at no time in history has this been more significant …"[26] For many, connecting with the Grail and the Quest offers a genuine wellspring of inner renewal, a beacon for a better world. But it comes at a price. The primary task of the spiritual seeker is to take responsibility for his or her own Quest. The Grail, now as always, remains enigmatically elusive, refusing to be pinned down or limited by mere human understanding, indeed, as all higher Mysteries should be.

CHAPTER 5

THE CATHARS

Historical Overview

The Cathars of the Languedoc were dualist heretics who probably presented the greatest doctrinal challenge faced by the Catholic Church in the twelfth and thirteenth centuries. The word "Cathar" comes from the Greek *katharos*, meaning "pure." The Cathars professed a philosophy of neo-Manichaean dualism—a belief that that there are ultimately two principles, one good and one evil, and that this world, the material world, is evil. Similar views were held in the Balkans and the Middle East by the medieval religious sects of the Paulicians and Bogomils with whom the Cathars were closely connected.

The Fourth Municipal Seal of Toulouse showing the Chateau Narbonnaise (dexter) and the Jacobins (sinister). (Castles and Manor Houses website)

Organization and Beliefs

The Cathars were dissident, pacifist Christians, who, when called before the Inquisition, spoke of their "Church of Love." As gnostic dualists, they would not accept the orthodox position of Rome that an omnipotent and eternal God could possibly have been responsible for the material world of matter. They believed this world, the earth. was the product of an evil creator. In their view, such a Creator was "either a being fallen from the perfection of Heaven who had seduced a proportion of the angelic souls there and then entrapped them in matter, or, he was a co-eternal power, quite independent of the Good God of the spirit. The only release for those souls encased in the material prison of the body was through the Cathar ceremony of the *consolamentum*, which was the means by which they could return to their guardian spirits in Heaven."[1] They did not believe in a Last Judgement, maintaining instead that this material world would end only when the last of the angelic souls had finally been released from it. They believed in reincarnation and that souls could take many lifetimes to reach perfection before their final release.

Because the material world was evil, Man was an alien sojourner. The main aim of Man was to free his spirit—which was in its nature good—and restore it with God. Towards that end, like many living a devout monastic life, they fasted, prayed, and meditated frequently, exalted celibacy, and shunned all luxury and material possessions. They were vegetarians although they ate fish. The Cathars were known to be successful healers and doctors, practiced the laying on of hands, and had a great store of herbal knowledge.[2] They also had their own system of hospitals and social care. Both girls and boys had equal access to education.

Catharism, the troubadours, and courtly love grew together in the same overall cultural climate of the Languedoc—a climate that placed a high value on the feminine and women. This was a relative rarity in medieval times and contrasted with the policies of the Church of Rome. Both the Cathars and the troubadours were in agreement that true love—from the soul—purified from the false love associated with earthly marriage.

It is not surprising that the Cathars would eventually collide with the Church once their movement grew large enough and obtained more influence, respect, and wealth. Nearly everyone in the Languedoc, including a number of Catholics, agreed that the Cathars' behavior merited their "nickname" (so to speak), "the Good Men" (or "Good Women"). The Cathar clergy were much admired as they prayed, taught, healed, and traveled around the countryside.

Catharism represented a near-total opposition to many of the primary beliefs and dogmas of the Church of Rome—an institution which they saw as largely having lost its way, gradually succumbing over time to become a bloated, luxury-loving, pompous, and highly corrupt organization. Cathars believed the Roman Church had turned its back on its true spiritual integrity and "sold out" for power and money in this world, the material realm. They were also motivated by a great disdain for what they perceived as a highly corrupt Catholic clergy, a situation noted by others in Europe at the time. For example, in 1145, the highly revered abbot Bernard of Clairvaux had visited the Languedoc to investigate the Cathar heresy. Even he agreed that there was much laxity and a high degree of corruption among some of the Roman clergy, which he utterly despised. Regarding the Cathars themselves, Bernard acknowledged that although one could say they were heretical, "No sermons are more Christian than theirs, and their morals are pure."[3]

Stone Stele—Deodat
Roche Museum, Arques.
(Ani Williams)

Due to their spiritual beliefs, the Cathars simply could not accept orthodox Catholic beliefs regarding the holy Eucharist and the other sacraments of the Church. These implied that Christ would have actually lived on this earth in the flesh, been crucified, and resurrected from this evil, material world. Cathars believed this was something that a divine spiritual being like Christ would never do in the first place. God (i.e. Christ, in the orthodox Christian sense) would never have existed in this material world at all, but only in Heaven. So in addition to refusing the sacraments, the Cathars rejected a fundamental tenet of Catholicism—the Incarnation. Again, a situation where all roads did *not* lead to Rome ...

The Cathar priesthood: the Perfecti and the Believers

The Cathar church was organized into dioceses whose bishops presided over an order of succession consisting of elder and younger "sons," deacons, and their esteemed priesthood, the *perfecti*. It was a popular organization with all levels of society; many supporters of Catharism were drawn from the nobility of the Languedoc, one of the most sophisticated, wealthy and cosmopolitan civilizations in all of Europe.

The *perfecti* were the Cathar elite priesthood. They included both men and women. They attained their spiritual state by a special initiation ceremony called the *consolamentum*.[4] A small minority within the Cathar movement as a whole, the *perfecti* vowed to live lives of exceptional purity, with far stricter standards than those required of the general membership. They traveled in pairs when conducting their ministry in the countryside and were highly dedicated to preaching, conversion, healing, and contemplation.

Prominent noble women, such as the Cathar heroine of the siege of Montsegur, Esclarmonde de Foix, the daughter of Roger-Bernard I, the Count of Foix, were among the devoted *perfecti*. The *perfecti* were generally warmly welcomed by the populace, such was the effect on others of the living example they provided of their sincere dedication to spiritual ideals.

The next level down of the priesthood—officially called *credentes*—were the more numerous but highly devout believers. They were not required to take the stricter vows required of the *perfecti*, but were allowed to more fully integrate into the society around them—marry and have a family, conduct business, and so on. They were usually drawn from the general population and were highly dedicated, assisting the *perfecti* in many ways: for example, by supplying food or shelter for members, or obtaining money or other assistance.

At a later point in their lives, a select few of the believers would eventually be allowed to take the *consolamentum* and become *perfecti*. The Cathars believed that the way to salvation was to be found through the release of the soul from the material prison of the body, so that the soul might rejoin its guardian spirit. The priesthood rejected marriage and had a strict code of celibacy.[5] It followed logically that they should reject a society that they perceived as being primarily based on materialism. With Catharism's celibacy, attitude to marriage, and other policies, the religion was perceived by Rome as being subversive of the entire social order of medieval feudal Christendom. "The interpenetration of church and feudality which characterised the north, and which ensured the subordination of women, was rejected by Catharism for its materialist base … the family with its hierarchy of the wise ensuring good order was of no relevance if one believed in a transmigration of souls in which the sex and social class of the bodies concerned were of no consequence."[6] It would appear there were a number of reasons why the Cathars were targeted by the church with a vengeance, above and beyond mere heretical theological concerns.[7]

A secret heretical network for protection

As many Cathars were forced to become fugitives during the decades of oppression by the Inquisition, the more integrated and often less conspicuous role of the believers was often very important. During these difficult times, providing safety and shelter for fellow Cathars were imperative, so an effective clandestine network inevitably developed. Some believers would transport another believer to a secret hiding place or safe house, away from the prying eyes of the Inquisition and its spies. This clandestine network was evidentially quite extensive, for—as the Inquisitional records tell us—a *perfecti*, "Austorgue, was told by Guillaume Salamon, a deacon of the heretics at Toulouse, of a certain female weaver in Toulouse, who would show her where heretics could stay, and indeed, when Austorgue visited the weaver's house, she was taken through the building to another house in which a *perfecti* was hiding."[8]

As there were many believers, the entire Cathar network available for potential assistance was quite extensive. We know that a number of the Cathar communities had expert craftsmen; Papermaking, for example, was a highly skilled activity. It become even more important because it enabled Cathars to develop secret watermark symbolism incorporated into the paper. Other craftsmen may have used similar methods of concealed visual symbolism to communicate safely with each other and with other heretics. As even orthodox monasteries often used secret hand signals, especially at meal times, it is not altogether inconceivable that the Cathars may have utilized such measures to avoid arrest and ensure their safety when traveling to and from their secret places of worship.

Foix Chateau.
(Ani Williams)

One Cathar craftsperson was sentenced to go on a gruelling pilgrimage in 1241 as punishment for providing two female Cathar heretics with thread, from which they made head-bands, which was forbidden. Similar examples exist in the inquisitional records, and, interestingly, many involved were spinners and weavers.[9] Believers also owned books and scriptures which they safeguarded against the Inquisition.[10]

The participation of women in all levels of Cathar society was very commonplace. This encouraged the authorities to hire female informants. Evidence from 13th century Inquisitional records from the Collection Doat in the Bibliotheque Nationale states, "there is a case of a female spy having been used by the Inquisition."[11] Agents of the Inquisition gave her money to buy food for the heretics and then reveal information about their activities and where they were hiding fugitives.

Hotbed of Heresy: The Languedoc in the 13th century

By 1208, the people in the Languedoc region had been chastised by the Pope for a number of unorthodox beliefs and heretical practices for some years. The tension was growing. However, the Languedoc itself was unique at a time of relative barbarity in much of Europe. By the early 13th century, this area in the south of France had spawned a sophisticated, prosperous, and cultured civilization where philosophy, the arts, courtly love, Hebrew, Greek and other foreign languages were studied, and a policy of definite tolerance of other religions was the norm—a situation quite similar to Byzantium in the east. The Languedoc region had roughly the same basic parameters as the earlier 8th-century Jewish kingdom of Septimania, under the Merovingian leader Guilhelm de Gellone. So it may be no surprise that major kabbalistic schools, such as that at Narbonne or Lunel, became centers of learning and cultural stimulation at the time of the Cathars. Interchanges occurred between Christians, Jews, Muslims, and other heretics in the area, where creative discourse and learning were the rule—not religious warfare. Troubadours spawned a culture of greater appreciation of music, poetry and storytelling.

The powerful Counts of Toulouse and the house of Trencavel especially supported the Cathars, as did others in the Languedoc and Spain. The Languedoc region was culturally more connected with Catalonia than it was with the rest of France—something that did not sit well with either the Church or the French crown. International trade was growing in the region as well. As the great wealth, culture, and power of the Languedoc continued to blossom and flourish, the envy of the far less civilized northern barons increased. In addition to the Cathars' perceived religious threat to the papacy, a potentially dangerous political powder keg was in place. Merchants in the region, who were often Cathar supporters, had grown weary of various trading restrictions enforced by the Church—such as what could or could not be sold, issues of increased charges and/or taxation, and the like. In time, the property, wealth and imposing castles of the wealthy and powerful lords of the Languedoc became definitive targets. As an example, the Cathar stronghold of Cabaret castle was specifically labeled "a fountain of heresy." Its powerful lord, Pierre-Roger, was dubbed "a veteran of evil days."[12]

Battle lines were forming within church circles about what to do about the Cathars. Although some churchmen were supportive, or at least tolerant, of Cathars, others were far less so. Prominent leaders, such as the formidable abbess Hildegard of

Arques Chateau.
(Ani Williams)

Bingen, composed rather stern sermons against the Cathars quite early on, especially following the 1163 burning of a group of heretics in Cologne. Other heretics, such as those sentenced to the stake in Vezelay, reportedly espoused Cathar-type beliefs by their rejection of the traditional sacraments. A group of dissidents was persecuted in Rheims around 1176–80, specifically because their ideas were said to far too clearly resemble those of the Cathars.[13] So the large and growing Cathar movement was increasingly seen as a heretical "cancer" that must be destroyed to avoid further infecting the Church as a whole and spreading its heresies further afield.

The situation in the Languedoc was a combustible cocktail. Various crusades were preached against the Cathars. At first, these calls were of no avail. Cathars were peaceful and continued to grow more popular and obtain more support, attracting a large following by the 13th century. Finally, the Inquisition was launched to exterminate them completely—culminating in a bloody and ruthless crusade.

Charges against the Cathars

Many of the charges leveled against heretics such as the Cathars in the first half of the thirteenth century—or variants of them— were similar to those later used during the European witchcraft trials from the thirteenth through seventeenth centuries. Most were focused on religious matters.

Some of the accusations had a highly sexual emphasis, as was the case with the Templars, witches, and others. The celibate Dominican inquisitors seemed to have had an unusual degree of interest in what they ascertained were "unnatural sexual practices" of the Cathars in certain areas of the Languedoc. Some scholars surmise that married Cathar believers (not the strictly celibate *perfecti* priesthood) may have devised a form of birth control, possibly including the use of medical herbs. In *European Witch Trials,* Professor Richard Kieckhefer comments that charges of sexual libertinage and unconventional sexual behavior were the norm for the Inquisition.[14]

There were many other heresy-related trials throughout Europe in medieval times. The French Cathar persecution was but one example of a wider phenomenon.[15] Kieckhefer also asso-

ciates the Albigensian Crusade with the political anxieties of the Capetien dynasty. It had held power in France since the tenth century, and due to a changing political situation, felt their future was threatened.

Montsegur, the famous hilltop citadel of the Cathars: looking outward at the scenic view below. (Simon Brighton)

A series of crusades against the Cathars

What provided the trigger for the brutal Cathar persecutions was an incident in 1208. Pierre de Castelnau, the Papal Legate to the Languedoc, was murdered by anticlerical assassins who were *not* Cathars. However, in spite of no evidence, seeing a good excuse to persecute the Cathars, the Church placed the blame for his murder squarely on their shoulders. Pope Innocent III threw down the gauntlet and immediately ordered a Crusade.

In 1209, the Albigensian Crusade was officially launched for the express purpose of eliminating the Cathar heresy. An army of at least 30,000 northern crusaders was quickly assembled under the leadership of Simon de Montfort, descending like a swarm of hornets upon the Languedoc. What motivated such numbers to immediately take up arms and murder their fellow Christians in the name of Christ? Quite simply, the Pope had made northern French noblemen an offer many could not refuse—if they joined the crusade to exterminate the Cathars, they would be given the valuable lands and luxurious goods of their victims. In addition, since the Cathars had been described by the Pope as worse than the Muslim infidel, this "sacred war" against the heretics was deemed holy, so spiritual benefits accrued. All who took part in the crusade were to be protected by the papacy, freed from the burden of paying interest on their debts, exempt from the courts, and granted full absolution from their sins. The price? One merely had to participate for a minimum of forty days.

Papal Inquisition and posthumous burning

By 1233, the formal papal Inquisition proceedings against the Cathars began. Inquisitional procedures involved committees, many of them staffed by the Dominicans, coming into local communities and setting up operations for a period of years. The Inquisitors often became a rather permanent, notorious fixture in the community—interrogating, imprisoning, and torturing the accused. A climate of fear, mistrust of one's neighbors, and a collective terror gripped the region.

During this period, like many unrepentant heretics, Cathars were burned at the stake. The initial Dominican emphasis was on burning heretics alive *and* dead, i.e, adopting a policy of posthumous burning, such as those that occurred in the village of Albi in 1234.[16] A heretic was never allowed to be buried on consecrated Christian ground, so if such a burial were discovered, the body would be exhumed and burned. Furthermore, all a heretic's property would be confiscated, ensuring that entire families would be destroyed.

The siege of Beziers—22 July 1209

On July 22, 1209, the feast day of St. Mary Magdalene, the strategically-located city of *Beziers* was pillaged and attacked with brutal ferocity by about twenty thousand northern nobles and other adventurers. The destruction of Beziers was the first major

military onslaught on a Languedoc city with a large number of Cathar residents. The army arrived enmasse, led by commander Simon de Montfort. No one was spared. The words of the Papal Legate Arnald-Amaury continue to live in infamy, "Kill them all. God will recognize His own."[17] Over 15,000 men, women, and children were slaughtered at Beziers. Arnald-Amaury victoriously gloated afterwards in a letter to the Pope that "neither age, nor sex, nor status had been spared."[18] If that were not enough, the fear and terror resulting from this single incident reverberated throughout the entire Languedoc. A series of attacks on other major Cathar castles would follow in the months and years ahead. Cathars fled for their lives into the hills, or, if they were fortunate, obtained shelter in a Cathar castle that had not yet been attacked.

The next target after Beziers was the beautiful port city of *Narbonne*, home of many Cathars and an eminent and sizable Jewish community. Both groups knew what awaited them after the example of Beziers. They strategically offered to surrender

Cathar Memorial—Minerve. A memorial with dove symbolism to commemorate the Cathar martyrs burned alive by the Abbot Arnaud-Armaury and Simon de Montfort. It is located at the only part of the Cathar castle left standing at Minerve. Carved on the monument are the simple words in Occitan: "Als Catars": To the Cathars. (Ani Williams)

Montsegur: view of
interior of fortress.
(Simon Brighton)

rather than face certain slaughter as they were totally outnum-
bered by the crusaders.

By 15 August 1209, the city and fortress of *Carcassonne* was
attacked. After they finally surrendered, crusader commander
Simon de Montfort declared himself Viscount of Carcassonne.

Chateau de Minerve - 22 July 1210

By July of 1210, the chateau of Minerve became a target. It was
here that many Cathars had fled, seeking refuge after the hor-
rific massacre of Beziers the previous summer. Located in the
Languedoc-Roussillon region of southern France, the ancient hilltop village was named for its beautiful temple to the goddess of
Wisdom, Minerva, that had once stood here. In 1210, it was the
site of a brutal, ten-week siege by Simon de Montfort's army, after
which some 180 Cathars were burned to death at the insistence

The Roman goddess Minerva, inspirer and protector of wisdom, arts, business, and defense. (Simon Brighton)

of Church leaders. The picturesque village of Minerve is a favorite Cathar pilgrimage site to this day.

Minerve is located above the River Cesse. Like other Cathar fortresses, the village was highly protected, located at the top of an isolated hilltop. But this did not stop the stormtroopers of de Montfort's army. They set up four catapults around the village. After they specifically targeted the town's water supply, Viscount Guilhem of Minerve and his entourage could not hold out for long. Guilhem was forced to negotiate. Minerve was surrendered to the Crusaders on 22 July 1210—again, on the feast day of St. Mary Magdalene.[19] Guilhem saved the villagers but he could not save the Cathars who had taken refuge in the town.

Minerve is especially known today for its impressive memorial to the courageous Cathar martyrs who were burned alive here by the Abbot Arnaud-Amaury and Simon de Montfort. The memorial was placed at the last remaining medieval Cathar castle ruins still standing in the town. Note the dove symbolism in the photo. It commemorates the Cathar "Church of Love" and the spiritual, peace-loving values of the 180 martyrs, who nobly went to their certain deaths in the flames. Eight hundred years later, residents and supporters of the medieval Cathar martyrs at Minerve installed another memorial stone to their ancestors at this site in July 2010, further preserving the memory of the Cathars for all posterity. That which is remembered, lives.

Carcassonne fortress, long range view. (Simon Brighton)

Cathar communities all over the Languedoc were terrified. Those who could fled for shelter. Others were arrested or hanged. By 1213, King Peter II of Aragon tried desperately to intervene on the Cathars' behalf; however, his army was crushingly defeated by the crusaders at the Battle of Muret. King Peter was himself killed.

DEATH OF SIMON DE MONTFORT AT NARBONNAISE (1218)

After Muret, the unruly hoard of crusaders headed for Toulouse, home of the powerful Counts of Toulouse, longtime Cathar sponsors. Here, the Château Narbonnaise, the prestigious citadel of the Counts of Toulouse for generations, was besieged for nine months.[20] It withstood the onslaught as long as possible, but in due course surrendered under treaty. The chateau was again the site of battle when Raymond IV of Toulouse re-entered Toulouse on 12 September 1217 to the tumultuous cheers of the population. He trapped de Montfort's wife and family within the Château Narbonnaise. Commander Simon de Montfort suffered a painful death here the following year. He besieged Toulouse for a third time and was struck by a piece of falling masonry from a catapult above.[21]

THE BRUTAL SIEGE OF MONTSEGUR (1244)

Probably the most famous siege of the Albigensian Crusade was of the formidable fortress of Montsegur. Below its high, craggy hilltop lies the "Field of the Burned" meadow. The information plaque standing there commemorates the brutal event that took place over 700 years ago. On 16 March, 1244, after a determined and courageous standoff, 205 Cathars were burned alive on the site, refusing to surrender and renounce their creed—voluntarily accepting death.

A lengthy and complex process of negotiations had taken place earlier between the Cathars and the Crusader army, a topic that has been addressed in a number of books. The Church and the crusaders believed the Cathars possessed a treasure(s), relics, or precious artifacts. Was it something of a highly spiritual, magical, or esoteric nature? In January 1244, two Cathar *perfecti* were known to have escaped from Montségur with what is generally considered to have been the monetary treasure of the Cathars, which they may have hidden in the complex system of caves nearby But the legendary Cathar treasure—whatever it may have been—has never been located—or if it was, has never been publicly acknowledged. On 16 March 1244, after the surrender, historians know that four other Cathar *perfecti*—who had remained hidden in the ruins while the other Cathars were being burned— somehow managed to escape with other object(s) of an unknown nature. Again, circumstances are unclear as to what was taken away, when it was removed, and where it may have been hidden. The circumstances surrounding the siege of Montsegur are an enduring "mystery of history." It is one that historians, archaeologists, and serious esoteric researchers continue to discuss.

Mysteries of Montségur

Here are some of the questions surrounding the fall of Montségur. It has never been clear why Montségur surrendered precisely when it did; nor why the specific terms of surrender were so lenient (at first); nor why the Cathars, under such trying circumstances, had asked for, and been given, a two-week break at a very specific point during the negotiations. It is widely believed they held a religious ritual that was crucial to them for some purpose. This

Montsegur: View of
interior archway ruin.
(Simon Brighton)

request was granted by the church fairly quickly. Why? It was an action never considered at the sieges of other Cathar strongholds.

There has been, and undoubtedly will continue to be, much speculation as to exactly what treasure(s) the Cathars may have possessed. If they did possess a treasure, what was its nature? Did it consist of material artifacts, ritual or sacred relics, a book such as their own special version of the Gospel of John, or something else of a spiritual nature? Was the reputed Cathar treasure of such interest to the Church that it was willing to negotiate more flexible terms than would normally be the case?

Despite this mysterious eleventh hour interlude, the Cathars who had survived the long-term siege, utterly refused to back down from their faith and principles. They willingly chose to go to the flames rather than recant. Some of the crusaders were so impressed by this display of spiritual strength and purity, they themselves converted to Catharism. History awaits more clarification about this most intriguing and disturbing incident of 1244.

Today, visitors can still see the ruins of Montsegur and walk up the steep incline to view the Cathar memorial and its cross on the hilltop summit, taking in the stunning views of the landscape. The simple stele memorial imitates an ancient Cathar marker. It was erected in 1960. The upper encircled solar-style cross is a traditional Cathar symbol; the lower cross is the heraldic cross of the county of Toulouse.[22] The Puivert Museum at Arques also has a Cathar cross stele on display in its interesting collection.

Cathar Bible—Rituel Cathare de Lyon, Bibliotheque de Lyon— Deodat Roche Museum, Arques. (Ani Williams).

CASTLE QUERIBUS: THE "LAST CATHAR FORTRESS" (1255)

After the fall of Montsegur, the defeat of remaining Cathar fortresses would follow. The very last, official fortress that managed to hold out against the Inquisition was at Queribus in the Corbieres region of the Languedoc. We do not know for certain what happened in the siege of 1255. However, its determined owner, Oliver Termes, did manage to save the life of Chabert of Barbera, his Cathar co-lord, through careful negotiation. Some of the fugitive Cathars who had been sheltered here for some time also escaped.[23] Yet, after the demise of Queribus, Catharism was largely finished in an official sense. Cathar survivors fled to the mountains or caves for safety. Some researchers maintain that the survivors of Queribus, seeking anonymity after such trauma, may have fled to northern Italy to seek the company of other Cathars and fellow dualists such as the Waldensians.[24]

PEYREPERTUSE CASTLE AND THE "FIVE SONS" OF CARCASSONNE

Peyrepertuse is a stunning ruined fortress and former Cathar citadel, located in the French Pyrénées in the Aude. The castle is one of the famous "Five Sons of Carcassonne," which include Peyrepertuse, Queribus, Termes, Aguilar, and Puilaurens. These castles were strategically placed to defend the new French border against the Spanish. They were associated with the Counts of Barcelona and later the kings of Aragon.[25] Built in the 11th century, Peyrepertuse is an example of a Cathar citadel that was never subjected to an attack during the crusades against the Cathars, although it did surrender in May 1217.

Walking down the steep trail of Montsegur, descending from the citadel ruins. (Simon Brighton)

Castle Queribus. (Anneke Koremanns)

Peyrepertuse Castle. (Anneke Koremanns)

The Church of Love—Amor—will rise again

Catharism was a popular and enduring heresy. As we have seen, it took many decades to formally eradicate it from the Languedoc. The last Cathar bishop was killed by Inquisitors in 1321, yet there were small lingering remnants of the Cathar movement reported to have survived in hills or caves as late as the 15th century.

Today, there are Cathar groups and sympathizers in France who continue to honor and preserve the memory of the medieval Cathars. A Cathar community lives in Arques, where the Deodat Roche Museum is located. It preserves interesting artifacts such as the Cathar stone stele. In recent years, the subject of the Cathars has become more popular than ever—a resurrection of interest after some years of dormancy. Diverse strands of Cathar beliefs survive.[26]

Cathar Cross—Puivert Museum. (Ani Williams)

Catharism has provided a focus for a positive sense of local pride and independence in the Languedoc region. Its courageous martyrs offer a universal symbol of nonviolent resistance and spiritual ideals against persecution and near-genocide. The Cathars have often been dubbed the "Church of Love"—Amor—symbolized by the dove; whereas the Inquisition and the medieval Church of Rome—Roma—symbolizes its inverse.

Are we collectively and symbolically entering a time of greater appreciation for spiritual values and cooperation? We are here reminded of the old Languedoc legend that says that since the fall of Montsegur in 1244, "after seven hundred years, the laurel will grow green again," implying that a "greening of the spirit," the renewal of the values of the Church of Love is at hand. At this time in history, in a world largely dominated by fear, war, and environmental destruction, could we be collectively witnessing the symbolic return of some form of Cathar spirituality, like a Phoenix rising from the ashes? Only time will tell. But the memory and courage of the medieval Cathars will endure, yet another illuminating thread in the gnostic tapestry of the ages.

Chapter 6

The Medieval Guilds

Historical Overview

Medieval guild draftsman at work

People marvel today at the beauty of a Gothic cathedral or an exquisite piece of medieval craftsmanship. But who created and built such magnificent works of art? What were the guilds about? A medieval guild (or "gild") was an association of craftsmen or merchants formed for mutual aid and protection, and to further their professional interests. The major examples were the craft guilds and merchant trade guilds; there were also parish guilds associated with cathedrals and local churches.

Merchant guilds

Merchant guilds were associations of nearly all the merchants in a particular town or city, whether they were local or long-distance traders, wholesale or retail sellers. A modern-day analogy might be a local Chamber of Commerce. By the 13th century, as medieval towns rapidly grew, the merchant guilds began to be officially recognized by many town governments. Guild members often included the wealthiest and most influential citizens. In the larger towns, a beautifully designed Guildhall might be provided by the merchants' guilds, where meetings and other events would take place.

The merchant guilds were intimately involved in regulating and protecting their members' business interests—both out-of-town trade and local commerce—ensuring that they or their ships and wagons would not be attacked or their products stolen or endangered when travelling abroad. Major ports, such as Venice, became key European crossroads. Here guild members from different countries would end up together in the same trading environment, resulting in great competition between them.

To illustrate the lengths to which some merchant guilds would go to protect their members, employees, secrets and goods, here is a rather amusing-but-true account about the savvy German traders at Venice. Resorting to what we would call today more elaborate "security measures," they installed bloodhounds on the scene:

Traders had to be able to protect themselves; they formed guilds or leagues; the members took a solemn oath to be true to one another until they returned home safely—or, until death. After making such perilous journeys, traders wanted to rest in peaceful surroundings and they built houses of their own in the important foreign trading centers.[1]

London Guildhall engraving by E. Shirt, after a drawing by Prattent, c. 1805

The German establishment measured about 180 x 100 feet … the same size as the houses with courtyards of the rich boyars. The buildings were surrounded by a high stockade of wooden stakes. It had only one gate, which was shut at night by the watchman. Bloodhounds were used to keep 'friends' at a safe distance from the valuable merchandise…. a watchdog began to growl angrily as soon as it heard anyone speaking any language other than German![2]

The medieval guilds eventually controlled the distribution and sale of most food, cloth, and other staple goods; so they gained a powerful monopoly in a given area. Similarly, the Knights Templar were known to be fiercely protectionist of their toll roads and the flow of goods into the prestigious Champagne Fairs.

In Scotland, from at least the reign of David I (1124–1153), and possibly earlier, "Edinburgh had been a royal burgh; that is, its rights, privileges and monopolies were held directly from the crown without any intermediary. Royal burghs had the valuable privilege of trading with foreign ports, which was denied to most lesser burghs of regality or of barony. As a result, the merchants of the burgh dominated the burgess-ship and membership of the Guild."[3] Scottish guilds soon grew in power. They also had specific policies to protect their trade, i.e., one statute stipulated that no one might buy hides, wool or wool-skins for resale nor to cut cloth, "unless he be a guildbrother."[4]

Crafts guilds

The medieval craft guilds were associations of all the artisans and craftsmen in a particular branch of industry. Craft guilds included skilled stonemasons, weavers, bookbinders, painters, bakers, dyers, embroiderers, leatherworkers, hatmakers, vintners, metalworkers (the "Hammermen"), and so on, in every country in Europe.

Edinburgh Hammerman, ritual costume. 1555. (The Brydon Collection)

Although they had roots in earlier times, the medieval craft guilds became much more widespread in the 11th century with the growth of European towns. The word "craft" comes from the old English word "craeft," meaning "skill."[5]

Stonemasons were heavily involved in building the Gothic cathedrals. The Knights Templar had their own "mason brothers" as per Templar Rule number 325, which states that other than chaplains, the mason brothers were the only members of the Order who had specific permission to wear leather gloves to help prevent injury due to the difficult work they did.[6]

It is interesting to realize that our modern concept of an "architect" was not the same as it was in the medieval period: "The word 'architect' was rarely used in the Middle Ages, the usual terms, 'lathomus' or 'caementarius,' indicating his association with quarries and the stone industry. In the eyes of the Church, the one true architect was God Himself, the architect of the universe, and mere men had to define themselves in other terms."[7] However, well before the end of the 11th century, the function of a master mason was becoming differentiated from that of a working mason, "to the point where the master mason had begun to operate and be recognized as a lay architect."[8]

Structure of the Craft Guilds

The skilled craftsmen in a town usually consisted of a number of family workshops in the same neighborhood. The prestigious Masters of these workshops related to one another as equals—specialized experts in their chosen areas. They would train young people, often sharing apprentices between them. The crafts masters would agree as a group to regulate competition among themselves, promoting their own as well as the town's prosperity. Craft guild members would agree on basic policies governing their trade, setting quality standards, and so on. From local beginnings, the early craft guilds gradually developed into larger, more sophisticated networks and associations of highly skilled craftsmen.[9]

Members of the guilds were divided into three grades: *Master, Journeyman,* and *Apprentice.* The master, a very accomplished craftsman, took on apprentices under his tutelage. Usually, these were boys (or girls, in a few cases, depending on the craft) in their teens. In lieu of wages, they were provided with food, clothing, shelter, and an education by the master in exchange for working for a fixed term of service that could last from five to nine years.

After successfully completing stage one, a qualified apprentice became a journeyman, who was allowed to work for one or another master and was paid with wages for his labor. The stonemason Journeymen traveled about far more than members of the other crafts in order to learn their trade with a number of Masters at different building sites. "There is no lack of evidence in the records of almost any period between 1270 and 1530 or later in which masons are described as having lodges where they may work, and 'mansiones' where they can eat and sleep."[10]

One medieval legacy we have inherited today is the famous "Tour de France" cycling race. Its namesake originated from the concept of the guild "tour" that a medieval journeyman would embark on, traveling around to various sites in France to learn his craft: "The *Compagnonnages* of France seem to have developed from the groups of Masons working on the great French cathedrals in the 12th century ... as in England, French Masons traveling from place to place were given lodging by fellow-Masons and helped with money to get them to the next Lodge. It would seem that itinerant Masons, be they French, English, or German, were able to grant and receive benefits only when passwords and signs were given ..."[11]

Once a journeyman could provide proof of his technical and artistic skills by illustrating his finished "masterpiece" for his final exam, he might be permitted to rise higher in the guild and become a Master. If successful, he could set up his own workshop

Old oxen yoke—an example of practical skills and details of the metalworkers projects for use in everyday life. (Simon Brighton)

Milners Patent Brass Safeplate; fine example of modern-day English metalworking. (Simon Brighton)

Misericord of St George
slaying the dragon (1390),
St Botolph's church,
Boston, Lincolnshire.
(Simon Brighton)

and hire and train apprentices on his own. But the path to becoming a master was long and difficult. Masters in any particular craft guild tended to be a highly select inner circle who possessed not only extraordinary technical competence, but also proof of their wealth and social position.

Some towns became famed far and wide for producing high quality work in their crafts workshops, with their skilled masters becoming particularly well-known. Each country's regional guilds tended to favor certain themes, characters, or religious figures in their exquisite stone, wood, or other carvings. In England, St. George slaying the dragon was a perennial favorite of many craft guild projects, as exemplified by the example of a 1390 wooden Misericord carving in Lincolnshire shown above.

Legends of gifted builders

Worldwide legends abound about the special knowledge, powers, or magical abilities of exceptionally talented craftsmen, such as metalworkers or stonemasons. Tubal Cain, Asmodeus at the Temple of Solomon, the Hiram Abiff legend in Freemasonry, and the "murdered Apprentice" at Rosslyn Chapel are well-known examples.

Medieval master stonemasons with exceptional skills would often inspire great respect, and, on occasion, a degree of fear among their guild colleagues. One English account demonstrates that exceptionally talented builders were sometimes assumed to have a magical connection, or, in this case, to be "of the Devil." Bloxham church's is famed for having the tallest church spire in all of Oxfordshire. The building itself is a tribute to the artistry of a group of exceptionally gifted north Oxfordshire masons who flourished in the 14th century. But apparently, one among their number was a bit unusual:

> Local tradition tells how a medieval mason of exceptional genius worked at both Bloxham and Adderbury. One day he tripped and fell, shedding a barrowload of stone which created Crouch Hill on the outskirts of Banbury. Then the man mysteriously vanished, leaving the lingering odour of sulphur in the air. Suddenly his fellow masons realized the truth—they had been working alongside the Devil![12]

Craft guilds guarded their trade techniques and initiation rites very closely. Apprentices would flock to be trained by certain masters, hoping to be fortunate enough to be chosen for an apprenticeship. Yet many apprenticeships were hereditary, and other masters might accept only a very few apprentices each year. Apprenticeship was thus an extremely selective process. It is difficult to overstate the great importance of these guilds in trade and commerce prior to the industrial revolution. As history has shown, in many areas in the Middle Ages, they literally *were* the economy.

Shipbuilders and other talented craftsmen building the façade of the Basilica di San Marco (St. Mark's Basilica), Venice.

Chartres is a case in point. Located in north-central France, it has been especially famed for its Gothic cathedral since the 12th century. But during the Middle Ages, it was also an important market town and a center of the wool industry. While it wasn't quite the rival of Paris or Bruges, it was a major part of the commercial network of northern Europe. It was also connected to the Mediterranean world through the cloth trade and its proximity to the famed Champagne fairs, where many exotic luxury goods and crafts were displayed. The oldest reference to a guild in Chartres is contained in a charter that count Thibaut IV issued to the innkeepers in 1147 before he departed on the Second Crusade.[13]

Esoteric aspects of medieval guilds

People ask today: What were the more esoteric traditions of the western European craft guilds? Did they truly have special secrets

A 19th century Scottish metalsmith student's Green Man "masterpiece" for his exam. (The Brydon Collection)

Example of metalworkers' skills with this woodland sprite head carving, high above, off a street in the Old Town of Edinburgh, Scotland. (Eric Wallace)

of initiation? Yes. We know that the trade "secrets" of the various crafts were most jealously guarded by the guild masters. But as these and other mysteries were not written down but passed on *orally*, historians do not know for certain what the specific nature of most of these secrets were. Some secrets and knowledge were passed down symbolically as well, i.e., by visual, not literary means.

For example, the masters of the stonemason's guilds recorded every member's name and his individual mark. In many surviving medieval (and other) buildings in parts of Europe, original mason's marks can still be seen, such as the mason's marks in various Gothic cathedrals or churches. Other guilds had their own unique marks and symbols to identify work done by their workshops in their area. Perhaps a contemporary analogy might be the individual mark or stamp of a customs or Assay office to indicate proper quality control and approval of certain high standards of workmanship in silver or gold.

Papermakers included arcane symbolism into their paper, and bookbinders often carried on secret guild knowledge by means of visual symbolism:

Usually the printers included secret marks in their books or engravings to indicate the presence of a cipher or double meaning. Large and intricate intial letters, including curious designs, sometimes served the same purpose. ... we should pause to consider the bookbinders, for these men also belonged to a guild and were in a position to perpetuate many curious emblems and figures on the covers of books...as a result of a certain confraternity which included within itself the various trade guilds, other landmarks were left to guide the observing searcher.[14]

Regarding the carvings on certain public buildings:

European public buildings, especially cathedral, libraries, and tombs, were adorned with innumerable devices in no way parts of the approved designs. Often these embellishments were concealed in obscure places, but scarcely a medieval structure has survived which does not include the symbols and signatures of the secret societies...This broad dissemination was only possible because the separate guilds and unions were aware of the high purpose for which the guild system had been established. The guilds formed a link between the troubadours and the trade unions. The trade unions were societies of artisans nourished by the apprentice system.... The guild Masters used the language of their crafts to conceal the mysticism of the great Humanist Reformation. Each guild taught the Universal Mystery in the language of its own art.[15]

In addition to their marks and symbols, the guilds had other ways of communicating their more specialized concepts. Such concepts included spiritual teaching. Although not an official part of the Church, each craft guild had its own patron saint. And, because of the intensity of the religious climate during the Middle Ages, they often propagated a religious message in addition to craft training programs. In some cases such spiritual knowledge was carried on by traveling troubadours, meistersingers, and musicians, which we will explore in chapter 8.

Papermakers guild members at work.

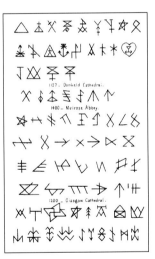

Examples of various mason's marks from Rosslyn, Dunkeld, Melrose and Glasgow. (12–15th century) (The Brydon Collection)

Parish Guilds and the medieval miracle and passion plays

One avenue for the religious and social teachings of the medieval parish guilds were the plays and pageants—colorful dramas that were also called miracle or passion plays. The guilds staged these activities, becoming even more intertwined with the culture as a result. The performances were fundraisers for the guild's charity works in the community, and they provided a symbolic way to help educate a largely illiterate populace about biblical stories from both the Old and New Testaments. Nearly all the guilds put on special dramas for the public at certain times of the liturgical year.

In medieval York, miracle plays performed by the parish guilds became especially well known, particularily the Corpus Christi play.[16] Other centers of colorful medieval pageants, like Chester and Wakefield were as widely known as York, and all were part of a large circuit of performances. Many of these plays have survived or been revived in some form, such as those presented at York today.

In medieval times, nearly everyone in the community came to see the plays. Performances would be done at specific points around a town on large elaborate wagons or platforms called *pageant wagons*. The crowds followed them around the circuit. These performances were quite an investment for the sponsoring guild:

> The pageant-waggons, e.g., in Chester, were large, ornate and expensive, and an expert on this city's drama, F.M. Salter, has estimated that it cost about £4000 (in 1967 values) to stage the play of the Chester Smiths in 1554 and this did *not* include the hiring, fitting, moving, and repairing of the basic waggon or cart. Of the Coventry Smiths Sidney Clarke records that their pageant was 'solidly and carefully built of wood and iron' with platforms, steps and trapdoors.[17]

Medieval guilds became famed for their own "specialty" drama. By way of example, the Goldsmiths favored "the Adoration of the Magi," while the Shipwrights preferred "Noah's Ark."

Mary Magdalene and the Mercator

During the High Middle Ages, many of the guild plays were supported by the Church since they usually featured the scriptures and various Easter or Christmas themes. Among the most popular medieval guild stage plays were those that featured Mary Magdalene. Her popularity was unparalleled.

Most medieval Easter conversion scenes, either in a guild play or at a secular function, would begin with the classic scene of Mary Magdalene visiting her Mercator—a local merchant much like a cosmetics, pharmacist or herbal business today. A typical scene would go much like this:

> One day Mary Magdalene walks into a merchant's shop in search of the most expensive and luxurious perfume oil possible, and should he have it in stock, the special new mascara, lipstick or perfume that she had heard about recently. Before her conversion, this thirteenth century Easter drama assures us, this would have all been done only to impress her latest love interest, a handsome young man named Amor. But this time, she came home tired from a rather exhausting day, and fell asleep on the sofa. A beautiful, loving angel enters the room, whispering in her ear, telling her all about Christ's presence at Simon's house, a well-known New Testament scriptural event. A bit startled upon awakening, Mary is initially defiant, laughing and singing her seductive songs while waiting for Amor to arrive. But then, in classic medieval style, she suddenly and dramatically converts. Clutching her richly embroidered clothes and sobbing profusely, she is portrayed as immediately tossing away her beautiful mirror, cosmetics and expensive jewelry, realizing that she truly wishes to completely change her life there and then. The next time she goes into the merchant's shop, she wears all black. Rather than buying her usual sultry perfumes and cosmetics—to his surprise—she solemnly orders only healing ointments and oils. Demonstrating her transformation from a previously "sinful" life to a

new "holy" one deserving of sainthood, the repentant sinner *par excellence* was a perfect theme for the medieval audiences of her day.

Sudden conversion scenes, like the one above, were rather common themes in medieval parish pageants. Medieval dramatists also loved to deliberately insert a touch of humor and melodrama to scriptural portrayals in an attempt to provide a more comical feel to an otherwise solemn scene. Due to her great popularity, Mary Magdalene's humanizing presence helped ensure that the guild plays were well attended. We find her here associated with cosmetics, perfumes and herbs. Her alluring beauty and the symbolism of the contents of her alabaster jar never far apart in medieval times.

Gradual decline of the Guilds and the Mystery plays

The guild plays were so popular they continued for over 250 years—from just after 1300 to about 1575, a sizable slice of English history.[18] Other European countries had their own guild performances and circuits. It is impossible to explain briefly the transition in dramatic presentation following the late 1500s. But due to a changing political and economic situation, many of the guild Mystery plays ceased to be regularly staged. In York, for example, they ended in 1572. Plays were known to be staged in some places as late as 1620. The most widespread of English calendar customs in the 19th century were the much-loved mumming plays, which are still performed in many places, and are especially popular at Beltane.[20]

But a final straw for the decline of the parish guilds occurred during the latter part of the reign of King Henry VIII. The relative wealth of some guilds undoubtedly became a factor for his targeting them. Professor Ronald Hutton states that for the rest of Henry's lifetime, England had not so much a reformed Catholic Church as a mutilated one in decay, being picked away piecemeal:

No more royal orders were issued for the removal of images, but the threat of such a step had been made in 1538. Largely because of it, but also probably because of a loss of faith in divine intercessors, only one new statue of a saint is recorded as being erected after that date, in comparison with the dozens purchased in the 1520s. The same combination of factors probably accounts for the rapid decline in the number and importance of parish guilds. This was certainly warranted, for in his last year Henry took the first measures for a survey of the wealth of these bodies, intending to confiscate at least some of it.[20]

Medieval popular plays

It is important to realize, that not all medieval guild plays were church-sponsored or even civic-related. A number were simply good entertainment. Ironically, God and the Devil might appear on stage together, with a fair amount of humor and good fun utilized to illustrate certain points. Delightfully notorious characters such as the Abbot of Unreason (Friar Tuck) became beloved figures of satire—and, in later times, a distinctly increasing irritant to church authorities.

The famous Feast of Fools is now usually discussed in terms of its later abuses. "Attempts at reform, it is true, specified that … not more than *three* buckets of water be poured over the Fool Precentor at Vespers! There are reports of old shoes being burnt on the altar in place of incense, and of riotous assemblies in the streets at night. It was excesses such as these that led to the feast's suppression, in England by the end of the 14th century, in France, a century later. But everywhere it left behind it a rich and lasting legacy."[21]

Maid Marian & the Robin Hood plays

We have all heard of the most famous pagan May Games play—Robin Hood and his sweetheart Maid Marian. This popular drama was performed in May and part of June in late medieval and Renaissance Europe, including much of England, Scotland, and France. The figure of Robin Hood is legendary. His myth started quite early on through ballads and, later—having undergone a series of changes before the more final version emerged—ended up as a favorite performance theme in late medieval times.

Caves at Creswell Crags, Nottinghamshire. Local legends say that Robin Hood and his merry men escaped from the Sheriff of Nottingham into this large, ancient complex of local caves at times.

But who was "Maid Marian"? This enigmatic figure is frankly of unknown origin. As historians note, her story appears to have been around for quite some time, even *before* the main Robin Hood tale became widely known or solidified. Of course, today we associate Robin Hood with not only Maid Marian, but also with lively characters like Friar Tuck, the Abbot of Unreason. Scholars believe the origins of Friar Tuck also came from an earlier mythic substratum than Robin Hood's, and that his details were later grafted onto the main Robin Hood legend.[22] But it is not known specifically *where* Marion's tale came from in England. There are no specific references to her, and like all such characters in medieval dramas, there are often several different versions of the story. But as we will see, there are many elements to the Robin Hood plays in various places in late medieval and Renaissance times. One cannot simply group them all together and generalize; their specific context must be taken into account.

Robin Hood was a traditional figure of the annual English May Day festivities and of the Morris Dance. Although they were certainly performed earlier (and all throughout medieval Europe), in England, some of the best documentation about the Robin Hood plays comes from the 15th and 16th centuries.[23]

The earliest Robin Hood plays were probably based on tales and concepts of an indigenous, pagan nature. This is understandable, given the ancient folklore and history of Beltane celebrations and later, of a Queen of May tradition. Other elements of pagan myths were gradually added to the central Robin Hood legend, culminating in the "primary tale" for the plays. The Robin Hood story should be viewed as a composite comprising different mythic elements.[24]

Robin Hood's name initially appears in William Langland's long poem, *The Vision of Piers the Plowman*, in 1377. But no definitive conclusions can yet be drawn as to precisely where the original Robin Hood figure came from, nor *who* "Robin Hood" was.

In the earliest Robin plays, there is no specific mention of a "Maid Marion." She only made her way into the legend via the May Games in the 16th century. In the Robin Hood tales that do mention Marian, there is no mention of her family—the primary emphasis being on the outlaw and his "merry band" of men. By the 16th century, however, Marian was the Queen of May and Robin becomes her King—of that there is no doubt.

However, throughout the period of Robin Hood/Maid Marian tales, there were numerous variations as to how she might be portrayed. The Marians in the colorful Elizabethan May games could be quite bawdy and flamboyant, as Professor Ronald Hutton has shown.[25] Indeed, there was also an English "Marian," a comic figure played by a man in drag, who accompanied English Morris dancers. This character was usually linked to the enigmatic figure of the Fool who, according to a manuscript of 1589, "dances around him in a cotton coat, to court him with a leathern pudding," a mock sausage—no doubt a portrayal that did not amuse church authorities, as British folklorist Jacqueline Simpson rightly observes.[26]

Robin Hood and Little John plays in Scotland at Roslin Glen

The highly popular May Games and the Robin Hood plays were also an integral part of life during the 15th and 16th century in Scotland at Roslin Glen. Here a huge gathering of gypsies would be invited by the St. Clairs of Rosslyn to congregate in the fields below Rosslyn Castle, where they were allowed to perform their plays each year.[27] The Romany Gypsies had been in Scotland for

Beautiful Roslin Glen in Autumn. (Karen Ralls)

Asmodeus, Rennes-le-Chateau church. (Simon Brighton)

quite some time, and the head of the noted gypsy family of Faa found protection under the hand and seal of James V as "our lovit Johnne Faa, Lord and Earle of Littil Egipt."[28]

Even after a strict act by the Scottish Parliament on 20 June 1555—which legally banned the specific play entitled *Robin Hood and Little John*—Scotland's Chief Justice, a St. Clair, was sponsoring plays on his estates in direct defiance of the ban. The specific historical details of these particular Scottish plays are largely lost to us as a result of the 1555 act. But the names of the key characters were mentioned in the act when it "ordained that in all time coming, no manner of person be chosen Robert Hude, nor Little John, Abbot of Unreason, Queenis of May, nor otherwise, under various severe pains and penalties."[29] Most of these plays had the figure of the "King of the May" as their focus.

We learn from the following excerpt that from at least 1492, the Edinburgh guilds were giving direct financial support to Robin Hood plays:

> But to whatever source he owed his origin ... the name of Robin Hood was well known in Scotland by the early years of the 15th century. It seems therefore perfectly

natural that this hero, whose deeds were on the lips not only of the professional minstrel but of the folk, should be adopted as the lord of the May feast. At any rate, it is noteworthy that the Scottish records have so far revealed no trace of Maid Marian, who, says Sir Edmund Chambers, is inseparable from Robin Hood in the English May game ... We do find a few references to the Queen of the May ... from at least 1492 onwards, the Edinburgh Guildry gave financial support to 'Robertus Hud', who, by 1500, if not earlier, was joined by his associate Little John ...[30]

ABBOTS BROMELY HORN DANCE

There were also many popular Mummers plays, minstrel plays, various folk dramas, puppet plays, and more. Some of these were performed all over Europe. A number of these earlier traditions and customs have continued to survive into the present day.

One of the most interesting celebrations, still performed in England, originated in the 13th century. The Abbots Bromely Horn Dance represents the modern-day continuity of a medieval English folk dance. It was originally performed at the Barthelemy

Abbots Bromely Horn Dance with Musicians. (Simon Brighton)

Abbots Bromley Horn Dance, in Staffordshire, England. An important example of modern-day continuity of medieval guild drama, pageantry, and related customs. (Simon Brighton)

Fair in August 1226, and is one of the few ritual rural customs to survive the passage of time. Today the Horn Dance, which takes place annually on Wakes Monday, offers a fascinating opportunity for visitors from all over the world. After collecting the horns from the church at eight o'clock in the morning, the Horn Dancers—comprising six Deer-men, a Fool, Hobby Horse, Bowman and Maid Marian—perform their dance to music provided by a melodian player. The action moves throughout the village and its surrounding farms and pubs, a walk of about 10 miles (or 16 kilometers). At the end of a long and active day, the horns are returned to the church.

A Word on the Medieval Fool or Jester

The origins, social and literary history of the Fool in the courts of 12th–16th century Europe is fascinating. The colorful figure of the court Fool or jester still resonates with us. But who were these strange, enigmatic figures in colorful motley dress—sometimes acting as top advisers to royalty? Why were they considered especially "wise"? Where did this custom come from? And why did their role eventually decline?

In the meager historical medieval sources that have come down to us, the Fools are generally little more than names in accounting books. They are remembered as colorful, but anonymous commentators on the "follies" of mankind—including those of the kings and queens whom they served. No one, it seemed, was immune from their wisdom and sometimes barbarous wit, and many a medieval ruler would carefully ponder their often enigmatic counsel and act on it accordingly. As many kings and queens were surrounded by mere sycophants, having the Fool present to ensure that a contrary view or perspective was offered had a valuable function.

By the time of the Renaissance, however, it was becoming culturally more fashionable to be interested in individual personality. Thus, some of the wittiest, even the most despised "men in motley" became more individually distinguished, some having followings of their own at royal courts much like modern-day celebrities. From the Fool of Charles I's court, the antics at Frederick II's court, to the dilemmas of Philip II of Spain as to what to do about his Fool's difficult advice, the power and ultimate influence of these complex figures was unquestioned in many royal palaces. On occasion, a woman could also serve as a jester, as evidenced by the presence of Nicola Ambruzzi La Jardiniere at the court of Mary, Queen of Scots. The figure of the Fool later appeared in Elizabethan drama, evolving yet again, at times, into the mime and clown ... even "Punch"!

By the mid-17th century, however, the era of the western European court Fool largely came to an end. Even by the early 17th century, amidst signs of declining influence of the Fool at

A modern-day Jester depiction, with blue and red motley.

Reclining Fool playing bagpipes, All Saint's church, Elm, Cambridgeshire. (Simon Brighton)

Will Sommers, court jester for King Henry VIII; from Robert Chambers' (d. 1871) *Book of Days.*

many European courts, a German preacher blessed the famed Fool Hans Fiesko with an extraordinary sermon and funeral with much pomp and circumstance. Yet this event was also the beginning of "the end of an era." The Fool would recede into the background of history as dramatically and mysteriously as he had emerged.

A labor of love that lasts forever

We have seen on our Quest that the world of medieval guilds was a complex and fascinating one. In its wake, it left many traces of beauty, craftsmanship, and customs for us to build on. In spite of the banning of certain medieval plays and their eventual decline, their creative spirit has carried on. The ethics, symbolism, drama, plays, and sites that relate to guilds will continue to inspire as long as human beings can appreciate fine craftsmanship, mutual aid fellowship, community service organizations, educational systems imparting hard-won skills, and the raucous laughter of the stage.

CHAPTER 7

HERETICS AND HERESIES

Historical Overview: A "sea of heresy"

What was "heresy" in the High Middle Ages? And who were "heretics"?

In the Middle Ages, a heresy was a religious belief or opinion in opposition to the orthodox doctrine of the Roman Catholic Church. It was seen as an "error of the faith." A heretic was someone who was accused of heresy—someone whose beliefs or practices differed from the beliefs of the Roman Catholic Church, thus making him or her a target. There were as many different kinds of heresies as there were heretics.[1] Obviously, those accused of heresy saw themselves not as "heretics," but as believers of their own faith and creeds. Throughout history, precise definitions of exactly what was "heretical" and what was "orthodoxy" have differed quite dramatically. It may be said that orthodoxy was largely decided by who held the sword.

In the 16th century, the Stonegate area of York became famous for its book shops and printers. From the Middle Ages the top of the street fell under the jurisdiction of York Minster and was home to related trades and many guild craftsmen. Goldsmiths, printers and glass painters all had businesses here; the Red Devil outside No. 33 is a traditional symbol of a printer. (Simon Brighton)

It was not only non-orthodox or allegedly "heretical" groups that were affected by direct accusations of heresy. Even within the church there were growing arguments developing between 1100 and 1500 over issues like piety, reform, dissent, and the institutional church organization itself.[2] Major controversies that sparked confrontations between Christians within the church included topics like access to scripture, policies on poverty, preaching, women, the Eucharist, and clerical corruption and wealth.

The war against heresy resulted in the development of a complex set of brutal inquisitorial procedures and resources to identify, label, and repress "heresy" all over Europe. In practice, this was largely regional in nature. Local eruptions of heresy in "hotspots" like the Languedoc, for example, would occasionally emerge like bright flames. As a result, a series of inquisitional and judicial processes were created to vigorously stamp them out at every possible opportunity. Many heretics were burned at the stake while proclaiming their beliefs. It was a powerful time with many changes—religious, political and economic, all contributing their own ingredient in the mix.

Although the terms "heresy" and "orthodoxy" used by medieval church authorities seem to imply a definitive, clear-cut division between right and wrong, there were often vigorous disagreements over exactly what was "heretical" and what was "orthodox." The debate raged on for some time prior to the formal Inquisition. The Fourth Lateran Council was a watershed in the religious life of the Middle Ages. In the fall of 1215, Pope Innocent III (1160–1216) painted an alarming picture of a church gone awry, of a heretical ship rapidly losing its anchor and moral compass.

The Church had always dealt harshly with strands of Christianity it considered heretical; but before the 11th century, these mainly clustered around individual preachers or localized popular sects—such as the Arianists, who did not accept the doctrine of the Trinity. The diffusion of the almost Manichaen sect of Paulicians westward gave birth to many of the now-famous 11th and 12th century dualist heresies of Western Europe. The first was the Bogomils. The dualist doctrine gradually gained more followers and increased in popularity—with groups such as the Cathars, the Waldensians, the Hussites, the Beguines, the heresy of the Free Spirit, and others increasingly becoming targets of the Church.[3] As we know from early 14th century accounts in Toulouse, a definitive and irrational fear of lepers, Moslems, and Jews also developed, often concurrently with the Inquisition's direct attacks on heretical groups.[4] It was not long before nearly any group or individual who did not completely "toe the party line" became a target of the Inquisition—or, barring that, was carefully watched by informants in each community, ever alert for new targets and information. The orthodox Church, as well as members of the political power structure felt threatened by such movements for various reasons. In response, they officially established the Inquisition.

Heretical groups were directly targeted and lists of charges created prior to their arrests. Accusations of heresy and heresy trials were carried out by the Roman Catholic Church and its inquisitional committees. In a few cases—such as with the Order of the Temple (Knights Templar)—the king and his court were directly involved. However, once condemned by the church, heretics were generally always then turned over to the political authorities for punishment.

Charges and Trials

At a trial for heresy in the Middle Ages, the main objective for the prosecutors of the Inquisition was simple: to *prove the charges* of the Church. Today, the primary purpose of a legal trial is, presumably, to obtain evidence and ferret out the truth. Our modern-day concept of a fair "trial by jury" did not exist in a medieval heresy hearing. Policy regarding arrests and trials of heretics was normally conducted solely by the Church; "the usual procedure was for a Church court to arrest and have custody of heretics, for it to try them under Church law, and at the end of the trial to release them for punishment by the secular arm if this was the verdict of the court."[5] Legally, at least, most matters involving heresy charges, heretics, or heretical movements were seen to be primarily under the Church's jurisdiction and not that of the state.

In a heresy trial, the normal procedures for examining suspected heretics by the inquisitional committees were already severe—in short, a basic "no-win situation" in nearly every instance. The accused in a heresy trial "had no right to know the names either of his accusers or of the prosecution witnesses, nor did he possess the right to be defended by counsel."[6] Third party witnesses were often not used at all, as was notable in a number of Templar trials. Following official procedure in a heresy trial, all inquisitional lines of questioning were supposed to be reasonable—with the goal of obtaining a confession or admittance of guilt using only the *threat* of torture. But as history has shown, beatings, torture and rape often occurred early on if the accused did not immediately confess.

Torture in a medieval heresy trial was legal in many (but not all) European countries. In France, it was used against the Templars, where a much higher proportion of "confessions" were obtained. Initially in England, any torture of Templars by ecclesiastical authorities was illegal, a policy which resulted in only a handful of confessions by comparison. Although Church policy stated that torture was legally to be applied according to a standardized procedure and not taken so far as to actually create permanent injury, in many cases this was directly violated. In an attempt to force a confession or elicit further information, brutal methods of torture would include: the accused being put "in tubs of scalding hot water, or extremely cold water; being beaten or having one's skull cracked; the use of notorious devices such as the

The cruelty of the Inquisition was supplemented by an unholy creativity in methods of torture. (*The Scarlet Book of Freemasonry*)

rack, which stretched the limbs to the breaking point; the thumb-screw, which, lined with metal studs, would gradually crush a heretic's thumb in a painful grip; or, the strappado, a device which would raise the victim, to whom heavy weights were attached, up into the air by a rope tied to the victim's hands."[7] One of the more gruesome accounts involving the Templars was of an Order priest being tortured by having fat smeared on the soles of his feet and then holding them to the flames. Several days after surviving this ordeal, a number of his bones simply dropped out of his feet; the unfortunate prisoner brought his bones to the hearing before the papal commission.[8] Clearly, as Dr. Peter Partner observed, the Templar arrests, in particular, made these already harsh procedures into "an instrument of savage terror."[9]

All in all, it was not a good climate for any group who did not see eye to eye with Roman orthodoxy, or had issues with kings or nobles. On Friday, 13 October 1307, the famous dawn arrests of the medieval Knights Templar took place in France, followed by later arrests of other European Templars in neighboring countries. English Templars (and other heretics) left their mark in the form of various "graffiti" symbols at sites where they lived or were incarcerated at locations like Temple Bruer, Byards Leap, and parts of Royston cave. In later centuries, other victims of the Inquisition would add their own marks at the same locations.

The Inquisition was initially staffed by the Dominican order in the mid-thirteenth century and designed to exterminate the Albigensian heresy in the Languedoc. It later extended its influence into Italy, Spain, and Germany. In England, direct pursuit of heresy was fairly rare until the late fourteenth century when the authorities attacked the Lollards—the followers of John Wycliffe, an influential theologian and Bible scholar who was dismissed from Oxford University in 1381 for his criticisms of the Church, and, especially, his desire to see the Bible translated into English.[10]

Women were accused in many of the earlier medieval heresy trials particularly against Cathars and Waldensians. Of course, women were often the primary victims in the much later witchcraft trials, the bulk of which occurred in the 15th, 16th, and 17th centuries.

Ironically, at the beginning of the Inquisition, a certain amount of skepticism seems to have prevailed regarding some of the charges commonly associated with the more lurid accusations about sorcery, magic, and "night-riding," i.e., attending secret meetings at night at which the Devil and other evil spirits were summoned. However, by the later Middle Ages, all this was to change. The public had been skillfully manipulated into believing such charges against individuals or heretical groups.[11] This public gullibility enabled the church to adopt a more aggressive policy against any vestiges of paganism in many areas.[12]

Image of the masonry fragment of a "cat" carving collected from the site and later sealed into the altar area of what became known as the "Grand Master's Chapel" on the ground floor of the tower at Temple Bruer, Lincolnshire. It is not known for certain today from precisely where on the original medieval site that this carving was originally located, but it remains a fascinating enigma today. (Simon Brighton)

Example of some of the Temple Bruer 'graffiti' carvings etched in stone, many of which have been left here over the centuries by persons unknown. This particular carving is sited on a stair window, with many of the letters reversed; its ultimate meaning remains undeciphered. (Simon Brighton)

Early signs of alleged "devil worship" coming into trials against heretical groups were occurring more frequently in the 12th and 13th centuries. For instance, a German chronicle of 1231 at Trier comments on various heretical groups in the area, where "tenets of the Waldenses, Cathars, and other sects may be recognized, and the rumor of nocturnal assemblies for devil worship is repeated, all prefaced by a narrative of the reckless and unrestrained conduct of heresy hunters in Germany at that time."[13] In England, there were laws related to witchcraft, including use of the death penalty. The first major witchcraft trial was held in 1589 at Chelmsford, Essex, starting an era of persecutions in England. "Fear became so intense that, in England, people, mainly women, began to be persecuted as witches and killed. An activity that we might associate with medieval superstition or the Inquisition occurred here much later and was the product not of Catholic, but of Protestant, zeal."[14]

In Scotland, which had a different legal system than England, it is believed that as many as 4,400 executions of witches took place.[15] Other types of heresy charges involved the use or possession of magical objects or artifacts, gemstones, divinatory arts, scientific knowledge, alchemical experimentation, and so on. Some

Mother Ludlam's Cave,
Moor Park, near Farnham.
(Simon Brighton)

of the trials of the late Middle Ages seem to have been directed specifically against necromancers, for example the case before an ecclesiastical court south of Paris in 1323 which "involved a group of monks, canons, and laymen, who were apparently plotting to invoke the demon Berich from inside a circle made from strips of cat skin."[16]

Women clergy among groups like the Cathars and Waldensians were especially troubling to the heresy hunters. But even within orders of the Church, learned older women show up in a surprising number of heresy trials, as we find in this rather intriguing-but-true account from the city of Reims in the late 1170s:

A so-called *erroris magistra* (mistress of error) humiliated her clerical interrogators with a display of knowledge of both the New and Old Testaments. She went on to escape her captors by jumping out the window, allegedly assisted by demons and a ball of thread ...

Royston Cave carvings, Hertsfordshire. (Simon Brighton)

[this] probably conceals a far more embarrassing truth such as that she was liberated by the crowds assembled to see her burn. Reims was a clerical city and it may be that the woman already had her education in the scriptures before joining the heretical group, usually identified as the Cathars.[17]

Modern historians have put great effort into recovering the true beliefs and knowledge of heretical groups. This effort is complicated by the fact that much of the history that has survived about heresies, heretical groups, and individual heretics was chronicled through the eye of the opposition, be it Church or state. Many of the writings of heretical groups were destroyed, scattered, mutilated, or remain as yet undiscovered. Perhaps in the future more records may emerge and clarity provided.

Accusations of heresy often "took the form of constructing and even inventing individual heresies as well as linking these heresies with one another."[18] The Inquisition essentially created the heresies they chased as the tortuous process continued—this insidious technique only served to elicit further points of ammunition to be used against other accused heretics. As the list of heresies grew exponentially, the use of torture increased so that more confessions could be obtained. This leads us back to the initial purpose and primary role of the prosecution in a heresy trial. The entire point was to prove the charges on behalf of the Church; to obtain a confession or admittance of guilt; and to force the accused to implicate others who would go on to widen the chain of victims. If one was not willing to confess, torture and death by hanging, fire, et al would be one's fate.

The memory of burned heretics is preserved in many areas today. The Villerouge-Termenes holds a medieval festival specifically commemorating the death of the "last Cathar perfect," William Belibaste.[19] In Paris, a commemorative plaque exists to honor Jacques de Molay, the last Templar Grand Master. Similar examples exist throughout Europe.

Perhaps the words of Cathar preacher Peter Authie best sum up the dichotomy of the severe clash of ideologies, as, in his view: "one church takes possession and flays, the other takes refuge and forgives."[20]

Some medieval heretics were famous in their own day and remain well-known; others were anonymous, courageously facing their death; some became known only long after they lived. We will now examine a few of the more famous medieval heretics, and let their stories be heard once again: Jeanne d'Arc, Roger Bacon, and Michael Scot

Joan of Arc: Heroine and Heretic

For nearly six centuries, Joan of Arc has been a source of inspiration and continuing fascination. Catholic saint, national icon, female prophet and martyr, some of the details of the life of Joan of Arc have remained a mystery. Little is known for certain about the early life of this young illiterate country girl—who became one of the world's most famous military leaders and a gifted mystic.

Early prophecies claimed that a "maid from Lorraine" would rise and save France. She led the French to victory under great odds against the English and the armies of the Duke of Burgundy

Statue of Jeanne d'Arc at Place des Pyramides, Paris.

Birthplace of Jeanne d'Arc, Domremy la Pucelle.

during the difficult Hundred Years' War over the English claim to the French throne. The young Joan inspired her men like few other leaders in history. However, she is perhaps most famous today for being burned at the stake by the Inquisition in 1431 for heresy—while demonstrating extraordinary courage and unflinching resolve, Joan's memory and legacy live on. Captured and sold to the English for 10,000 crowns by her treacherous Burgundian captors led by John of Luxembourg, she was tried for the controversial—and dubious, to many—charge of witchcraft in Rouen. As Eliphas Levi states in *The History of Magic,* "the greatest magical prosecution to be found in history, after that of the Temple [i.e., Templars], was the trial of a maid who was, moreover, almost a saint."[21] Many centuries later, in 1920, she was in fact finally declared a Catholic saint. Joan was at last vindicated.

Lingering questions remain about her. For instance, many ask: Why was Joan so readily accepted by the Dauphin Charles as his "God-given" savior and allowed to lead an army while a mere teenager? Why was she "burned three times" by the English, as history asserts? Why did the Church, in the end, under great pressure from the English, burn this young girl?

While we may never know the answers for certain to some of these questions, historians know that the "maid of Orleans" was born in 1412 in a village on the borders of the duchy of Lorraine in northeast France. Devoutly religious and of a decidedly mystic inclination, at age 13 the young Joan began hearing voices near a special tree. She claimed her messages came from a trio of saints.

It was also said that she had been seen dancing around a maypole. Clearly, she had what she believed to be a number of otherworldly contacts from which she drew inspiration. Especially in the 15th century, such claims could be downright dangerous, if not deadly, should one suffer from the accusations of witchcraft—often a sure route to imprisonment, torture, and death by burning. Joan's family grew more concerned as the voices continued.

Joan's "voices" insisted she present herself directly to Robert Baudricourt, leader of the French royal forces at Vaucouleurs and ask to see the King. Not unexpectedly, Baudricourt dismissed the girl's claims, believing she was merely delusional at best. Yet Joan persisted. She made a number of correct predictions, including that the French would experience tremendous defeat at the battle of Herrings, near Orleans. After this proved true, Baudricourt allowed her to go to Chinon in 1429 to see the King, Charles VII.

When the teenage prophetess arrived, in an effort to test her abilities, the Dauphin Charles VII hid among his courtiers. But Joan identified him right away, impressing all that were present, especially Charles. He gave permission for Joan to join the royal

Ruins of great hall at Chateau du Chinon, where Jeanne d'Arc met with Charles VII.

army. The English were attacking Orleans, morale was low, and defeat seemed inevitable. Joan made her own suit of armor and carried her own battle standard. She rode her white horse into the battle of Orleans, taking ultimate direction from what she called her divinely-inspired source. She rallied the French like never before, the battle culminating in a resounding victory at Orleans in May of 1429. The English were turned back and their hegemony over half of France significantly weakened. Joan then urged Charles and his army to capture Troyes, which they did, followed by marching on to Reims, where Charles was crowned with Joan of Arc at his side. This was Joan's "finest hour."

But the year 1430 would prove quite different for her. King Charles and his courtiers seemed less than enthused about going further, in spite of their successes. Yet Joan continued to listen to her voices, and told the king he must take action. Charles response was meager to say the least. She was given a small contingent of 500 men to defend the town of Compiegne; pressing on, they were simply unable to withstand the larger English force.

Joan was captured by the pro-English Burgundian John of Luxembourg and sold to the English, who were certain this young girl was a witch and a sorceress. She was imprisoned and put on trial for heresy and witchcraft at Rouen in 1431. The Church authorities and judges questioned her at length about her voices and visions. From the records of her trial, it appears that, as Marina Warner comments, the inquisitors were strangely "obsessed with determining the extent of Joan's sensual experience of her voices, the extent of her bodily contact with them."[22] The words of Joan at her trial, preserved in one of the key documents, strikes one as being those of a totally sincere, direct, honest young person. Nonetheless, because she was adamant about what she saw as the clear *heavenly and otherworldly* source for her mysterious voices, she would not submit to the authority of the court. She was found guilty of insubordination and heresy, condemned to die by burning at the stake, and executed in May 1431.

After the initial fire burned out, it is said the English soldiers raked over the coals and burned her remains twice more to ensure that she could never be rumored to have survived the flames—so afraid were they of her "sorcery." Her executioner, Geoffroy Therage, admitted that he feared being damned for burning the body of a holy woman. But it took almost 25 years after her death before her own mother could convince the Pope to order a retrial, which ultimately found her innocent.

Clearly, Joan's courage, resolve, strong faith in God, and conviction that the messages she received were true guides were an indication of her extraordinary depth of character. Her memory lives on today. She can still be seen in the series of stained glass windows at the Holy Cross Cathedral in Orleans, which depict ten key scenes from her life. The display in the final window quotes what the voices told her at the trial as the verdict of death was delivered: "Do not bewail your martyrdom when you shall come in time to the Kingdom of Paradise."

Unfortunately, our last opportunity to have better understood Joan was lost shortly before her execution. The most trusted chronicler of the age, Georges Chastellain, whose eyewitness *Chronicle* remains today one of the most reliable sources of events and key people of the 15th century, was given permission to visit her prior to her burning. His last words were written the night before he was to meet Joan of Arc in person. And apparently, he did meet her the very next day. But, strangely enough, all of the pages of the manuscript beginning on that day were cut out. The official record of the trial ends at this point, with the judges' signatures and the notaries' official seals. It does not specifically describe how Joan was burned.[23] But, centuries later, beatified at Notre Dame cathedral and later canonized in 1920, St Joan of Arc lives on—her memory continuing to inspire people—religious or not—all over the world.

Roger Bacon

Roger Bacon, dubbed "Doctor Mirabilis" in his day, was born in 1220 at Ilchester, Somerset (or, some claim, Bisley, Gloucester) in England and died 1292. An English churchman, philosopher, and educational reformer, he was a major proponent of experimental science. Bacon was a renowned lecturer on Aristotle at Oxford, and had extensive knowledge of a number of fields: including mathematics, optics, astronomy, alchemy, and languages. He read Latin, Greek, and Arabic works and was the first Europeans to describe in extensive detail the process of making gunpowder, the steamship, the motor car, the aeroplane, the submarine, and the cantilever bridge—all this in the 13th century. He proposed

Roger Bacon in his Franciscan observatory at Oxford. (1897 engraving)

flying machines, described eyeglasses, observed lenses and mirrors, studied reflection, refraction, and spherical aberration, and used a camera obscura to observe eclipses of the sun. He later lectured in Paris, greatly impressing colleagues and students alike.

A contemporary of leading Paris churchmen Albertus Magnus and Thomas Aquinas, Bacon had an interest not only in philosophy and theology, but in the serious study of alchemy. He sought for a broader knowledge of Arabic and other eastern sources. Albertus Magnus's astrological work, *The Mirror of Astronomy,* contains a solemn warning that its teaching should be kept secret. It appears that Bacon quoted this text, and others against the breaking of secrets, and "then suggested a series of ways to preserve the more hidden character of nature's own knowledge."[24]

He produced his three major works, the *Opus Major, Opus Minor,* and *Opus Tertium,* which outlined a scheme for further research in languages, optics, mathematics, and so on. His dream was to introduce the natural sciences to the universities of Europe. He became a Franciscan in Oxford in 1251. He was a Christian who genuinely believed his scientific work would contribute to a greater understanding of the world and so of God—through understanding His divine creation.

Perhaps not unsurprisingly, he soon ran into trouble with the Church. Clearly a lodestar of his time, in 1277 and 1279, Bacon was condemned to prison by his fellow Franciscans because of alleged "novelties" in his teaching. The condemnation was probably issued because of his strong attacks on some of the orthodox theologians of his day and his serious interests in alchemy and astrology. Exactly how long he was imprisoned is unknown, but some believe it may have been as long as fourteen years. Little is known about his life from this point on; his last work was in 1292, the year of his death. A commemorative plaque exists in Oxford in his memory. There is also a statue of him outside the University of Oxford's Museum of Natural History.

Michael Scot: The "Wizard of Midlothian"

The ruins of the magnificent medieval Melrose Abbey in the Scottish Borders stood very close to the large Roman fort of Trimontium on the Great North Road from London to York up to Stirling in central Scotland.[25] Melrose Abbey has a fascinating his-

Long Meg and her Daughters, Cumbria. Folklore says that Scottish wizard Michael Scot turned a coven of witches into this group of stones. (Simon Brighton)

tory. It was built by the Cistercians and it is said that the heart of Robert the Bruce is buried there. Another association with Melrose, although more unusual, is the mysterious and gifted Michael Scot—dubbed the "Wizard of Midlothian" in medieval times.

Born in 1175 in the Borders of Scotland (or, as others claim, in Balwearie Fife), Scot was a brilliant scholar, mathematician, and philosopher, widely known for his translations of Aristotle from Arabic and Hebrew into Latin. Records show that he was in Toledo in 1217, a major ecumenical center at the time where Christian, Jewish, and Moslem scholars would work side-by-side on certain projects. In this environment, for example, he translated the famed treatise of al-Biruji (Alpetragius) on the sphere, as well as the great Arabic philosopher Ibn Rushd ("Averroes"), and more works of Aristotle from Greek into Latin.

Scot was so esteemed by his colleagues in Europe that he was summoned to be a scholar at the court of the famed Frederick II of Sicily. By 1220, we know Scot was in Bologna, Italy. From 1224–27, he may have been in papal service. He was one of the most famous medieval astrologers and magicians, well-known to those at all levels of society. His reputation was that of a very effective "wizard."

Scot's grave is said to be at Melrose Abbey, in the south transept chapel nearest the presbytery. It has a cross on it as Scot was a cleric. According to Sir Walter Scott, writing several hundred

Kits Coty House, Aylesford, Kent; stones legends claim were "erected by witches." (Simon Brighton)

years later in *The Lay of the Last Minstrel,* Michael Scot was buried there with his books of magic. The cross is portrayed as driving away the wizard's allegedly demonic followers:

> I buried him on St Michael's night,
>
> When the bell toll'd one, and the moon was bright,
>
> And I dug his chamber among the dead,
>
> When the floor of the chancel was stained red,
>
> That his patron's cross may over him wave,
>
> And scare the fiends from the Wizard's grave.

Michael Scot is also particularly remembered in Scotland as a powerful local wizard. Legends say he was aided by a "devilish spirit" for whom he was constantly inventing new tasks: splitting the original Eildon Hill into three, bridling the River Tweed with a curb of stone, and weaving ropes out of sand. Borders legends persistently link him with ownership of Aikwood Tower. These same legends recount his transformation into a hare by the neighbouring Witch of Fauldshope, and his subsequent magical revenge on her. A man of extraordinary intellect, many gifts and magical abilities, Scot was known throughout Europe. He remains as fascinating and elusive today as he undoubtedly was in medieval

Pendle, Lancashire; the region where the famous Pendle Witch Trials were held in the 17th century. (Simon Brighton)

times. Although Dante assigned him to the eighth circle of Hell in his *Inferno*, others, like Boccaccio, admired him.

The Museum of Witchcraft, Boscastle, Cornwall

No visit to the north Cornish coast would be complete without a stop at the Museum of Witchcraft. An interesting place to learn more about the history of witchcraft in England, it may be found along the coast at Boscastle, north Cornwall. It is one of Cornwall's more popular and unique attractions. It is also near to Tintagel, another favorite with visitors today. The museum has an outstanding collection of witchcraft and related folklore artifacts, dating from the time of the witch-hunts until the present day, illustrating how witchcraft, cunning folk, and folklore and

Plaque in Exeter commemorating the Bideford Witches, said to be the last three witches to be executed in England, late 17th century. (Simon Brighton)

certain magical traditions developed and evolved in England over the centuries. Its well-maintained, extensive library holds a vast collection of books and archives about English witchcraft and related topics.

Commemorating the Outcast Dead: Cross Bones cemetery, London

Another place not to miss when you are visiting London is the Cross Bones Cemetery. From the Cross Bones website, we learn about an interesting, if long forgotten, aspect of London's history. On Redcross Way, a tranquil back-street running parallel to Borough High Street, there is a plot of land surrounded by London Underground hoardings. There is a big rusty iron gate adorned with ivy, ribbons, flowers, feathers, jewelry and other curious totems. It bears a bronze plaque with the epitaph: "R.I.P. The Outcast Dead." This is Cross Bones, a pauper's burial ground with a legend going back to medieval times.

In his 1598 *A Survey of London*, historian John Stow (1525–1605) refers to a burial ground for "single women"—a euphemism for the prostitutes who worked in Bankside's brothels or "stews." The age of the graveyard is unknown. By 1769, Cross Bones had become a pauper's cemetery, servicing the poor of the parish. Up to 15,000 people are believed to have been buried there.

Beginning in 1996, local writer John Constable revived the story of Cross Bones. *The Southwark Mysteries* is a cycle of poems

Cross Bones Gates plaque. (Simon Brighton)

and mystery plays inspired, he writes, by the spirit of a "Winchester Goose" (prostitutes licensed by the Bishop of Winchester) and "the outcast dead." Constable's work has been performed in Shakespeare's Globe and in Southwark Cathedral. Interest generated by *The Southwark Mysteries* inspired the Cross Bones Halloween festival, celebrated annually since 1998 with a procession, candles and songs.*

Cross Bones Gates, Southwark, London. Memorial ribbons commemorate the Outcast Dead from medieval and later times. (Simon Brighton)

Conclusion

As we have seen in this chapter, many medieval heretics were burned at the stake for their beliefs. Their endurance, courage, and perseverance under such circumstances is often breathtaking—if not heartbreaking—for us to contemplate today.

---

* For more on this, please visit *http://en.wikipedia.org/wiki/Cross_Bones—cite_ note-Constablewebsite-8*

The Frensham cauldron, now in the Church of St Mary, The Virgin, Frensham, Surrey, England. (Simon Brighton)

Among the most famous martyrs to religious intolerance are the last Templar Grand Master, Jacques de Molay and the Preceptor of Normandy, treasurer Geoffrey de Charney. Upon denying the guilt of their Order, they were classified as "relapsed heretics." Given the earlier confessions, their retraction greatly shocked everyone present, including the most eminent churchmen. To recant a confession of heresy (even one made under torture) automatically identified the person as a "relapsed heretic." This was to commit yet another crime, assuring one's ultimate fate.

They were then ordered to be immediately burned on an island in the Seine by the French King Philip IV in March of 1314. The reverberations of their execution have remained with us down the centuries. Let us pause to contemplate de Molay's last words as he was being led to the stake:[26]

Before heaven and earth and with all of you here as my
witnesses…I declare, and I must declare, that the Order
is innocent. Its purity and saintliness is beyond question.

One of the most interesting vagaries of history comes from
an official who was present on that fateful day. Having witnessed
their burnings in person, the 14th century chronicler Geoffroi de
Paris ended his customary bureaucratic report of the entire matter
with these immortal words:

> One can easily deceive the church,
>
> But one can never in any way deceive God.
>
> I shall say nothing else
>
> Whosoever desires may add more.[27]

And that, as many today might well add, truly says it all.

Dr. Faustus in his Magical
Circle commanding a
demon. Woodcut from
Christopher Marlowe
(1636)

CHAPTER 8

TROUBADOURS

A red Rose is univerally associated with love, the Feminine, and is often portrayed in paintings and symbolism about the troubadours and the courts of love.

> … it is agreed that there is no good thing in the world, and no courtesy, that is not derived from love as from its fountain head
>
> —Andreas Capallanus[1]

Who were the medieval troubadours?

The famed musicians and poets of Love, pageant and song continue to cast their fascinating allure today. Their intense celebration and longing for true love is a universal theme. In the High Middle Ages (1100–1350), a *troubadour* was a professional composer and performer of music and poetry, an especially gifted contributor to medieval society.

Much of this movement was from Occitania—a region covering the southern half of France, northern Spain (Catalonia), and parts of Italy—where many believe the troubadour tradition had its earliest late 11th century roots. From Italy, related branches from this universal musical tree of Love began to spread its influence throughout nearly all of Western Europe: the *troubadours* in the Languedoc, the *minnesangers* in Germany, the *trovadorismo* in Portugal, and the *trouveres* in northern France, to name but a few.

The texts of troubadour songs deal mainly with themes of courtly love, courtesy, and chivalry. Some were serious; others were humorous, clever satires; but all had love as their focus. Troubadour songs can be grouped into three major styles: the *trobar leu* (light), *trobar ric* (rich), and *trobar clus* (closed). Likewise there were many genres of troubadour music. The most popular were the *canso,* but the *sirventes* and *tensos* were especially popular in the later troubadour period, especially in Italy and among the female troubadours, the *trobairitz.*

> The troubadours' principle song genre, "Le Canso" was, according to Dante, (Occitan poetry's greatest enthusiast) "worthy of the highest honours to those who practice it with success—and a source of acute embarrassment to those who could not."[2]

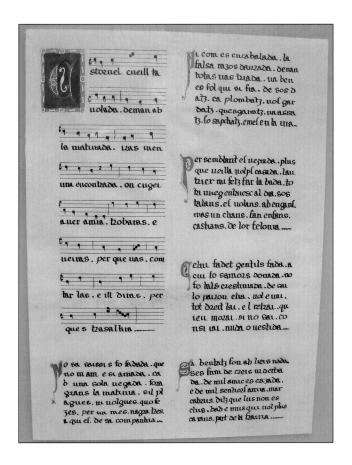

Example of a sheet of medieval Troubadour music from the Puivert Museum, in Puivert, a village in the Aude department in the Languedoc-Roussillon region in southern France. (Ani Williams)

Duke William IX and his granddaughter Eleanor of Aquitaine (1122–1204)

The earliest troubadour whose work has survived is Guilhèm de Peitieus, better known as Duke William IX of Aquitaine, who lived in the late 11th and early 12th century. The medieval work *Orderic Vitalis* refers to William composing songs about his experiences on his return from a crusade in 1102, with some experts claiming this may be the earliest reference to troubadour lyrics known today. This manuscript may also be the first description of a troubadour performance, an eyewitness account of the gifted and charming William of Aquitaine "in action" in a troubadour role.

After his death, his now-famous granddaughter—the extraordinarily influential, spirited, and wealthy heiress Eleanor of Aquitaine, lover of arts, learning, and culture—carried the troubadour torch further, spearheading a major development in

Modern-day depiction of decorative troubadour instrument motif, suspended from a building's architecture, Toulouse, France. Here, the lingering memory and historical legacy of the medieval troubadours remains in varied forms, a creative witness to their contribution to society and the community. (Ani Williams)

medieval history. One of the most powerful women of the Middle Ages, Eleanor was a duchess of Aquitaine in her own right. She would go on to become queen-consort of France and later, queen of England. She brought the ideals of courtly love from Aquitaine—first to the court of France, then over to England where she was queen to two kings during her lifetime. Her talented daughter Marie, Countess of Champagne, was a patron of Chretien de Troyes, and she played a key role in bringing courtly behavior to the Count of Champagne's court. The role of a medieval *courtier* was varied:

> Courtly love became a part of courtly life and its customs and special forms came to dictate what was expected of a *courtier,* who was usually a knight of lower rank than the *seigneur* who might, in this region, be a woman. In the Languedoc, privileged women could enjoy the respect and indeed love expected from a vassal. The basic form of Fine Love is woven into this relationship of vassal to lord,

hence the romantic custom of getting on one knee before the loved one …[3]

This energetic early seeding and flowering of the troubadour movement was culturally important in Western Europe. However, it was in the latter half of the 12th century and the earlier part of the 13th when a virtual "boom" in troubadour activities flowered—consequently, almost half of all of the troubadour works that survive today are from this peak period.

Major regions of courtly love and troubadour activity

Where did the troubadours sing, charm, and entice? Images of medieval troubadours and jongleurs of southern France are quite familiar, their songs and legendary fame known to us today. But we must also examine the extraordinary culture of Occitania, Majorca, Andalusia, and Sicily that earlier spawned this great cultural experiment, which then spread further through the Languedoc, and all over the Continent.

Many scholars maintain that the troubadour tradition in France began in western Aquitaine, especially at Poitou, and also in the Gascony region. From there, it extended into eastern Aquitaine and Provence. The troubadour movement was especially influential in the Languedoc and Toulouse regions. By the early 13th century, it stretched out to Italy, then, to Catalonia, and then to the rest of Spain—a "movement" dubbed the *rayonnement des troubadours*. The peak period of troubadour activity lasted from

Tournament shown in René d'Anjou *Livre des tournois France,* Provence 15th century. (Wikimedia Commons)

Musician playing seven-stringed lyre at Puivert. (Ani Williams)

about 1170 until about 1220, the famous half-century "heyday" of the troubadours. Here, their lyric art reached the height of its popularity and the number of surviving poems is greatest. This is the period when the *canso*, or love song of the troubadours, became distinguishable as a distinct musical genre all its own. For example, one of the key medieval troubadours and star performers of the Languedoc—Bernart de Ventadorn—was highly regarded by his contemporaries for his songs and performances.

Nearly four hundred and fifty historical troubadours are known to musicologists today. Records show that they came from a variety of backgrounds and traveled to many different courts. They were cultural ambassadors of sorts. Contrary to popular belief, the troubadours were generally not mere itinerant wandering entertainers. They were of the musical elite and were often invited to stay at one court or another for a fairly long period of time under the patronage of a wealthy nobleman or woman.

At first, most troubadours were of the nobility, but later records show that talented troubadours could also belong to a lower class. Many troubadours are described in their *vidas*—a type of medieval *resume* or CV—as "poor knights," though they were of minor nobility status. The *vidas* are the only near-contemporary writings available attesting to the existence of the troubadours and their distinctive individual personalities.[4] Some possessed a clerical education and were quite learned, which provided them with a greater understanding of musical styles and vocal training. For instance, there are similarities between Italian and Catalan troubadour culture: "Broad trends such as the spread of lay literacy, the rise of written production in the vernacular, and the growth of courts and their administrative staff resulted, in both Catalan and Italian courts, in a series of paraliterary troubadour activities."[5]

Difference between a "troubadour" and "jongleur" or "minstrel"

A professional troubadour was a composer who wrote his own songs or poetry. He or she did not merely sing or play the works of others—this was a key factor. By the middle of the 12th century, a definite distinction was made between the creator of original songs and one who simply performed the work of others. The latter category of entertainers was called *joglars*, the French *jongleur*, the English *juggler*, etc., so technically speaking, the medieval *jongleur/joglar* is really more properly defined as an entertainer or *minstrel*, a singer.

In the peak era, we read that professional troubadours often found fault with some of the *jongleurs* and minstrels. Serious questions about performance standards and exactly what some entertainers were actually doing arose. *Jongleurs* often performed the troubadour's songs in a courtly setting, not only by singing or playing musical instruments, as might be expected, but also

"Swan lovers." (encaustic painting by Dawn Gaskill)

by adding in additional skills like dancing, juggling, acrobatics, or other humorous antics. At times, some of these performances were described as either trivial buffoonery, untasteful, or, at times, downright vulgar.

By the late 13th century, we witness troubadour Guiraut Riquier complaining about the growing lack of definition as to exactly what constituted a proper troubadour, as opposed to a minstrel entertainer. He wrote a letter to King Alfonso X of Castille asking for royal clarification on the proper reference for the terms *trobador* and *joglar*. Riquier argued, and the king seems to have agreed, that on the whole a *joglar* was not a troubadour but a courtly entertainer, as opposed to an intinerant popular minstrel; and that a professional troubadour was *both* a poet and a composer.[6]

Even so, many troubadours were known as jongleurs, either before they began writing their own songs or at the same time. Some well-known troubadours even had their own jongleurs who would travel to perform their songs at other courts on their behalf:

> Raimon de Miraval employed two *jongleurs* who would travel to welcoming courts to perform his works … Bayona and Forniers … While [they] headed for the court of Alfonso II of Castile, Miraval was on his way to his friend and patron Raimon VI, count of Toulouse. While Peire Vidal, the greatest voice of them all, took 'Fine Love' to Syria, Raimon de Miraval offered five years of love-service to … Loba de Pennautier. This great dame was also courted by Peire Vidal …[7]

A court was not the only setting for troubadour performances. There were intensely competitive music and poetry contests held in the north of France, especially Brittany. Troubadours, like modern musicians, poets, and writers, often met and traded tales and techniques with each other: "It is nevertheless incontestable that Chretien [de Troyes] had close and sustained contact with the court of Poitiers. Where else would he have gained his extensive knowledge of British legend if not at Poitiers, where a person was as likely to meet a Celtic bard as an Occitan troubadour?"[8] In Germany, the *minnesangers* sang of love and con-

Carving of medieval troubadour and his instrument at Puivert, a village in the Aude department in the Languedoc-Roussillon region in southern France, an area still famous today for its enduring legacy of the medieval troubadours. (Ani Williams)

tributed to the growing Arthurian corpus, such as Wolfram von Eschenbach's famous *Parzival*. "In the late 12th century, we find the German *minnesinger* taking up the themes of the Provencal troubadours in their lyrics. We find other writers, such as Hartman von Aue and Wolfram von Eschenbach reworking and elaborating the material that they found in French texts to compose the first German versions of the Arthurian story."[9]

Secular musicians and minstrels in England

Due to the vagaries of history, politics, and the ravages of time, only about thirty secular English or Anglo-French songs have survived with their music from the two hundred years up to 1377. "They include *Angelus ad Virginem* (mentioned by Chaucer) and *Maiden in the Moor*, which is still sung as a folk song today. It occurs in the famous Red Book of Ossory compiled by the 14th century Franciscan Richard de Ledrede, but this friar gave it Latin religious lyrics so that his clerical readers would not 'pollute their throats with popular, immoral or secular songs.'"[10] Much secular music was simply not written down at all, and frankly, did not need to be. The talented bards of old had long improvised and sung from memory. Their music was also played by traditional methods.

Later, music flourished under Edward III, who reigned in England in the mid–14th century. He founded the illustrious Order of the Garter. Several compositions are associated with his

Chapel Royal, and with St. George's Chapel, Windsor, St. Stephen's, and Westminster; one description of the great variety of musicians and instruments at the time of Edward III is insightful:

> But here come the musicians after eating, without mishap, combed and dressed up! There they made many different harmonies. For I saw there, all in one circle, viol, rebec, gittern, lute, micanon, citole, and the psaltery, harp, tabor, trumpets (*cornemuses*), flutes (*flajos*), bagpipes (*chevrettes*), krumhorns, cymbals, bells, timbrel, the Bohemian flute, the big German cornet, flutes (*flajos de saus*), flute (*fistule*), pipe, bagpipe (*muse d'Aussay*), little trumpet, buzines, panpipes, monochord where there is only one string, and bagpipe (*muse de blef*) all together. And certainly it seems to me that such a melody was never seen or heard, for each of them, according to the tune of his finger, and feather, and bow, I have seen and heard on this floor.
>
> —Guillaume de Machaut (1300–77)[11]

One of the most amusing-but-true stories from England is how the Earl of Chester was rescued from a brutal Welsh siege of Rhuddlan Castle by a relief force of terrifying minstrels!

> In 1212, when Randulf, Earl of Chester, was besieged by the Welsh in his castle of Rhuddland in Flintshire. He sent an appeal for help to Roger de Lacy, justiciar and constable of Chester, afffectionately known in the local dungeons as 'Roger of Hell.'. Roger, casting around for the most effective, vicious and altogether intimidating relief force he could find, realised that Chester was full of jongleurs who had come for the annual fair. He gathered them up and marched them off under his son-in-law Dutton. The Welsh, seeing this fearsome body of determined musicians, singers and prestidigitators bearing down on them ready to launch into an immediate performance of their terrifying arts, fled. Who but Roger of Hell would have been so ruthless? The event gave rise to the old English oath, now sadly forgotten but well worth reviving ... Roger, and by all the fiddlers of Chester![12]

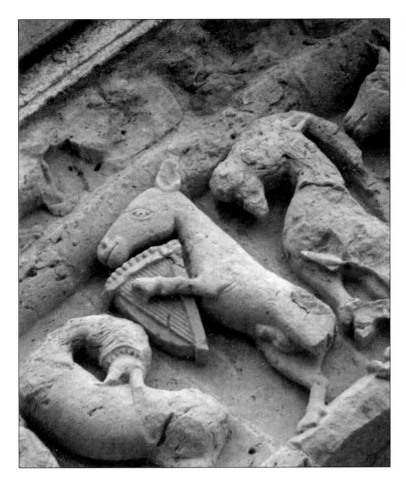

Carving of a donkey
playing a harp, exterior,
Chartres cathedral.
(Karen Ralls)

Wandering minstrels were not bound to a specific lord nor allowed to wear his livery. "A minstrel without a livery was a bit like a band without a record contract. Livery indicated that a minstrel had both status and a regular income, and made it easier for him to be accepted in the right castles and earn a decent reward. But he still needed a full range of entertainment skills." (13)

John of Salisbury, Bishop of Chartres, historian, and elegant Latin stylist of the twelfth century, seemed to have found certain jongleurs quite appalling, as "even they whose exposures are so indecent they make a cynic blush are not debarred from distinguished houses…they are not even turned out when with more hellish tumult they defile the air and more shamelessly disclose that which in shame they had concealed. Does he appear a man of wisdom who has eye or ear for such as these?"[14] As in France and other areas, in England, too, it seems that some jongleurs could be quite daring indeed!

Carving of sow and piglets playing harp, Notre Dame cathedral.

Women troubadours: the Trobairitz

One classic question often arising today is: were there women troubadours? Yes. Historically, the *trobairitz* were the female troubadours, the first women composers of secular music in the Western tradition. Many were from Occitania, and a number were of noble heritage. The word *trobairitz* was first used in the 13th century *Romance of Flemenca.* It is the feminine form of *trobaire,* the Provencal root of "Troubador"—"to find" or "to compose." The number of trobairitz varies between sources: there were twenty or twenty-one named trobairitz. There are a number of anonymous texts ascribed to women; musicologists believe the total number of trobairitz texts varies from twenty-three to around forty.[15] Sadly, only one melody composed by a trobairitz has survived the ravages of time. Out of a total of about 450 troubadours and 2,500 troubadour works in all, the trobairitz and their corpus of material form a minor but important sub-genre of their own, so they are quite well-studied by experts today.

Fin' Amors: "Fine Love," the famous code of love

The famous **Fin' Amors** ('Fine Love') of the medieval troubadours was what we know of today as "courtly love"—a noble attempt at a higher level of chivalric behavior, courtesy, and unique way of expressing love.[16] Many love songs and spirited discussions took place in European courts about love, types of love and lovers, and how to be a good lover according to the *Fin' Amors* code. As most medieval noble marriages were arranged purely for political and economic reasons, courtly love was a concept and way of acknowledging love beyond the ordinary, rigid constraints of the time.

To the troubadours, courtly love was an experience between erotic desire and spiritual attainment. Ironically, the actual term "courtly love" was first popularized by Gaston Paris as late as 1883. Ever since, it has come under a wide variety of definitions and uses.[17] Paris said courtly love was an idolization and an ennobling discipline. The lover (idolizer) accepts the independence of his lady—often the married wife of his lord, for example—and tries to make himself worthy of her by acting bravely and honorably and by doing whatever deeds she might desire, subjecting himself to a series of tests to prove to her his love and commitment. Sexual satisfaction, Paris said, may not have always been the goal or even the end result; but courtly love was not entirely Platonic either. It was initially based on attraction. Therefore, with marriage essentially removed from the courtly love issue, "what remains in fine amor is love. But what kind of love?"[18]

And that, for the troubadours—and for all of us—is an important question! The troubadours would sing and wax lyrical about this: what kind of love, what type of love, and so on. Some scholars believe that the troubadour movement may have been as much or more about *the lover's longings* as it was about love itself. "Troubadour poetry is not about women, their beauty or charms; it is about the lover and his longings. The highest praise is measured in terms of the lady's influence on the admirer, and so the qualities of the love loom large in their philosophy."[19]

Musician playing the bells at Chartres, stone carving. (Karen Ralls)

Others directly refer to the powerful, subtle eroticism in much of troubadour poetry, commenting on its possible relevatory and initiatory function: "In fact, there is a very subtle eroticism in the poetry of the troubadours and in the romances by Chretien de Troyes—in particular, in *The Knight of the Cart* ... this eroticism, which Rene Nelli has proved is genuine, can be readily summarized: Everything is based on revelation and initiation. The act of revelation is important in that it involves a choice."[20]

Experts still debate whether courtly love was purely literary or was actually practiced in real life, adding that there are no surviving historical records that offer specific evidence of its presence in reality. But others maintain that "courts of love" were held within Eleanor's orbit—her own unique network of sophisticated, cultural "salons." Medieval *courtesy books* from this period have been found.[21] The 1405 book of Christine de Pizan called *Book of the Three Virtues* expresses some disapproval of courtly love, namely, the author felt the convention was often being used to justify and cover up illicit love affairs. Clearly, all was not as platonic as some today insist.

Yet love, as we know, is universal. The troubadours' concept of *Fin' Amors* had its own "rules," principles, stages, and art that a proper courtier would learn and know well. Barbara Tuchman, in her groundbreaking study of the 14th century, summarizes the medieval stages of courtly love beautifully:[22]

STAGES OF COURTLY LOVE

- Attraction to the lady, usually via eyes or a glance
- Worship of the lady from afar
- Declaration of passionate devotion
- Virtuous rejection by the lady
- Renewed wooing with oaths of virtue and eternal fealty
- Moans of approaching death from unsatisfied desire (and other physical manifestations of lovesickness)
- Heroic deeds of valor which win the lady's heart
- Consummation of the secret love
- Endless adventures and subterfuges avoiding detection

Fusion with the lover explains fairly well the attitudes claimed by the code of love to be those of the genuine lover:

Misericord, St. Botolph's Church, Boston, Lincolnshire. Depiction of a mermaid in her siren guise, said by legend to lure sailors with her recorder or pipes. (Wikipedia Commons)

"He who is dying of love's passion neither sleeps nor eats." (twenty-third rule). Love must imbue his entire life, each second of his existence, because love is perpetual renewal. The fifteenth rule states: "Every lover must grow pale when in his lover's presence," which can seem an exaggeration, but which is actually the obvious transposition of an internal movement, because, as said by the sixteenth rule: "At the sudden sight of his beloved, the heart of a lover should tremble."[23]

Another tenet was that love can never make the person experiencing it feel terribly safe or secure, with another rule stating quite clearly, "those in love are always fearful." "In fact, there is a constant fear of losing one's lady, losing one's love, losing one's reason to live."[24] Jealousy, in the noble sense of the word, is ever present, as is the fear of displeasing one's lady. "The pains taken to respond to the desires of one's lady spur one's action, and everything must be brought into play so that the couple becomes the union of two beings isolated on this earth, thereby re-creating, although they may not know it, the famous dyad, the sacred couple, the mythical androgyne, which some feel may have been the very origin of life."[25]

Once the signs have been decoded and the traditional values turned upside down:

There is no reason for 'baseness' to exist. Courtly love is, in short, a rule for life that allows one to go from low to high. It is in this regard that Catharism has often been mentioned in connection with the poetry of the troubadours. And it is a fact that the renunciation of baseness and the exaltation of the primordial couple, freed from the illusions of this world, and also the attempt to overcome ego in order to attain a perfect fusion are all familiar themes of the Cathars.[26]

Some argue that the ultimate point of courtly love was indeed of a physical nature. They insist that physical love is but a doorway to a spiritual Otherworld that is in a state of perpetual becoming. That courtly love is a medieval form of sacred Western Tantra:

> The intimate relationship that develops between the lover-knight and his mistress-lady necessarily happens through sex. But here the sex is not a final end but a necessary method of acting in order to gain awareness of an Elsewhere that is in a constant process of unfolding … Orgasm is only a form of passage …[27]

Medievalists who have delved into the theme of courtly love "have, and continue to, diverge wildly in their opinions—some regard it as a simple social game, others consider it an attempt at spiritualization, others have seen it as the symbol of Cathar asceticism, and still others as the result of platonic theories in Christian thought. The least that can be said, in any case, is that the problem of courtly love is not a simple one. Even during the 11th, 12th, and 13th centuries, courtly love was discussed and dealt with in various manners, according to circumstances and the people involved."[28]

De Amore ("On Love") by Andreas Capellanus

In addition to *Fin' Amor,* one of the most famous medieval love books is the late 12th century *De Amore* ("On Love"), written by the priest Andreas Capellanus.[29] Scholars maintain it was composed around 1185 at the specific request of Marie de Cham-

pagne. (Interestingly enough, this is right before Chretien de Troyes wrote his most famous Grail romance, *Percevel*, circa 1190. Chretien, likely a native of Troyes, is known to have served at the court of his patroness, Marie of France—Countess of Champagne and daughter of Eleanor of Aquitaine—between 1160 and 1172.)

Andreas Capallanus in *De Amore* gives a listing of the *four major stages of love* that have been consistent through the ages:

In medieval lore, swans were often associated with love, as well as the healing waters, as this lovely swan swims towards its mate amidst the lily pads. (Simon Brighton)

> The first consists in arousing hope;
>
> The second in offering kisses;
>
> The third in the enjoyment of intimate embraces;
>
> The fourth in the abandonment of the entire person.

De Amore deals with several specific themes that were the subject of spirited debate among the troubadours of his day. The underlying concept of Capellanus is that courtly love ennobles the character of both the lover *and* the beloved, provided that certain codes of behavior are respected. (30) In this work, the most ennobling kind of love is generally portrayed as held in secret, often extremely difficult to obtain and could often remain unconsummated, thus fueling the fires of ardor even more.

De Amore begins with a preface in which the author addresses an unidentified young man named Walter. Though Capellanus' relationship with the young man is unclear, he describes Walter as relatively new to love and offers to teach him with this book. Book One of *De Amore* sets out a series of nine imaginary dialogues between men and women of different social classes, from bourgeoisie to royalty. In each dialogue the man is pleading inconclusively to be accepted as the woman's lover, and in each he finds some small reason for optimism.

Book Two takes love as already established, and begins with a discussion of how love is maintained and how and why it may come to an end. Following this comes the series of now-famous thirty-one medieval "judgments of love," said to have been pronounced in contentious cases by great ladies in the famous "Courts of Love" judgments. (The "Courts of Love" were mentioned by Capellanus. They were reputed to consist of some 10 to 70 women convened to rule on questions of the propriety of various interactions based on the etiquette of courtly love. They are discussed in more detail later in this chapter.) Some were attributed to Eleanor of Aquitaine, and the others to noblewomen in her elite circle.[31] Capellanus continues by setting out some of the basic "Rules of Love" for his medieval reading audience. A few of his more famous examples include: "he who is not jealous cannot love"; "no one should be deprived of love without the very best of reasons"; "when it is made public, love rarely endures"; "a true lover is constantly and without intermission possessed by the thought of his beloved."

Book Three of *De Amore* is called "The Rejection of Love," a shorter diatribe that seeks to remedy the natural affection of men for women, by painting all women as difficult as possible in so few words. Quite a surprise after the first two parts! Capellanus' final conclusion, is that, in the long run, it may simply be best to simply forego it all in favor of the love of God. Some scholars have puzzled over why Capallanus seems to suddenly and vehemently "turn on love"—and women—in this last third of the book. One comments that his work may, in fact, have been written as a parody of the scholastic method of argumentation in vogue at the time:

> It was written at least in part as a sophisticated satire on both his society and recent intellectual trends ... as a commentary on the then-current vogue for scholastic argumentation and categorization, as well as on the romances that were becoming popular ... Arguing both for love, as Andreas did in the first two-thirds of his book, and against it, in the last third, has confused many scholars ... This division in his work, however, makes much more sense as a parody of the scholastic method of argumentation, in which the philosopher or legal scholar was required to provide arguments both for and against a proposition.[32]

The Courts of Love

Some further insights about Capellanus' work, and courtly love in general, include the fact that the author of 'The Art of Love' was, in fact, a frequent guest of Eleanor of Aquitaine. He knew her quite well. "In his treatise on amorous casuistry, which was vaguely inspired by Ovid, he records themes and debates that must have been dear to the queen-duchess and her companions. It is he who mentions the courts of love, those female tribunals of which Eleanor was, both literally and figuratively, the uncontested sovereign."[33]

> These courts of love probably date from as early as 1152—the beginning of Eleanor's reign, if not in Paris then at least in Poitiers. Here she lived alone for many months after her marriage to Henry, at a time when he was greatly occupied with the succession of Normandy and England. The new queen's Courts of Love took place during her expeditions to the different cities of her vast domain. We should note that out of the 31 'judgments of love' mentioned by Andreas Capellanus, six are attributed to

Swan misericord,
Magdalen College
Oxford. (Nina A. Thune)

Eleanor, five to Ermengarde (viscountess of Champagne),
and seven to Marie de Champagne, who appears to have
excelled in this art.[34]

Raimon de Miraval: Troubadour of the Languedoc

Miraval is a tiny village in the Cabardès, some twenty miles north
of the walled city of Carcassonne. It was the birthplace of Raimon
de Miraval, esteemed poet of love and honor. Born between 1160
and 1165, Raimon died between 1216 and 1229. "According to
his *vida*, Raimon de Miraval was a 'poor knight' of the Carcasses,
who owned a fourth part of the castle of Miraval. [Raimon de]
Miraval enjoyed the favor of Raimon VI's magnificent court of
Toulouse and was, with his few possessions, able to avoid extreme
poverty."[35] Raymond VI's court was extremely influential, so Raimon's being invited there so often was indeed a special honor.

Miraval further refined his own system of *Fin' Amors* principles. For Miraval, defending a lady's honour was a particularly
important aspect of proper troubadour behavior. Loyalty was a
cardinal virtue in his ethic of love, "and was absolutely essential to
the proper conduct of the 'Fin' Amors'. It was, in the troubadour
world, a serious moral issue ..."[36]

The Rules of Love: Miraval's guide to successful courtship

First of all, the ideas that love is the cardinal virtue and that love makes you a better person were underlying assumptions. Tobias Churton explains:

> The Fine Love provides the energy for spiritual vision… The world without the Fin' Amors is implicitly vulgar since it resists the moral of Love. This gives Miraval's vision a clear logical parallel with that of the Cathars among whom he spent most of his life. For Miraval, the agonies of this world can be borne and even redeemed by projecting the inner world upon the state of things about him; love takes him beyond himself. He can love the wise and the mad simultaneously … opposites are reconciled as he and his lady are reconciled. This was his way to wholeness. The Fin' Amors has a religious, that is, ordering character, which takes it far beyond the mere sexual romanticism which provided the opening key. Troubadours like Miraval did not just dream their way to a better world, they put their law upon the world and lived it out, regardless of the consequences.[37]

Miraval on Jealousy:

> Jealousy is a prime virtue of the Fin' Amors. Jealousy exacts fidelity from the lady, and from the lover also. Miraval sang: 'Jealousy teaches me to consecrate myself exclusively to the service of a lady, so that I want no other and abstain from paying court to them.[38]

On the agony of being in love:

> Love is necessarily accompanied by torments, but the good things compensate for the bad with a noble lady. Miraval asks: 'What value has Love if one does not suffer evil from it?' Love must be tried in the alembic of experience and time.[39]

Equally agonizing it must have been even with some churchmen. The illustrious Ramon Llull commented on how difficult
and demanding it was to maintain his later monastic life: "… in
later life, having turned away from his profligate youth, confessed
that 'the beauty of women, O Lord, has been a plague and a trib-
ulation to my eyes …'"[40]

ON YEARNING, HOW LONG LOVE COULD TAKE:

> Before the absolute fulfillment of the Fin' Amors must
> come the customary favors of courtesy: affection, kind-
> ness, presents and friendship: the sound basis for rec-
> ompense after long service—and service could be very
> long indeed. It was for the ladies to prove, by a thousand
> means and tests, patience and fidelity. It is this time-fac-
> tor that gives many troubadour *cansos* that edge of frus-
> tration and yearning which is often mistaken for ritual
> sublimation of sexual desire.… If there were any doubt
> about the joyfully carnal aspect of authentic troubadour
> aspiration, one only need read Miraval's *canso* dedicated
> ironically to 'the one who does not want to hear songs.[41]

ON TO LOVE … AND TO LOVE WELL:

The troubadours of the 12th century all saw Fine Love as the privileged way—to those who surrendered themselves to it without
reserve—of becoming a better person.

> When the troubadour loved *well*, when he cultivated
> within himself the courtesies that refined heart and deed,
> he ennobled and raised up his merit or value and his
> consciousness. As Miraval sang: "It's thanks to her that
> I love the fountain and the stream…" Troubadour con-
> temporary Arnaut Daniel: "Always I become better and
> more pure / because I serve and honour the most kind
> …" Miraval again: "Because it is from Love that proceeds
> the highest value …" This love does not simply come
> from out of the troubadour, rather, everything good in
> the world comes from love; love is the source. Transcend-
> ing his *natural* limitations, yearning for the highest: these

were the dynamics shared by Miraval and the Good Men and Good Women.[42]

Bouquet of roses.

How the Lady opens hearts and minds:

> The true "mysterium coniunctionis" remains to be achieved in everyone. In liberating the extraordinary and revolutionary vitality and mystery of the feminine— divine and human—the troubadours set a luminous example for their own, for our time, and for the time to come. The Lady opens hearts and minds; without Her, we are spiritually dead.[43]

Roman de la Rose: a medieval courtly love bestseller

The author of the earlier part of the hugely successful *Roman de la Rose*, written in the 13th century, drew heavily on the *De Amore* of Andreas Capellanus for his material. Presented as an allegorical dream-vision about love, this compelling tale was the work of two French authors, "Guillaume de Lorris who wrote the first part in about 1230–35, and Jean de Meun who almost forty years later embarked on an extensive continuation which he completed around 1275 … The enormous popularity of this work in its own day and for many years that followed provides us with confirmation that courtly love and its principles continued to be a preoccupation for medieval society throughout the entire Middle Ages … For about 300 years after its first appearance … it seems to have been one of the most widely read and influential vernacular poems of its time."[44] Presented as an allegorical dream:

> The tale is an account of the narrator's quest to pluck the rose, a representation of the young woman who becomes the object of his love. In the walled garden of 'Deduit' or Pleasure (said to represent courtly society), the dreamer meets the god of Love, who causes him to become enamoured of a rosebud glimpsed in the fountain of Narcissus. Rejecting the advice of Reason the lover resolves to approach the rose, but encounters a number of setbacks, personified in figures such as Danger, Jealousy and Fear. Finally he succeeds in kissing the rose before Jealousy constructs a fortified tower round it, the point at which the contribution of Guillaume de Lorris ceases. The implicit sexual metaphor or the lover's quest is developed to a final conclusion in the continuation of the poem, added many years later by Jean de Meun, where the dreamer finally succeeds in entering the inner sanctum of the rose before awakening at daybreak …[45]

The Decline of the Troubadours

The great variety of poems and songs of the Occitanian and Catalan troubadours survived by the foresight of a few enlightened patrons, who, sensing the end of an era, began feverishly collecting these manuscripts as best they could, in spite of the Inquisition.

Chivalry and the knightly chivalric code

It is important to keep in mind that not all troubadours were knights, and not all knights were troubadours. *Chivalry* is the traditional code of conduct associated with the institution of medieval knighthood. The chivalric code was more like a cluster of concepts that emanated from individual training and service to others, often having spiritual overtones. Over time its meaning evolved to emphasize ideals such as knightly virtues, courtly love, and courtesy, along with the skills and behavior of the warrior. A knight's code of chivalry was a moral system that stated all knights should protect others who cannot protect themselves—such as children, widows, the handicapped, and elders. All knights were expected to have the strength, valor and skill to fight wars and to be exceptionally disciplined.[46]

Scholars have lamented the lack of any oral tradition sources about chivalry, but have had other sources to consult in learning about the historic chivalric code:

> We can … only regret that no medieval writer went from one castle, tourney field, court, siege camp, battle line or raiding party to another, observing and interviewing knights of all particular social claims to record their commonplace attitudes and beliefs; with such evidence, we could easily differentiate their attitudes in varying degrees from the ideal statements and reform tracts which we possess in abundance. Lacking such a record, we have no oral history of chivalry, although that is precisely what we want … Almost unnoticed, our assmption can easily become that this is what chivalry was and how it actually worked in medieval society. The hard truth is that we must reconstruct the living reality of chivalry from the entire set of text available: the vast corpus of imaginative chivalric literature, as well as ecclesiastic and lay legislation, legal records, contemporary chronicles, handbooks for knights, the details of chivalric biography.[47]

One historian remarks that the chivalrous idea "is pride aspiring to beauty, and formalized pride gives rise to a conception of honor, which is the pole of noble life."[48] Let us recall that the "troubadour code of Love" is not identical to "the knightly code of Chivalry." On the other hand, both flourished at the same time and were often followed by the same person.

Tournaments

> Imagine a world where vivid color was a luxury; where music was heard only at fairs, courts and suchlike great gatherings; where entertainments might be seen at rare intervals, and then only in towns and cities, a world where after nightfall the darkness was broken by no more than a few feeble gleams.[49]

Tournaments were often the central feature of medieval pageantry. Familiar to us from both literature and Hollywood, the image of the famed "jousting tournament" remains with us today. Lords and ladies, knights in their shining armor, music and feasting. Medieval tournaments combined the spectacular with the excitement of a dangerous, skillful sport and the attendant hero-worship of its "stars." Coupled with this "was an element of idealism, for the tournament was central to the world of chivalry, and the ladies who watched from the stands were there to inspire as well as admire, to strengthen their knights' courage by their presence. By the end of the Middle Ages, tournaments were immensely expensive to stage, and hence were aristocratic, exclusive rarities, usually associated with some great occasion of state."[50]

GIFTS FROM A LADY, MINSTRELS, AND JUGGLERS

Medieval legends, art, and the lore of today often mention the ladies watching these colorful tournaments. They would often give their knight a special gift either before—for "good luck"—or after, if he won or did well in the competition. Some accounts say that it was for the love of a lady that a knight would fight diligently and endure the most hardship. One of the most prized gifts a lady could bestow was her special belt, girdle, or scarf. This was given to a knight after a successful tournament: "Sometimes these gifts given as prizes at tournaments would contain the lady's hair woven into the girdle or a bracelet. Like the green girdle that the mysterious lady gives to Sir Gawain in the Middle English

Der herzoge von Anhalt.

Tournament from medieval Codex Manesse, Herzog von Anhalt, 1305-1315. (Wikimedia Commons)

poem *Sir Gawain and the Green Knight,* and which binds him within the circle of female control, these items of dress were also associated with women's semi-magical protective power."[51] They would sometimes be made by the lady or her staff, but always had a personal touch, a favorite color or design. "From the belt would hang the purse, a major accessory in both the male and female wardrobe, since clothes did not contain pockets at this period …"[52] So the girdle as well as the purse could be part of a tournament prize.

Occasionally, at or near medieval tournament sites, minstrels and jugglers would entertain the crowds. But clowns and harlequin figures as we think of them today came much later. (In England, we have the famous early 17th century image which

English Elizabethan clown Will Kempe dancing a jig from Norwich to London 1600.

portrays one of the best known early comic actors in the early Shakespeare dramas—Will Kempe—dancing a jig from Norwich to London (1600)! Some experts believe Kempe may have been the model Shakespeare used for Falstaff.)

Puivert Castle: A famed troubadour citadel

Chateau du Puivert, a Cathar citadel in the Aude, is one of the most famous Cathar—and troubadour—castles in medieval France. As the French tourist website informs us, it is twenty minutes from Quillan, towards Foix. This stately residence with its 35-meter high keep and six towers dominates the Puivert-Nébias plain. Its huge courtyard evokes the jousting tournaments so loved by knights, while its great hall calls to mind the troubadours' poetic songs. In the 12th century, the Congosts, the lords of Puivert, were Cathar protectors. Captured during the Albigensian Crusade in 1210, Puivert castle became the property of two northern French Lords. During the Occitan counter-conquest in 1220, the site was liberated by Loup de Foix. At the beginning of the 14th century, a new castle was built. The sculpted decoration in the Musicians' Hall in the keep demonstrates that the sophisticated new castle was intended to be a stately residence rather than a fortress. The sculptures depict a bagpipe player, a drummer, a hurdy-gurdy player, a lutenist, a harp player, and a zither player.

The Quercorb museum, dedicated to everyday life in the region, is also in the village of Puivert. The second floor houses a gallery of troubadour musical instruments with reproductions of eight instruments of the medieval period. The last gallery presents a model of Puivert castle and moulds of the sculptures in the Musicians' Hall of the castle. The construction of the present chateau dates from the 13th century. The castle was classified as a *Monument historique* in 1907. It is privately owned. Puivert Castle has also been a location for major films, including *The Ninth Gate*, starring Johnny Depp.

Puivert Castle. (Anneke Koremans)

Legend has it that the town of Puivert welcomed a great gathering of troubadours in about 1170. At this meeting, troubadour Peire d'Auvergne penned a satirical Occitan poem which concluded with the words:

> *Lo vers fo fats als enfobatz*
> *A puich-vert tot jugan rizen*[53]

> "This poem was composed to the sound of bagpipes
> At Puivert among song and laughter."

King David playing harp, stone carving, at Freiburg cathedral, Germany.

King David playing the harp at Chartres, stained glass window. (Jane May)

Carvings at cathedrals and chapels of troubadours, musicians and minstrels

Images abound of musicians in medieval buildings. Most often they are carved in stone or wood—often as misericords in cathedrals. They portray not only human musicians, but a fair amount of animal/mythic musician symbolism as well. Medieval bestiaries would often have similar images. In various cathedrals, chapels, or private homes, we note symbolism of a musical animal or myth in carvings—a donkey or ass, monkey, mermaid, siren, sow and piglets, the Fool, angel(s), and so on.

1297 1298

1299 1300 1301

Five examples of medieval troubadour "Foolscap" watermark images. (From Harold Bayley's *Lost Language of Symbolism*, vol. II, p. 320.)

Classic Christian themes of angel musicians are common. Old and New Testament stories were often portrayed in medieval buildings with musical instruments accompanying the image—King David is a perennial favorite in this regard, as are clerics portrayed playing bells.

Non-human or animal symbolism often accompanies troubadour or musical themes in the art of medieval buildings; described in medieval poems or court documents; and in heraldry. An example of an animal image on a heraldic shield includes ***the Swan***, symbolizing love and fidelity:

The Foolscap image in Troubadour watermarks was used at times by Albigensian papermakers—reminiscent of a cluster of ancient themes relating to music, harmony, the wisdom of The Fool and a higher, universal Wisdom.

The Lion and the Unicorn

Lion and Unicorn symbolism, especially exemplified in the famous series of tapestries now in the Cluny museum in Paris, are among the most interesting that relate to the theme of Love.

Lady and the Unicorn tapestry, Puivert. (Ani Williams)

The Paris tapestries [i.e., now in Cluny] were rediscovered in 1841 on the walls of the sub-prefect's dusty offices in the castle of Boussac at Creuse. It was the writer Prosper Merimee who first drew attention to their value. In 1844 George Sand saw them and wrote about them in her novel *Jeanne* and in articles, in which she correctly dated them to the end of the 15th century on the basis of the ladies' costumes. Yet they remained at the castle for a long time, threatened by damp and mould. Not until 1863 were they brought to the Thermes de Cluny in Paris, carried by the wave of Romanticism. Careful conservation has now restored them almost to their former glory.[54]

And on the fascinating symbolism of the Unicorn in these tapestries:

Above all the scene is dominated by the Unicorn. It is invariably near the lady's left-hand side—the side of the heart—now reclining, now standing and always attentive to her actions. It radiates a self-consciousness which gives it a different dimension from the lion. It thinks its own thoughts and could leave the scene if it so wished. But it stays there. Its attitudes are those of devotion, and the intimacy between lady and animal is reflected … It is as if the two poles of the animal have merged … which binds them together. Over all of the pictures [i.e., tapestries] there is a refined grace, bordering on decadence.[55]

The unicorn theme was commonly found in medieval bestiaries, which were "… used among other things as inspirations for carvings in medieval cathedral and church architecture, especially that of the order of the Cluniac monks who were prodigious builders."[56]

Rosslyn: *Song, Sonnet and Pageant*

As we learned in chapter 6 (Medieval Guilds), Roslin Glen in Scotland was a popular venue for summer plays. (See chapter 10 for more on Rosslyn.) As part of these festivities, a number of "strolling players" and musicians gathered for the famous Robin

Rosslyn Chapel musician playing the bagpipes, flanked by two Green Man images. (Karen Ralls)

Hood and Little John plays. We mentioned that there was a large gypsy population in medieval Scotland. As a minority, they often suffered from legal prohibitions against practicing the skills for which they were well-known: as artisans, metal workers, horn-carvers, and so on. Thus a number of gypsies turned to entertainment to earn their living. They had long been valued as talented, traveling storytellers, so they were easily welcomed to join native "strolling players" and "minstrels," performing at the St. Clair festivals held at Roslin.[57]

In chapter 10, we also discuss the St. Clair family connection to the esoteric brotherhoods in more detail. But here, let us quote an authority who compares the symbolism of the old artisan guilds and fraternities with the message of the music and poetry heard at medieval gatherings: "There lay a ritual symbolism involving a search for something remote, hidden or lost … Bards, troubadours, Meistersingers, and strolling gypsy players, by way of song, sonnet and pageant, carried onwards just such an esoteric doctrine."[58]

The End of the Troubadours

The Knights Templar, Cathars, Sufis, and similar groups liaised with troubadours, contributing to the overall flowering of the troubadour movement at its peak. Yet, in time, the culture, language and music of the troubadours were wiped out by a combination of the Inquisition and the Bubonic Plague.

By the 14th century, in Toulouse, the mere possession of a troubadour manuscript was enough to land one before the terrible tribunals of the Inquisition. Of the Occitan troubadours, only a few hundred sparse melodic frames have survived. (These were not records of actual music, but were intended as mnemonic devices for those who knew the songs and wanted to recall a specific sequence of codes—a musical "Art of Memory.")

Europe lost a great treasure when the last troubadour died in 1292. He was Guiraud Riquier of Narbonne (1254–92). But by the time he reached maturity, the art was already failing. The Inquisition targeted the troubadours and worked feverishly to suppress them. At the same time, a transition was taking place from the idolization of the chivalric Lady to the Christianized feminine archetype:

There was a slow process in action whereby religious lyricism aimed at the Virgin Mary was substituted for that of the lady. Consequently, heterodox persons since that time have tended to see 'Our Lady' not as the Virgin Mother but as Mary of Magdala, Christ's true lady friend. Furthermore, genuine love-poetry aimed at real ladies became hidden within the cult of the Virgin with all the inevitable results for the repression of woman entailed in this. Ladies were virgins or safely married; *women* were fallen.[59]

In 1323, a group of merchants, bankers, and clerks got together in Toulouse to codify rules of language and versification to encourage the remaining poets to perfect their art, to purify morals, and—in a climate of religious rigor—to edit works and submit them for the approval of the Grand Inquisitor.

The social status of troubadours varied considerably … In northern and central France aristocratic poets known as *trouveres* wrote poetry, largely about love, for royal and princely courts. The language they used was the *langue d'oil*, the ancestor of modern French. Like the troubadours, they died in the 13th century.[60]

The Black Death in 1348 hastened the decline of the noble art all the more. This pandemic wiped out an estimated one-third of the population of Europe. The zeitgeist no longer favored either the expression of self-centered emotional aspirations or large gatherings for entertainment. Among any troubadours who still remained in the final period of the 14th and early 15th centuries, famous troubadour competitions were held—a desperate effort to keep the tradition alive in the aftermath of the Inquisition and the Plague.

However, the medieval troubadour could not survive the rigidity imposed upon the creativity he had celebrated. As the primary message of the troubadours was love: "one is looking at an archetypal poetic process which, while illuminated by Jungian psychology to some extent, is foreign to what was apparently a spontaneous and fertile effusion of people who lived by their own moral, erotic, and spiritual categories."[61]

While the famous troubadour Miraval died in a heart-breaking downturn of civilized life, his spirit has truly survived. "We can find echoes of our man in Renaissance Platonic love poetry, in 18th and 19th century romanticism, and in the best of the rock & roll and folk tradition. The *Fine Love* was ecstatic but not mindless. Its disciplines were never easy since their aim was an elusive unity of flesh and spirit, requiring a commitment to self-purification alien to exploitable hedonism. Nothing guaranteed love."[62]

Ever since, the legacy of the troubadours—and love—have continued, beckoning to us, challenging us all to see Love in a new light and as a higher truth all its own.

"To recover the Joy which we have lost"

But, perhaps best of all, for both Western civilization and in our own lives and the lives of those we love, we may still ponder the last words of the last remaining song of the troubadour Raimon de Miraval:

> So that, before long, we shall be able,
>
> ladies and lovers
>
> to recover the Joy which we have lost![63]

Chapter 9

Arthur and Merlin
Glastonbury and Other Sacred Sites

"Listen. Strange women lying in ponds distributing swords is no basis for a system of government ...."[1]

Detail of St Kentigern and Merlin stained glass window, Stobo church, Scottish borders. (Dr. Gordon Strachan)

Stories, legends and myths continue to inspire—perhaps none more so than the tales of King Arthur, Merlin, and the Knights of the Round Table. Like all great myths, the Arthurian legends are told and retold, ever weaving their spell, inspiring lives, minds, and hearts through the ages.cross

Today, their popularity continues unabated. I have long noted that, for young and old alike, a key to enjoying these tales and adventures often comes from visiting Arthurian-related places in person. In the Recommended Reading section at the end of this book, there is a list of books about Arthur, Merlin, and Guinevere. It is a good place to find resources to continue your studies. Here we will mainly focus on places you can visit.

King Arthur: Historical Introduction

The quest for an historical Arthur has been a challenging task for scholars for centuries. Many have studied the Arthurian tales—historians, archaeologists, Celtic scholars, Jungian analysts, theologians, and mythologists, among others. Arthur is one of the most enduring legends of all time: "the power, durability and adaptability of his legends suggest that 'universal truths' may be discovered by an exploration of the legends."[2] Indeed, universal truths are the animating soul of enduring myths, stories, songs, and legends.

King Arthur is an important cultural figure in early Celtic literature as a leader, warrior, chieftain, hero, and champion against the invaders. Certainly no other hero of the Dark Ages is featured so prominently in such a vast amount of literature as King Arthur. But not all that has come down to us speaks in consistent glowing terms of Arthur, Lancelot or Guinevere. Perhaps the fact that they are portrayed with their imperfections may have humanized them

and helped ensure their survival. Little was heard of a historical Arthur figure after 542, so the mid–6th century has been assumed to be roughly when he died. After that time, youths of noble and royal birth in various parts of Europe began to bear the name Arthur as parents would have wanted to name their children after a great warrior hero.

By the 12th century, Arthur became a Pan-European figure, a dominant motif in literary and artistic culture, a focal point for the cults of chivalry and courtly love and for esoteric mysteries such as the Holy Grail. Numerous versions of his tales were written in Old French, Latin, Old Welsh and others. Also by the 12th century, prominent historians like William of Malmesbury, Caradoc of Llancarfon, and Giraldus of Wales were trying to sort out fact from fiction about him. One author tells us about the power of the "Arthurian mythos":

> The potency of the Arthurian legends may reflect the remarkable achievements of the historical King Arthur. But undoubtedly a factor in their cultural power and adaptability was that from the earliest stages the mythos of Arthur absorbed aspects of Celtic religion and deification, such as the mysterious birth, the sword in the stone, the water deities, (ladies of the lake), the cauldron of immortality and the Other World, and, most importantly, an element found in many religions, the Second Coming … The Arthurian legendary material has attracted many of the great writers of European civilization—Taliesin, Geoffrey of Monmouth, Wace, Chretien de Troyes, Gottfried von Strassburg, Wolfram von Eschenbach, Geoffrey Chaucer, Sir Thomas Malory, Edmund Spenser, Alfred Tennyson, Thomas Hardy, T. S. Eliot …[3]

As scholars have pointed out, the figure of Arthur that has come down to us in English history as an active, heroic king was largely the creation of Geoffrey of Monmouth. Geoffrey, a Welshman, wrote *Historia Regum Britanniae* (History of the Kings of Britain) in 1132. The Arthurian legend is believed to be rooted in Celtic tradition, but "it only achieved its prodigious popularity when it became a dominant theme of medieval literature in

OPPOSITE: Statue of King Arthur, Hofkirke, Innsbruck, designed by Albrecht Durer and cast by Peter Vischer the Elder, 1520s. (Wikimedia Commons)

Glastonbury Tor, Somerset, a site of many legends through the centuries, including those about the powerful faery King Gwyn reigning from his domain within. Other lore in earlier times claimed that it was here that Melwas kept Guinevere prisoner for a time, and that Merlin devised his Round Table. Today, the threads of many traditions intersect in this extraordinary place. (Eily Nash)

Continental Europe, first and foremost in France. However, Arthur was a known figure in Welsh tradition at least as early as the 8th century. In one of the earliest references, that of Nennius in his *History of the Britons*, Arthur is a war leader who defends his country against Saxon invaders."[4]

On the Continent, Chretien de Troyes introduced a different Arthur: the *roi faineant* hovering in the background while his knights dominate the action… In England … the version of Arthur which prevailed … was basically that of Geoffrey of Monmouth. Only at the very end of the Middle Ages did Thomas Malory supplement Geoffrey's whole account of the rise and fall of the kingdom with materials from the French romances.[5]

Early Arthurian folklore is mainly associated with the areas of Wales, lowland Scotland, Brittany, Cornwall, and parts of

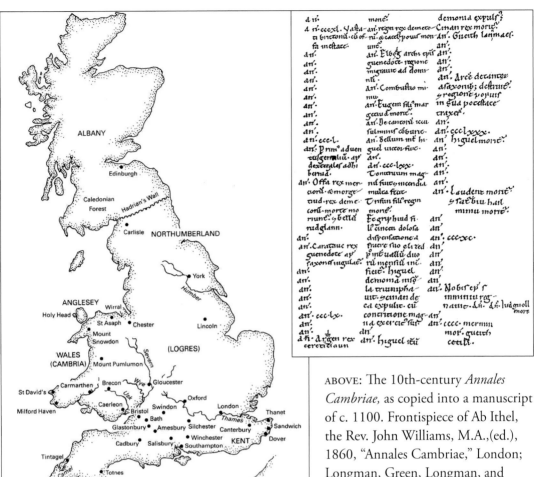

ABOVE: The 10th-century *Annales Cambriae,* as copied into a manuscript of c. 1100. Frontispiece of Ab Ithel, the Rev. John Williams, M.A.,(ed.), 1860, "Annales Cambriae," London; Longman, Green, Longman, and Roberts.

LEFT: Map of 6th century Arthurian Britain. (J. Ralls)

Cumbria, England. Sites in southern England, such as South Cadbury in Somerset, eventually also became focal points for archaeological excavation. Archaeologists confirm that very early on, hill forts developed in Britain in the late Bronze and early Iron Age (roughly the start of the first millennium BC).[6] Arthur's literary entrance into English culture comes much later—immortalized by works of the 12th and 13th centuries, when the longstanding oral tradition of the Arthurian and Grail stories were written down.

Arthur and scholarship

King Arthur has been thought of as a Celtic hero, as much of the earliest references to him come from Celtic areas. Academic scholars have said that the Latin version of his name, Arturus, does not seem to have been found anywhere else. They have come to the inevitable conclusion that it must be a name that commemorates the great deeds of a lost king or chieftain of the Dark Ages. An interesting, but more controversial, alternative view has recently been advanced by other scholars who claim evidence that a second century Roman officer named Lucius Artorius Castus, prefect of the VIth Legion, may have been the historical Arthur.[7]

Theories abound and the search is still on even now, as more theories and concepts about Arthur, Merlin, and Glastonbury continue to be exchanged in academia.[8] Ideas continue to be expressed in a number of interesting non-academic publications and forums as well. Worldwide interest in all matters Arthurian remains as popular today as it ever was.

Arthur Through the Ages

The Arthurian tradition was carried into more modern times through the arts—exemplified by the great interest in and revival of Arthur during the Tudor period, by later poets such as Tennyson and his famous *Idylls of the King,* and in the Pre-Raphaelite

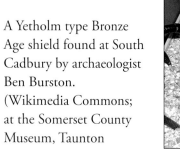

A Yetholm type Bronze Age shield found at South Cadbury by archaeologist Ben Burston. (Wikimedia Commons; at the Somerset County Museum, Taunton

Engraving of Cadbury Castle, drawn in 1723 by William Stukeley and captioned *Prospect of Camalet Castle.* (Wikimedia Commons)

paintings of Burne-Jones and Rossetti. The composer Henry Purcell, who wrote the music for an opera entitled *King Arthur or the British Worthy* (produced in March 1691 at London's Dorset Garden Theatre with a libretto by John Dryden), also participated in the revival of Arthurian themes.[9]

Lord Edward Bulwer-Lytton, one of the most popular novelists in the late 1840's reworked the Arthurian tales in his 12-part epic poem *King Arthur.* In this series, Arthur, is a warrior-king of the Dark Ages who successfully leads the Cymrians—the Welsh or British—against the incursions of the Saxons, who are identified as Teutons. Arthur is both a national hero and a champion of Christianity, and is claimed by Bulwer-Lytton as the founder of the royal line that descends to Queen Victoria."[10] (Bulwer-Lytton is also known as the author of the fascinating novel *Zanoni*, which includes Rosicrucian themes.) Over the centuries, other artists and novelists continued to contribute to the Arthurian corpus.

The "Once and Future King"

The myth of the "Once and Future King"—the idea that Arthur is asleep in a grave, especially a cave, and will someday return to save the country in its hour of need—is found in various parts of Britain. A dormant, powerful protector prepared to arise and answer the needs of the community or nation is a well-known theme found in much world folklore. Merlin, too, is said to be waiting the right time to re-emerge.

Merlin as drawn by
Aubrey Beardsley for his
illustrated edition of *Le
Morte d'Arthur,* 1893–94.

MERLIN

Another fascinating Arthurian character is, of course, Merlin—
still an important figure lingering in Western consciousness.
"Merlin is forever." Readers worldwide still enjoy and find meaning in the many versions of these tales. Arthur, Merlin, and the
Grail have become archetypes, both Pagan and Christian, and
have grown in human consciousness for centuries.[11]

Philip Carr-Gomm reminds us about the key role of the wizard Merlin in the story of Arthur: "And behind this array of creative outpourings and obsessions stands the lone figure of Merlin,
the archetypal wizard who masterminded the birth and rearing
of King Arthur, who acted as his Druid, advising him from the
shadows during his reign. Indeed, it was Merlin who was responsible for the creation of the Round Table, and, ultimately, for the
knights' quest for the Holy Grail."[12]

A most unusual Birth

Merlin is a multi-faceted wonder—a wizard, bard, prophet, skilled
magician, and the key advisor to King Arthur. Almost everything

about him is outside of time and space, starting with his entry into this world.

Robert's de Boron's account portrays Merlin as a suspicious character with possible connections to evil spirits. On the positive side, de Boron mentions that thanks to the intervention of a priest who blessed his mother, Merlin used his powers for good in the end. De Boron claims that Merlin's mother was a lovely, virgin teenage girl of parents in great difficulty. This differs from the account of Merlin's mother as a princess by Geoffrey of Monmouth.

In de Boron's story, because she forgot to say her prayers one fateful evening, she was then raped in the middle of the night by a demon. Merlin's conception resulted.[13] Upon awakening after that fateful night, the girl knew she was pregnant. She contacted two friends and "confessed." She was then quarantined in a stone tower until the baby was born. Shortly after the birth, the baby was taken away from her and things took a very unusual turn. It was noted that the new baby had thick, black hair, could talk like an adult, and was said to be a prodigy during his early months. In medieval times, when Christian chroniclers such as de Boron were writing about a "hairy, talking baby" it would definitely imply a

Merlin's Cave, Tintagel, Cornwall. (J. Ralls)

very dangerous or "demonic" connotation. Heresy was something no one ever wanted to be associated with. De Boron's message is that Merlin—a "son of a widow"—even though his mother was blessed, *is still somehow dangerous, illegitimate, suspect, and heretical.*

De Boron taints the image of the famous wizard with accusations of black magic and horrible heresies. In medieval times, this tableau was a way of conducting what we now call a "smear campaign." His account states that a group of devils plotted and planned to create an evil Antichrist—a half-human and half-demon. This was said to be Merlin. But de Boron portrays a priest intervening, and blessing the girl chosen to give birth to this creature. Merlin later repays the priest by telling him how Joseph of Arimathea brought the Holy Grail to Avalon.

De Boron's portrait of Merlin was a dramatic change from earlier writings about Merlin where he is portrayed as an esteemed wise man, pagan era mage and seer.[14] Later medieval authors seem to have wanted to downgrade or destroy Merlin's reputation, while modern-day authors have expounded further on the "inspired seer" concept.[15][16][17]

But no matter which version you prefer about Merlin, in nearly all accounts he is directly associated with nature—having a special relationship with plants, trees, rocks, animals, and certain springs or fountains. He is continually portrayed as a "man of the forest" or as a "wild man of the woods" with the gifts of poetry, prophecy, and magic. His home is *the sanctuary of the forest*, harkening back to the earlier Celtic belief regarding the importance of groves of trees to the Druids. French Breton scholar Jean Markale comments that although Merlin's behavior in the Arthurian stories may have caused him to be labeled a "wandering madman," he is actually to be considered as a "wise man" or "sage":

> By taking refuge in the heart of the forest, or by agreeing to go to the invisible prison of the fairy Vivian, Merlin withdraws completely. He separates himself from the society of his time and affirms his discovery of a new reality, a new alliance. From this it is evident that Merlin, who is taken for a madman, is in fact a sage.[18]

In our modern industrialized society, we are cut off from nature. In these tales, Merlin seems to symbolize a vast knowledge of, and a special alliance with, nature—as well as more magical or spiritual types of advanced knowledge. His home is the earth. He is often portrayed as a solitary figure living in the forest, a tree, or a special tower that serves as his astronomical observatory.

Merlin was said to have written prophecies; but scholars today point out that none of his early poems have survived, only descriptions of them by others, such as Geoffrey of Monmouth.

> Geoffrey had published a long series of prophecies attributed to Merlin, called the *Prophetiae Merlini,* which he incorporated in its entirety into his *Historia.* About 1150 he finished the *Vita Merlini,* a biography in which he delved further into Merlin's origins. With these three works, Geoffrey created a character which has continually fascinated novelists, poets, artists and scholars through the centuries.[19]

It is impossible, of course, to say for certain what a historical Merlin may have said or written. But it is the legends of his prophecies that have lived and are known to many today—through novels, films, and storytelling.

St Michael's Mount, Cornwall, where legend says the archangel Michael appeared to a hermit here in the Dark Ages, the period of Arthur and Merlin. (Simon Brighton)

OPPOSITE: Dunbarton, Scotland, the Dark Age court of King Rhydderch and Merlin's sister, Queen Gwenddydd, where the prophet is said to have spent three enforced stays during his madness. (Simon Brighton)

Was Merlin Historical?

Was there a genuine historical Merlin? If he did exist, he seems to have come down to us as a composite of several historical characters—Merddyn Wyllt or Merlin Sylvestis, for example. Scholars suggest other candidates such as Merlin Ambrosius, who is believed to have been born in 450 and died about 536. He was named and described in Geoffrey of Monmouth's *Historia Regum Britanniae*. Geoffrey associated him with the British leader Vortigern and portrayed him as the Merlin of Uther Pendragon, involved in Arthur's birth and childhood. Merlin was also called Ambrosius in a ninth century work by Nennius called *Historia Brittonum*.

Another Merlin, based in Scottish territory, was known as Merlin Sylvestris (of the wood) and Merlin Caledonius (Merlin the Wild). He is portrayed as having lived in the forest during the second half of the 6th century, after Arthur's death. This is the Merlin mentioned at the battle of Arfderydd (Artheret) mentioned later in this chapter. His name is spelled as Myrddin. He is described as a mad man who fled to the forest sanctuary, the location of which some writers believe was the upper Tweeddale area of the Scottish Borders, near Stobo. Nicolai Tolstoy in *The Quest for Merlin* believed that the location where the original Myrddin, or Merlin Sylvestris, had his forest sanctuary was that of the summit of Hart Fell, a beautiful area near Stobo in the Scottish Borders. Another location suggested by Tolstoy is that of nearby Geddes's Well, near the top of Broad Law in the same general area. Stobo is only about 15 miles from Hart Fell and 8 miles from Broad Law.[20]

Merlin's "threefold death"

Tolstoy also notes similarities between the "threefold death" of Merlin and that of Christ:

> In some manuscripts, Merlin is said to have predicted his own death, and other accounts imply that the Lady of the Lake may have purposely killed him. But he is also believed by some as having had a "threefold death", as: 1) He was stoned by the Christian shepherds of King

Rhydderch Hael of Strathclyde; 2) He fell over a steep bank of the river Tweed by the foot of Dunmeller (Drumelzier); and 3) He fell into the river and impaled himself on a sharp stake, and so died from both impaling and drowning simultaneously.[21]

Merlin and the Goddess

Themes of the maidens of Avalon, the mother goddess, and the Feminine in relation to the Merlin mythos have also been addressed by an increasing number of modern writers, both fiction and nonfiction, including Caitlin Matthews, R.J. Stewart, Marion Zimmer Bradley, and others. Dolores Ashcroft-Nowicki discussed these connections at a Merlin conference held in Britain: "The Goddess still watches over these islands…The faith that was new in Merlin's time in its turn has faded, for to everything there is a season of fullness and increase followed by one of waning and decrease, but her symbol, the Great Cup that holds the Ocean of Time, will remain forever."[22]

GLASTONBURY

We will now turn to Glastonbury, one of the most important Arthur-related sites in English history. Since the 12th century, Glastonbury has been identified with Avalon, the mystical island of Arthurian lore. The turning point in what one scholar calls "the historicizing and anglicizing of Arthur" was the exhumation of his relics at Glastonbury Abbey in 1191:

> In that year, his body and according to some accounts that of Guinevere, too, was 'discovered' in a sarcophagus buried at great depth between two ancient pyramids in the monks' cemetery, a leaden cross revealing the identity of the remains … Why the discovery of Arthur's body took place precisely when it did appears to have been the result of several factors. The devastating fire at Glastonbury in 1184 created a financial crisis and the community would have been sympathetic to the kind of publicity Arthur's discovery would generate. According to Giraldus

LEFT: Glastonbury Abbey ruins. (Karen Ralls)

RIGHT: Glastonbury Abbey, side view. (Karen Ralls)

BELOW: Glastonbury Abbey, Lady Chapel, north door. (Karen Ralls)

Cambrensis, Henry II suggested the dig and in the 1180's Henry II would have had good reason for reminding the Welsh that Arthur was dead and buried (and in English territory at that). He might also have wished, in the aftermath of the Becket fiasco, to have promoted Glastonbury as an alternative site to Canterbury for the origins of English Christianity....[23]

Originally, it was said that *three* bodies had been found, including that of Mordred. This "fact" was later excised, as was that of the discovery of the remains of Guinevere once Richard the Lionheart became associated with this event. The inscription on the lead cross found with the bodies was said to have been discovered, in 1193 by Giraldus: "*Hic iacet sepultus inclitus rex Arthurus cum Wenneuereia uxore sua secunda in insula Auallonia*"

Glastonbury Tor, from inside St Michael's Tower at summit. (Eily Nash)

("Here lies buried the famous king Arthur with his second wife Guenevere in the Isle of Avalon.") Ralph of Coggeshall (c.1194) read it as "Here lies the famous king Arthur, buried in the Isle of Avalon." Writing a half a century later, another Glastonbury chronicler, Adam of Damerham, and, later, at the time of the Dissolution of the monasteries in the 16th century, antiquarian John Leland also had their own very similar variants of what they felt the proper wording to ultimately be.[24]

The lead cross itself is believed to have been lost in the 18th century. Some people ask today: did the monks perhaps "fake" this discovery to get more pilgrims and desperately needed revenue after the devastating Abbey fire of 1184? Yet without the cross itself, obviously nothing can be said for certain, fuelling further speculation through the years.

From very early times, Glastonbury was not only a key pagan sanctuary, but also, a powerful site in the landscape. The Tor, the hill rising above the area of the Abbey, has unique springs and a system of paths or terraces which are believed to be the remnants

St Michael's Tower at summit of Glastonbury Tor. (Simon Brighton)

of a prehistoric maze. In the Recommended Reading section, a number of books are listed that expand much further on these and other aspects of Glastonbury and the Tor.

Some legends suggest Glastonbury as a likely site where Joseph of Arimathea came to Britain with the young Jesus to visit his Cornish tin mines—embuing Glastonbury with early Christian affiliations.[25] In 597, St. Augustine was quite surprised to find a *pre-existing* Christian church in the west of Britain. Legends also say that Christ and some of the apostles came to the island of Anglesey in Wales after having survived the crucifixion.

Celtic missionaries were trained at Glastonbury, and there is a tradition that St. Patrick went there. *The Domesday Book* called Glastonbury "The Secret of the Lord," indicating that there was already an existing legend of some type already in place. The Holy Thorn at Glastonbury, which legend informs us to have been planted from the staff of Joseph of Arimathea, is, in fact, a genuine Levantine thorn variety—the *Crataegus Praecox* species. It mysteriously blossoms twice a year, in May and at Christmas. In Washington, D.C., on the grounds of the National Cathedral, there is a cutting taken from the Glastonbury Thorn tree.

Glastonbury is home to many legends of earlier pagan times. One pagan-Christian legend describes a "showdown" between St. Collen and the tenacious faery King Gwyn ap Nudd, who was long said to have reigned from under the Tor:

Glastonbury Tor, in particular, came in Welsh tradition to be associated with Annwfn [i.e. the Otherworld], and Annwfn's lord, Gwyn ap Nudd, in later tradition the fairy king … And it was on the eminence of Glastonbury Tor that he was encountered by Collen, the sixth-century wandering saint … Collen had come to live as a hermit in a cell on the Tor, and one day overheard two men talking of Gwyn, who had his palace there. He rebuked them for speaking of devils … they warned him that Gwyn would not overlook such an insult, and would certainly send for him. Sure enough, a few days later, a messenger came to Collen's cell to invite him to visit Gwyn. Three times the saint refused, but at last agreed to go, though taking the precaution of hiding a flask of holy water under his cloak. He entered the hill by a secret door and found himself in a

Chalice Well, Glastonbury. (Simon Brighton)

wonderful palace, where Gwyn sat in a golden chair. The king offered him food, but Collen refused it, no doubt because he knew that fairy food was perilous. 'I do not eat the leaves of a tree,' he said, and after further boorish remarks, sprinkled his holy water about him. King and palace vanished forthwith, and Collen found himself … alone on the cold hillside.[26]

This tale is from the 16th century *Life of St. Collen.* King Gwyn was portrayed as a god, a son of Nudd, the British god Nodens, who was honoured at an important shrine at Lydney near Chepstow. He was also connected early on with Arthur—as in the early Welsh tale of the hunting of the great boar Twrch Trwyth.

The *Chalice Well* at Glastonbury has also been the focus of books and pilgrimages. There are two famous springs—dubbed

Chalice Well, Glastonbury, its beautiful gardens and healing pool. (Simon Brighton)

the "Red Spring" and the "White Spring"—and much lore features them. Local author Nicholas Mann has this to say:

> One of the springs, on the side of Chalice Hill, flows through a grove of yew trees … The other spring, on the side of the Tor, once emerged from a cave in a small and verdant coombe. Its flowing water coated everything it touched with a white deposit. Because of their colours, the waters are known as the Blood Spring and the White Spring, and their symbolism and sacred nature has resonated ceaselessly throughout the traditions and myths of the ancient Isles of Britain.[27]

The Chalice Well gardens also has a famous cutting from the "Thorn Tree." In addition to the one at Glastonbury Abbey, several other cuttings were planted in the Glastonbury area. Today we occasionally hear in the media of deliberate destructive attempts on these trees made by vandals and youths. Professor

Ronald Hutton amusingly notes a 17th century incident about one such attempt:

> A royalist newsbook in December 1654 boasted of how churches were 'excellently adorned with rosemary and bays' and told a cautionary tale of how a 'Canaanite' had just tried to cut down the famous thorn tree at Glastonbury. This always flowered around Christmas and was popularly cited as testimony to the sanctity of the feast. The fanatic swung an axe at it (so the story went) but only cut himself.[28]

Saints such as St. Brigid, were a popular focal point for Irish pilgrims travelling in or near the Glastonbury area. Again, Hutton comments:

> Glastonbury, indeed, carefully nurtured its association with her, claiming to possess her relics in rivalry with Kildare, a process undoubtedly encouraged by the ambitions of the abbey's royal English patrons to extend their influence in the British Isles. For similar reasons Glastonbury also claimed to possess the bodies of St. Patrick, St. David and several Northumbrian holy men.[29]

The perennial appeal of Glastonbury to pilgrims—from those of "all faiths or none," so to speak—continues today. The Chalice Well remains a firm favorite.

Glastonbury represents the convergence of a number of Arthurian-related and other myths. It is interesting to note what one longer-term resident has to say about it today:

> In Glastonbury myths are being transformed and re-made all the time. Ancient customs and cults are re-discovered and revived here, threads are followed, webs are woven, boundaries of consciousness are pushed. Glastonbury is a natural sanctuary where the earth spirit is teacher. It comes alive in the weird and wonderful landscape, in the peculiar shades of light, in the changing seasons, in the air we breathe …[30]

But as with many places worldwide that have become associated with a powerful mythic, religious, or spiritual substratum, we tend to see a historic interplay of sense of place, time, and myth, all of which are ever-evolving, shifting and changing.

VISITING OTHER RELATED ARTHUR AND MERLIN SITES

Rather than merely reading about the Arthurian history—which is fascinating enough—travelers have learned that by visiting the Arthurian-related sites they can gain new insights and understanding into the wisdom of the Arthurian legends. The numerous Arthur and Merlin sites of Britain offer a modern visitor a magical experience for further exploration. Here follow some of the most interesting and accessible places you may visit for further inspiration.

Arthurian Sites in Britain

TINTAGEL CASTLE IN CORNWALL

Cornwall has a rich tradition relating to King Arthur. Most familiar is the legend of Arthur being born at Tintagel Castle on the north Cornish coast. The story of his birth at Tintagel comes from Geoffrey of Monmouth's 12th century *Historia Regum Brittaniae* (*History of the Kings of Britain*):

> [Geoffrey] mentions the birth of Arthur at Tintagel Castle, a scene which may be familiar to modern readers from the beginning of the well-known film "Excalibur." To summarize, at an Easter gathering, Uther Pendragon, the king: … was seized with an obsessive lust for Ygerna, the beautiful wife of Gorlois, Duke of Cornwall. His advances to her were obvious. Gorlois withdrew from the court, taking his wife with him. The King treated this action as an insult. He sent Gorlois an ultimatum ordering him to return, and, when this was rejected, marched to Cornwall to ravage the ducal lands. Gorlois put Ygerna in Tintagel Castle, on a coastal headland which could only be approached along a narrow, easily guarded ridge.

Having stowed her beyond Uther's presumed reach, he led a force to oppose the royal army, making his base at a fort some distance off. Uther surrounded Gorlois's weaker force and prevented its escape. Then, on a friend's advice, he sent for Merlin. The magician gave him a potion which turned him into an exact replica of Gorlois. Thus, effectively disguised, Uther passed the guards at Tintagel and found his way to Ygerna. Supposing him to be her husband, she caused no difficulties, and as a result of this encounter she conceived Arthur. Meanwhile, the real Gorlois had been killed in a sortie....[31]

Dozmary Pool, Cornwall, where legend says the Lady of the Lake is custodian of Arthur's invincible sword, Excalibur. (Simon Brighton)

Tintagel and the surrounding coastline is an extraordinarily beautiful area with several key links to Arthurian legends. "Merlin's Cave," on the shore below the castle, is where Merlin is said to have taken the baby Arthur from the sea. "King Arthur's Footprint" is a hollow in the rock "at the highest point of the Island's southern side. This is not entirely natural, having been shaped by human hand at some stage ..."[32]

Until fairly recently, scholars naturally tended to dismiss any Arthurian associations with Tintagel Castle as it was built in the early twelfth century for Reginald, Earl of Cornwall. It was assumed that Geoffrey named Tintagel mainly to please Reginald—the wealthy brother of his patron, Robert, Earl of Gloucester. Excavations had concluded that there had been a Celtic monastery on the site. More recent era excavations at Tintagel in 1990–1, however, tell a different story:

> ... that the site was never a monastery, and was indeed used in the 5th and 6th centuries as a stronghold, possibly on a seasonal basis since it would be all but uninhabitable in winter storms. Moreover it is now clear that the medieval castle was not started until a century after Geoffrey was writing, so he had no reason at all to name Tintagel unless there was a tradition already in existence.[33]

Pottery was found there that indicated a rather luxurious lifestyle, perhaps as a holiday destination! Originally the name Tintagel only referred to the Castle; the settlement nearby was called Trevena. This was changed to Tintagel following the opening in 1893 of the North Cornwall Railway to Camelford, which had obvious tourism implications for the area. The name of Tintagel is derived from the Cornish "Tyn-tagell." "Tyn," or "dyn," means fort, and "tagell" means constriction, which obviously relates to the neck of rock connecting the mainland with the "island." An alternative explanation for the origin of the name Tintagel is that the fortress was once known as *Tente d'Agel*, from the Norman-French.

OTHER CORNISH SITES

Other favorite Cornish sites associated with Arthurian legend are St Michael's Mount, and the haunting and evocative Dozmary Pool—famed for where Arthur's sword Excalibur was said to have been thrown by the Lady of the Lake after he was mortally wounded in the Battle of Camlann. It is located out on Bodmin Moor.[34]

King Arthur and nine kings are said to have pledged each other in the holy water from St. Sennan's Well after Arthur helped them slay the Danes near Land's End.[35] Robert Hunt, a folklorist writing back in 1881, commented that "not far from the Devil's Coit in St. Columb, on the edge of the Gossmoor, there is a large stone, upon which are deeply-impressed marks ... this is 'King Arthur's Stone,' and these marks were made by the horse upon which the British king rode when he resided at Castle Denis, and hunted on these moors ... King Arthur's bed, chairs, and caves, are frequently to be met with. The Giant's Coits ... are probably monuments of the earliest types of rock mythology."[36] There are many other early traditions associated with Arthurian lore and places in Cornwall.

According to Geoffrey, Cornwall is the site of Arthur's death. Legend states that Arthur succeeded in stopping a rebellion—led by his own traitorous nephew Mordred—at Camlann, which Geoffrey locates somewhere in Cornwall. In this battle, Arthur was mortally wounded and taken to the magical isle of Avalon for his wounds to be tended by the Lady of the Lake and her nine maidens. Sadly, Geoffrey doesn't elaborate more about Arthur from that point on.

North Cornwall Arthurian Centre

An interesting place to begin, if you have never visited Cornwall and are interested in Arthurian history, sites and folklore, is to have a look at the Arthurian exhibition at the North Cornwall Arthurian Centre, near Camelford. The Centre also has what has been dubbed the "Arthur's Stone" on its grounds, which some believe may be connected to Arthur's famous battle of Camlann.

Slaughterbridge

There is also a strong tradition that Arthur died close by at Slaughterbridge, near the river Camel. This site consists of two main elements. The first, on the hillside, is the earthworks of a small medieval settlement and post-medieval farm called Old Melorn. The second, in the valley bottom built in to the river cliffs is the mostly buried remains of a mid-eighteenth century garden created by Lady Dowager Falmouth (Charlotte Boscawen). In the center of a garden is the 6th century "Arthur's Stone" inscribed with Ogham and Latin. Both landscape features were also part of the grounds of the nearby Worthyvale manor house.

The Arthurian Center informs us that the Arthur Stone was erected as a memorial beside a road that ran across the site in the 6th century. In the medieval period, a settlement called Melorn developed here, possibly with a chapel. This settlement shrunk to a farm and was then demolished. One of the buildings was last in use as a smithy. There may have been a mill below the village. Charlotte and her husband Hugh Boscawen moved to Worthyvale Manor around 1700. The garden was built soon after, with a path leading from a "folly" on a low mound, via winding paths along river cliff terraces, rock cut steps. and a patterned cobbled area with seats. Paths lead to the relocated Arthur Stone in a natural "grotto" beside the River Camel. Charlotte died in 1754 and the garden was soon forgotten. However the fame of the stone continued to attract visitors to the site. A ticket office (now an earthwork) was built near the stone in the 19th century.[37]

Sixth century inscribed stone at Slaughterbridge, Camelford, Cornwall; it marks the legendary site where many believe that Arthur and Mordred met for the final battle of Camlann, which ended the Fellowship of the Round Table in 537. (Karen Ralls)

THE DRUSTANUS (TRISTAN) STONE, FOWEY, CORNWALL

The Drustanus (Tristan) Stone is an interesting standing stone site. Many claims are made about the legendary Tristan's possible origins—one of which is that he was born in Cornwall. British author Geoffrey Ashe adds:

> The real trouble is that the tales of Tristan and [King] Mark have other antecedents besides Cornish ones. 'Drust' in various forms was a Pictish name (though Britons were being called so as early as the sixth century), and one or two of Tristan's early adventures recall tales that were told of an eighth-century Drust in Scotland…Mark appears in other places—conspicuously, in Wales. It has even been maintained that the legend is not Cornish at all…However, so little is known of the way stories were

The Tristan Stone menhir is just outside Fowey (Cornwall). The plaque near it reads: "This stone was erected nearby about 550 AD. It has on its north side a raised T, an early form of christian cross. On its south side it has an inscription in 6th century letters. When translated this reads: 'Trystan here lies of Cunomorus the son.' Cunomorus was Marcus Cunomorus of the medieval life of St. Sampson and King Mark of Cornwall in the love story of Tristan and Iseult." (Karen Ralls)

spread and elaborated, in the two or three centuries after Arthur, that the assumption cannot be proved and the conclusion, even if jumped to, may have been right. The Tristan Stone could indeed be the memorial of the man himself.[38]

Arthurian legends in Wales

Wales has a longstanding Arthurian connection, both north and south, and has many important Arthurian sites and place-names. The first mention of Arthur is thought to be a reference in a line from the poem *Y Gododdin of Aneirin*, the earliest known work of literature in Welsh. This poem is dated from the 6th century, when parts of Britain (Wales, northern England and southern Scotland) spoke a variant of Welsh. The earliest surviving written form of the poem dates to the 13th century. The reference to Arthur may be no earlier than the 9th century, but it demonstrates the fame of

Arthur around at the time.[39] The most important of the historical texts is the *Historia Brittonum*, the "History of the Britons" dating circa 829–30. It gives the earliest written record of Arthur who "fought against them [the Saxons] with the kings of the Britons but he himself was leader [Duke] of Battles" winning twelve battles. The *Annales Cambriae*, or 'Welsh Annals' (probably compiled in the mid 10th century) records the date of one battle, the Battle of Badon, in 518, and Arthur's death at Camlann in 537–9.

Early Welsh literature has many wondrous tales which form an important strata of the Arthurian tradition. There are portrayals of Arthur in anonymous Welsh poetry found in 13th and 14th century manuscripts. In one of the poems in the Black Book of Carmarthen, *Englynion y Beddau* ('The Stanzas of the Graves'), Arthur's grave is described as a great mysterious wonder because no one knows precisely where it is located. One of the greatest of the Welsh Arthurian prose tales is *Culhwch ac Olwen*, and *The Mabinogion remains a continuous firm favorite today, as it has for centuries.*

Culhwch ac Olwen is among the earliest of the Welsh Arthurian tales. Some scholars continue to speculate that it may be even earlier—in its first compilation—than the famous Four Branches of the *Mabinogi,* which date to around 1100.[40] The Culhwch story is basically a quest tale—"a quest within a quest." Four other Welsh tales also focus on Arthur—the romances of *The Lady of the Fountain* (or *Owain*); *Peredur; Geraint son of Erbin*; and the *Dream of Rhonabwy,* which tends to present a more satirical view of Arthur and his world.

Arthur is also mentioned in the Old Welsh poem *Preiddeu Annwfn*, The Spoils of Annwfn. Here, Arthur visits the Otherworld to carry off a magical cauldron of the realm of the dead. Celtic scholar Miranda Green refers to the medieval Welsh texts, like the *Y Gododdin,* that specifically mention the name Arthur. The *Gododdin,* for example, describes the warrior Gwawrddur who, while heroic, "was not Arthur." A spate of young princelings appeared in several Welsh kingdoms in about 600; the sudden popularity of the name for these young noblemen may point to an early warrior named Arthur, who perhaps adopted the title "dux bellorum" when fighting against the Saxons. Obviously, Wales, too, has long laid a claim to Arthur.

In truth, many today would agree that ultimately, there is no hard evidence to link Arthur with any identifiable site for certain; for example, as compelling a case can be made for Caerleon as for anywhere else.[41]

SOUTH WALES ARTHURIAN LOCATIONS

Ten of the major Arthur locations in South Wales are given, along with a map, on the University of Wales Newport website. They have been arranged as a trail for visitors to explore the various Arthurian places and legends in the area. I briefly list them here:

CAERLEON

The Roman tetrapylon in Caerleon was almost certainly the gigantic tower described by Gerald of Wales in 1188 and destroyed in the Middle Ages. By then, it had become associated with revived Welsh kingship and tales of Arthur. The National Roman Legion Museum in Caerleon has much information about early Caerleon, including archaeological data.

LODGE HILL, CAERLEON

The Lodge Hill Silurian hillfort overlooking Caerleon was given royal status by Geoffrey of Monmouth's imaginative *Historia Regum Britanniae.* Archaeological work in 2000 showed that the Iron Age fortification had been reoccupied in the late Roman period—and possibly, during the "Age of Arthur".

HANBURY ARMS, CAERLEON

Alfred, Lord Tennyson had a life-long fascination with the legend of Arthur. In 1856, as he was working on his most important Arthurian work *Idylls of the King,* the Poet Laureate came to Caerleon for inspiration. He stayed at the Hanbury Inn and the window where he wrote is still known as "Tennyson's window."

GERALD'S PALACE LOCATION: ROMAN BATHS, CAERLEON

Gerald of Wales visited Caerleon in 1188. Convinced that this had been Arthur's court, he described several surviving Roman buildings. Among them were "immense palaces," probably including the fortress baths. These were demolished, almost certainly for political reasons, in the early thirteenth century.

The Round Table Location: Roman Amphitheatre, Caerleon

Regarding the perennial search for a location of the court of Camelot, many in Wales today believe it may have been at Caerleon. Its amphitheatre ruins are still to be seen. Nennius mentioned "Cair Lion" as one of Britain's thirty-three cities in the ninth century. It was the earlier site of one of Britain's three permanent Roman Legionary fortresses. Caerleon thus remains of continual interest to archaeologists from various perspectives.

In the later Middle Ages, the remains of the Roman amphitheatre were already being described as the "Round Table." In 1405, when French troops came to Wales to assist Owain Glyndŵr, chronicles claim that the combined Welsh and French armies encamped "at King Arthur's round table" in Caerleon. Of course, a number of contenders for the "Round Table" exist in Britain, and Caerleon is one of the better known.

Cadair Arthur Location: Cadair Arthur, Abergavenny

Cadair Arthur, or "Arthur's Chair," is found on one of the region's most imposing sites—the towering Pen y Fal or Sugar Loaf which dominates the north Gwent landscape. The mountain not only has Arthurian associations but also archaeological evidence of people in the Mesolithic, Neolithic, and Bronze Age.

Cist Arthur Location: Llanddewi Skirrid, Abergavenny

The Skirrid, Gwent's broken back Holy Mountain, has a geological feature known as *Cist Arthur,* or "Arthur's Chest." The ancient Welsh tales of the Mabinogi show Arthur acquiring a chest to keep the board and pieces for a Welsh variation of chess, a game called *gwyddbwyll.*

Chasing the Boar Location: Sudbrook, Caldicot

The hunt for the enchanted wild boar, Twrch Trwyth, in the tales of the Mabinogi shows us a very different Arthur from the chivalrous king of Camelot. Sudbrook Camp, near where the boar was forced into the mouth of the Wye, was an important Silurian and, later, Roman port.

Geoffrey's Window Location: Monmouth Priory, Monmouth

Geoffrey's Window in Monmouth priory is too late in date for the writer ever to have sat there. However his importance is confirmed by the folk tradition which says that he did. From the priory, it is only a short trek over to King Arthur's Cave. Here archaeologists have found Palaeolithic, Mesolithic, and Bronze Age artifacts.

Dubbed "King Arthur's Round Table" since the Middle Ages, the huge amphitheatre at Caerleon was originally built to serve the Roman legionary fortress of Isca around 90 A.D. It could once seat a whole legion, up to six thousand spectators; it is visited by many all year round today, and is occasionally used for events and re-enactments." (Wikimedia Commons)

The Living Legend Location: Old Tintern Station, Tintern

Historic Tintern, with its famous Abbey and other nearby archaeological sites, is a good base for the continuing Quest for the Legend in the Landscape. Arthur today can be found at the Victorian Railway Station where wood carvings create a "circle of legends," including both Arthur and Geoffrey of Monmouth.[42]

"Arthur's Stone sites" in Wales:

At least seven Stone Age megaliths all over Wales have been called "Arthur's Stone." Moel Arthur, near Denbigh, is one. And, according to another tradition, King Arthur and his knights lie sleeping in a cave below Craig y Ddinas, Pontneddfechan in South Wales. There are many more.

Arthurian Sites—North Wales:

Stunning North Wales, too, has a longstanding, very rich Arthurian history and a plethora of sites and place-names and history relating to Arthur, far too numerous to mention here in full. Among the major "must-see" sites to visit when exploring the area include **Moel Arthur**, or "Arthur's Hill," an Iron Age hillfort. One of the best known legends is about **Maen Huail** in Ruthin, associated with what might kindly be described as a famous "showdown duel" that was said to involve Arthur himself! Further north Welsh legends say that Arthur had a court at **Caerwys** (near Holywell), and a chapel called **Capel y Gwial**, the Chapel of the Sticks, is said to have been located at Nannerch, near Mold. In the hills above Llansannan, near Denbigh, locals still tell of **Bwrdd Arthur (Arthur's table)**. Another site with this same name can also be found on the Berwyn hills above Llanarmon Dyffryn Ceiriog. The sword Excalibur was said to have been buried under a rock near the summit of the adjoining hill **Pen y Cloddiau**. The Llangollen area has a number of Arthurian associated places, especially **Castle of Dinas Brân** high above the town, and remains a favorite today with hillwalkers and locals throughout the year as well as for summer visitors from all over the world. It has long been said to be the home of the "Holy Grail," hidden underneath its ruins. Arthur's final resting place is known to most as Avalon, but some Welsh texts record the name as Afallwch and at Rhosesmor there is a hillfort known as **Caerfallwch (Fort of Afallwch)**.[43] There are more Arthurian-related sites to explore in north Wales, of course, but these are some of the best-known.

Scotland: Arthurian sites, legends, and place-names

Scotland, too, has long had its own unique group of enduring legends, folklore and, especially, interesting place-lore. The Lothian and Borders area of lowland Scotland, near Edinburgh, in particular has a long tradition of place-names and legends relating to Arthurian topics even though much of Arthur's history has often been associated in the popular mind in more modern times with England, Wales, and Cornwall.[44]

Scotland offers yet another "take" on the Arthurian mythos through time. Strangely enough, as a number of scholars have pointed out, Arthur's battles are not referred to at all in the Anglo-Saxon Chronicle. It is now believed by a number of Arthurian scholars that at least one, and probably more, of his battles were most likely fought somewhere in the north. This may have been either in the Scottish lowlands, in northern England, or in north Wales. The problem is precisely where. Of course, archaeologists still do not agree and further research continues.

Back in the 5th century, at the end of the Roman period and right before Arthur's time, Scotland was an area of many different linguistic and racial groupings. At the time, the main language group in southern Scotland, near Edinburgh and the Borders, was what experts have designated the "P-Celtic" language family. This relates to the Welsh, Cornish, and Breton branches of the Celtic languages. The powerful Votadini (Edinburgh area), the Selgovae (Borders/Tweeddale area), the Novantae (south-western area), and the Damnonii (in the valley of the Clyde river, and Glasgow area) tribes were also all P-speaking tribes in early times.[45] The other major family of the Celtic-speaking languages, comprising the Irish, Scottish Gaelic and Manx branches and their variants, is called the "Q-Celtic."

"Men of the north": The Gododdin

The Welsh poem *Y Gododdin* takes its name from the Latin appellation of the Votadini (Goddodin), a powerful tribe who lived in and around the Edinburgh area. In this poem, the warrior Gwawrddur is praised as heroic, but it is stated that he "was not Arthur." Clearly, he is being compared to what sounds like a great warrior who was named Arthur. In the 6th and 7th centuries, it is believed by some scholars that several of the P-Celtic tribes from the Scottish lowlands and Strathclyde areas migrated into north Wales, taking their memories of Arthur with them. In this theory, what is left today in Scotland are the numerous place-names and legends commemorating Arthur and his great deeds from that earlier time.

One of the earliest initial advocates of a specifically Scottish location for Arthur was W. F. Skene, who believed that most, if not all, of Arthur's major battles were fought in the lowlands of Scotland. Most modern scholars do not accept this theory in its entirety, preferring instead to acknowledge that at least one or more of his battles were most likely fought in the north, which seems logical enough. To his credit, Skene did attempt to point out possible sources of remaining confusion: for example, the lowland Scottish tribe "Damnonii" being nearly identical to the Cornish "Dumnonii," implying that this was a mistake of the early manuscript translators regarding where Arthur's base was. Ironically, Arthur was never listed as a king, nor was he ever named on any kingship lists. Instead, he is described as *"dux bellorum"*—a very courageous war leader or warrior chief. Yet, through the ages the popular image of Arthur as a "king" has nonetheless persisted, inaccurate as it is.

The strongest contender for a Scottish-based location for one of Arthur's key battles is the Scottish wood called *Cat Caet Celidon*. It is listed as the 7th battle in the *Historia Brittonum*, and is one of the twelve major battle sites of Arthur. This was the famous Caledonian forest, where Merlin was said to have wandered. This is also spelled as *celyddon*, and is where the modern word "caledonian" is believed to have come from. People today generally think of Scotland when "Caledonia" is mentioned. In earlier times, those often referred to as "Scots" today were called the "Caledonians" by the Romans. The term "Scots" in medie-

val manuscripts generally meant the Gaelic-speaking Irish immigrants—a different people altogether. The "Picts" were listed as separate from both of these, and did not speak Gaelic.[46]

Arthur's Seat

Arthur's Seat, a huge, imposing, ancient volcanic rock that dominates the Edinburgh skyline, has a number of interesting traditions associated with it. In early times, all over Scotland, numbers of young people would rise before dawn on Beltane (May Eve) and go out to meadows or hillsides to bathe their faces in the fresh dew. In Edinburgh, such traditions survived well into the 18th century at Arthur's Seat each Beltane morning.

And indeed, even today, Beltane Eve is celebrated on top of Calton Hill in Edinburgh. Now a huge, lively evening festival—featuring drama, music, drumming and dancing—it began as a local gathering and is now a major civic event, organized by the Beltane Fire Society in Edinburgh. In recent years, up to 10,000 people have come from far and wide to attend this annual event on the evening of the 30th of April.

Stirling Castle

The Stirling area also has pervasive legends about the site of Stirling Castle and its famed turf "round table" below. According to tradition:

> This was one of the historic seats of the Celtic hero Arthur, the flat table-land which lies southwest of the Castle being identified with the Round Table on which

AT LEFT: Arthur's Seat, Edinburgh, south view. (Karen Ralls)

AT RIGHT: King's Knot, Stirling Castle grounds, Scotland; some believe this may be a key contender for Arthur's Round Table in Scotland. (Karen Ralls)

he trained his forces. (It is, in fact, so designated by Barbour in the 14th century and by Sir David Lyndsay in the 16th.) The Castle was a favourite residence of Alexander I and William the Lyon, and has associations with several of the Stuart kings.[47]

A local Scottish Borders legend says that Arthur never died, but still sleeps with his knights and their horses and armor under the Eildon Hills near Melrose until such time as he will be needed again. They were very nearly awakened by a local Borders horse dealer who had accidentally strayed into their cavern under the Eildon Hills, but, as the tale informs us, as he did not present a threat, the knights returned to sleep and still remain there, undisturbed, waiting for the "call" to return again.[48]

Scottish place-names

J. S. Glennie published an early gazeteer of Scottish place-names that had legends or traditions associated with various Arthurian legends. For example, in the Edinburgh and Lothians area, he listed a number of well-known sites such as the Firth of Forth, Culross monastery, Stirling Castle, Arthur's O'on, Stenhousemuir, the Carron, Camelon, near Falkirk, Bathgate, Linlithgow, the Avon, Abercorn, Dalmeny, Cramond, Edinburgh Castle, Kirkliston, Arthur's Seat in Edinburgh, Trapain Law, Bass rock, Kilduff, and Aberlady Bay. In the Borders/Tweeddale area, he listed sites such as the Gala Water, Stowe, the River Tweed, Peebles, Caledonian Forest, Drummelzier, the Teviot, the Eildon Hills, Melrose, Abbotsford, Earlston, Kelso, Jedburgh, and Berwick, among others.[49]

Glennie also listed place names in other regions of Scotland as well, and W. J. Watson, in his now-classic work *The Celtic Place-Names of Scotland,* also lists sites in the west of Scotland associated with Arthur, such as Arthur's Seat in Dumbarton, Loch Long, Arthur's Face, a rock on the west side of Glenkinglas, Struarthour in Glassary, and Argyll, among others.[50]

Queen Guinevere's Monument

One of the more popular Arthurian sites for visitors to Scotland today is the area of the so-called "Guinevere Monument," at Meigle, in Perthshire. A location long associated with lore relating to the Pictish queen Guinevere, possibly spelled either as "Guanhumara," or "Guenore." Today, the museum at Meigle has a number of important Pictish stones and other artifacts on display, some of which are associated with Arthurian legends.

MERLIN PLACES

Merlin sites in Cornwall

Cornwall also provides a rich ground of Merlin lore. Some of its more well-known places are *Merlin's Cave* near Tintagel, the extraordinary waterfalls of St Nechtan's Glen, and the Tristan (Drustanus) Stone, near Fowey.

Bardsey Island—Ynys Enlli—in Wales has also long been considered a possible candidate for the magical, elusive "Isle of Avalon". Merlin is reputed to still be there, encased in his glass castle with the Thirteen Treasures of Britain, waiting to return, when needed, in the future.

Guinevere's Mound plaque at Meigle churchyard, Perthshire, Scotland. Also known as Vanora, or Guenore, ('Guinivere') the wife of King Arthur, as early local Scottish legends have long maintained. A variant of Wannour or Wannore (an old Scottish form of Guenore, a name similar to 'Guinevere'), Vanora's mound is a grass-covered mound, in front of which two Pictish carved stones of Christian date are known to have once stood, to be viewed in the Meigle Museum nearby. (Karen Ralls)

Stonehenge, where legends say Merlin magically transferred the stone circle of Ushnagh from Ireland over to Salisbury Plain. (Karen Ralls)

St Nechtans Glen, Cornwall, the hidden waterfall in a valley near Tintagel. (Simon Brighton)

Merlin sites in Brittany

Brittany, too, has a long, extensive Merlin history, with much lore, and place-names, far too many to list here. A few of the most well-known sites to many English-speaking visitors today include the Barenton Fountain rock area, the Broceliande forest, the Mirror of the Fairies in the Val Sans Retour, Comper (Arthur's Oak and Viviane's birthplace), Merlin's Tomb dolmen, and stunning Mont St Michel.

St Kentigern and Merlin stained glass window, Stobo church, Scottish borders. (Dr. Gordon Strachan)

Merlin sites in Scotland

The battle of Arfderydd, Merlin, and St. Kentigern

The sole historical reference we have to Merlin is connected with a sixth century battle is the battle of Arfderydd. Now known as Artheret, it is located near the Solway Firth, about ten miles north of Carlisle, between the rivers Esk and Liddel, on the border between Scotland and England. This famous battle is believed to have occurred around 573, although details are unclear. It was fought between Gwenddolau, the Pagan King of the North and patron of Merlin, and the Christian King Rhydderch Hael of Strathclyde who was victorious. It is implied that Merlin was present at the battle, and "went mad" from losing his family, friends, and his patron, fleeing into a forest.

From that point on, Merlin lived in the forest, only to emerge at certain key junctures—to prophesy or to advise Arthur. His whole legend grew from this experience. After his victory, King Rydderch Hael recalled St. Kentigern, a follower of St. Ninian of Whithorn, back from north Wales to his domain in Scotland

Hart Fell lowlands in the Scottish Borders, an area with much lingering Scottish Merlin lore, even today. (Karen Ralls)

to help him re-evangelise the area. Many legends about Merlin and St. Kentigern have survived, mainly with a focus on how the wild, poetic man of the woods, the pagan Myrddin (Merlin), was eventually converted to Christianity by St Kentigern (now called St Mungo, the founder of Glasgow). According to local legend in the Stobo area of the Scottish Borders, Merlin met St. Kentigern just before he died.

Stobo Kirk, a local Borders church, is one of the oldest churches in Scotland, dating from Norman times. Tradition says it was built on an earlier site of a church founded by St. Kentigern in the 6th century. A persistent legend is that Merlin was baptized by St. Kentigern on its altar stone. Today, nearby Altarstone farm is very close to Stobo Kirk. The legend of Merlin and St Kentigern is portrayed on a stained glass window in Stobo Kirk where it may still be seen.[51] Whatever the ultimate truth of the matter, "the legend lives on" in Scotland, too, sustaining the memory of Merlin.

Merlin's Final Resting Place?

Where exactly, then, was Merlin laid to rest? As might be expected, through the centuries there have been several suggested legends and places. One Scottish Borders account says Merlin finally died at Drumelzier, where the river Tweed meets the Powsail Burn. This place is called "Merlin's Grave" today. Just upstream from there is a place called Merlindale. His death at Drumelzier is mentioned in a later vision by the famous 13th century Scottish seer, Thomas of Ercildoune, the famous "Thomas the Rhymer" of Borders lore.

The power of Myth and Time

Many today recall what Alfred Lord Tennyson said about Merlin in his famous poem *The Idylls of the King* (52)—that he was "the great Enchanter of the Time"—an idea that could also be said of the entire Arthurian corpus of myths and legends.

Ultimately, however, these timeless stories are far more, as they are perennial archetypal mysteries—the Enchanters of *All* Time. For many around the world today, they still exist in memories, stories, hopes and dreams, the custodian of secrets, of another Quest to come.

The late Dr. Gordon Strachan and Dr. Karen Ralls discussing the history of regional Scottish Borders Merlin sites and folklore, in Edinburgh (1995). (J. Ralls)

CHAPTER 10

ROSSLYN: CHAPEL, CASTLE AND GLEN

Detail of young Green Man carving at the northeast corner of Rosslyn Chapel. (J. F. Ralls)

Just south of Edinburgh, the capital of Scotland, stands Rosslyn Chapel, one of the most ornately-carved 15th century stone chapels in all of Europe. A visual cornucopia, a "library in stone," the unique symbolism of Rosslyn's exquisite medieval carvings— from the Green Man to the famed Apprentice Pillar—continue to intrigue visitors from all over the world.

Often dubbed "the Chapel in the Woods" in earlier times, Rosslyn Chapel is officially known today as the Collegiate Chapel of St. Matthew.[1] It stands on College Hill as part of the beautiful scenery of Roslin Glen—the North Esk river below, and as part of the stunning scenery of the nearby Pentland Hills. What is the actual history of this extraordinary chapel?

Rosslyn Chapel has been the focus of many a Quest throughout the centuries. Legends abound, inspiring young and old, from near and far to further explore its secrets. Rosslyn's vaults have been speculated to be a repository for everything from the Ark of the Covenant, the Holy Grail, a Black Madonna, the missing Holy Rood of Scotland, the crown jewels, to the lost scrolls from the Temple of Jerusalem. For years people have speculated about what—if anything—may have been hidden at Rosslyn, who put it there, and why. Others remain skeptical, saying that until the vaults are actually excavated, no one can say anything for sure. For hundreds of years, there have been theories about the chapel and the wisdom of the ages that it may hold—from sober analysis to wild speculation.

Countless visitors have passed through its doors, walked in its glen, and examined its impressive castle ruins. In the past, William and Dorothy Wordsworth, Queen Victoria, J. W. Turner, Sir Walter Scott, Dr. Samuel Johnson, Robert Burns, James Boswell, and Ben Jonson made it a point to visit Rosslyn Chapel and its beautiful environs. Indeed, Rosslyn Chapel remains a place of pilgrimage, intrigue, worship, and further exploration.

As stated by the Earl of Rosslyn in his recent guidebook, *Rosslyn Chapel,* work on this magnificent stone edifice began in 1446. It was an extraordinary effort directed by the founder himself, Sir William St. Clair, the third and last St. Clair Prince of

OPPOSITE: Apprentice Pillar, Rosslyn Chapel. (Simon Brighton)

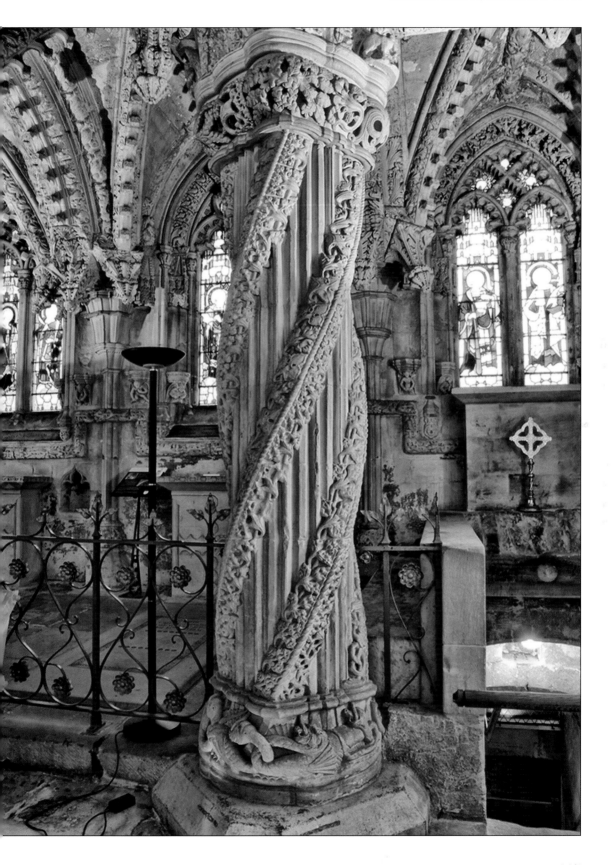

Old Roslin Inn, plaque, with famous vistors listed: William and Dorothy Wordsworth (etc). (Karen Ralls)

THE OLD ROSSLYN INN (CIRCA 1660-1866)
HERE COUNTLESS TRAVELLERS TARRIED AWHILE
AMONG THE DISTINGUISHED VISITORS WERE
KING EDWARD VII WHEN PRINCE OF WALES
DR SAMUEL JOHNSON AND JAMES BOSWELL
ROBERT BURNS AND ALEXANDER NAYSMITH
SIR WALTER SCOTT AND WILLIAM AND DOROTHY
WORDSWORTH

ERECTED IN 1950 BY MRS HERBERTSON OF MELBOURNE AUSTRALIA
DAUGHTER OF THE LATE CHARLES TAYLOR, CURATOR OF THE CHAPEL

Orkney. Historian Walter Bower updated Fordun's *Chronicle of the Scottish Nation* in his new *Scotichronicon* (1447), which says that *"Willelmus de Sancto-Claro est in fabricado sumptuosam structuram apud Roslyn"* ("Sir William St. Clair is erecting an elegant structure at Rosslyn.")[2]

Rosslyn Chapel is actually only part of what was intended to be a much larger cruciform building with a tower at its center. It took forty years to build, and the learned Sir William oversaw the entire process, personally inspecting each carving in wood before he allowed it to be fashioned in stone. That such care was taken is notable in and of itself, and assures us that nothing in Rosslyn Chapel is there by accident.[3]

One of the best sources about Rosslyn Chapel and the St. Clair family was a manuscript written in 1700, about 216 years after the chapel was completed. This extensive work is by Father Richard Augustine Hay, Canon of St. Genevieve in Paris and Prior of St. Piermont:

> He examined historical records and charters of the St. Clairs and completed a three-volume study in 1700, parts of which were published in 1835 as *A Genealogie of the Saintclaires of Rosslyn*. His research was timely, since the original documents subsequently disappeared.[4]

Father Hay described Sir William's great dedication to the building process:

> Prince William, his age creeping up on him, came to consider… how he was to spend his remaining days. Therefore, to the end, that he might not seem altogether

unthankful to God for the benefices he received from Him, it came into his mind to build a house for God's service, of most curious work … he caused artificers to be brought from other regions and foreign kingdoms and caused daily to be abundance of all kinds of workmen present as masons, carpenters, smiths, barrowmen, quarriers … first he caused draughts [plans] to be drawn upon eastland boards [imported Baltic timber] and he made the carpenters carve them according to the draughts, and he gave them for patterns to the masons …[5]

But exactly where these "other regions and foreign kingdoms" were that the builders came from is still debated, with a number from European countries such as France being most likely. Sir William St. Clair, was a "Renaissance man," a cultured, erudite, learned individual, certainly one of the most knowledgeable of his time, aided by his talented associate, Sir Gilbert Hay and others.

The chapel was generously endowed by Sir William, and by his grandson (also named Sir William) in 1523, with land for dwelling houses and gardens. But as the Reformation took hold in Scotland, it had a devastating effect on Rosslyn Chapel. In spite of this, however, the Sinclair family remained firmly Catholic. During this tumultous period in Scottish history, many churches

Green Man, Lady Chapel. (Simon Brighton)

and their altars and furnishings were deemed to be "idolatrous" and "Popish."

Then, in 1650, in one of history's ironies, fate intervened. Cromwell's troops, under General Monk, attacked Rosslyn Castle. Monk stabled his horses in the chapel. Given the exquisite beauty of this architectural masterpiece, it is rather hard to believe. But some think that using the chapel for such a practical purpose ironically may have helped to save the building from even further damage.[6]

On 11 December 1688, we know that a Protestant mob from Edinburgh along with villagers from Roslin beseiged and damaged the Chapel, smashing many of the statues and outer carvings. The chapel remained abandoned until 1736, when James St. Clair glazed the windows for the first time, repaired the roof, and re-laid the floor with flagstones. Sir John Clerk of Penicuik was instrumental in encouraging St. Clair to make these renovations. Given this turbulent history, we are very fortunate indeed to have Rosslyn Chapel available to us today.[7]

In a Chapel guide book written in the 1930s, the author refers to Rosslyn Chapel as resembling the Temple of Jerusalem, adding:

> Like Solomon's Temple, for which David, his father, made such ample provision, the 'Collegiate Church of St Matthew' was intended to be 'exceedingly magnificent, of fame and glory throughout all countries' (1 Chron. 22, 5) and such it has proved to be through the centuries.[8]

The *arcanum in stone* that Rosslyn was ultimately designed to be also contains a great variety of iconography, including many biblical scenes throughout. Some imagery, however, is not overtly Christian, hearkening back to earlier pagan wisdom traditions as taught by Plato, Pythagoras, and others. Many of these were later adopted by medieval Church fathers and philosophers in Paris and then re-explained in a Christian context. Pagan symbols at Rosslyn were no exception to this process of reinterpretation. However, Rosslyn also has unique carvings and themes not found elsewhere, including symbolic metaphors and allegorical stories. One of the most famous is the Apprentice Pillar.

The Apprentice Pillar and the "Murdered Apprentice" carving

The Apprentice Pillar at Rosslyn Chapel has been the subject of a number of books and articles. This beautiful pillar continues to intrigue researchers. Freemasons, historians, archaeologists, architects, members of modern chivalric Orders like the Knights Templar, the Rosicrucians, and others come from all over the world to marvel at its intricasies.

The Apprentice Pillar is an ornately-carved stone pillar with a unique legend all its own—that of "The Murdered Apprentice."[9] Briefly, the basics of this legend are these:

> The Master Mason, having received from the Founder the model of a pillar of exquisite workmanship and design, hesitated to carry it out until he had been to Rome … and seen the original. He went abroad and in his absence an apprentice, having dreamt that he had finished the pillar, at once set to work and carried out the design as it now stands, a perfect marvel of workmanship. The Master Mason on his return, seeing the pillar completed, instead of being delighted at the success of his pupil, was so stung with envy that he asked who had dared to do it

Head of murdered apprentice. (The Brydon Collection)

in his absence. On being told that it was his apprentice, he was so inflamed with rage and passion that he struck him with his mallet, killed him on the spot and paid the penalty …[10]

The master is said to have felt such remorse for this act that he took his own life. There are three carved faces in the vicinity near the pillar, assumed to be the apprentice, his grieving mother, and the jealous master. Later in this chapter, we will discuss the possible similarities between this story and that of Hiram Abiff, the legendary builder of Solomon's Temple celebrated by Freemasons.

The tale of the murdered apprentice had been told from at least the 1600s, but some believe it may have originated from the time of the building of the chapel itself. An early telling of the tale is given by a Yorkshire writer, Thomas Kirk, in his account of his travels through Scotland in 1671. He writes of his first encounter with the Chapel:

> Two miles further we saw Roslen Chapel, a very pretty design, but was never finished, the choir only and a little vault. The roof is all stone, with good imagery work; there is a better man at exact descriptions of the stories than he at Westminster Abbey: this story he told us that the master builder went abroad to see good patterns, but before his return his apprentice had built one pillar which exceeded all that ever he could do or had seen, therefore he slew him; and he showed us the head of the apprentice on the wall with a gash in the forehead and his masters head opposite to him.[11]

Around the bottom of the Apprentice Pillar are carved eight serpents—or dragon-like beasts—who are portrayed gnawing at the roots of a tree. This symbolism may be gleaned from Scandinavian tradition, where the eight dragons of Neifelheim were said to lie at the base of Yggdrasil, the great ash tree which bound together heaven, earth, and hell. The serpent-dragons are said to keep the fruit of knowledge from growing on the tree of life. The idea of divine knowledge being suppressed or kept from man by his own ignorance—which the serpent-dragons likely represent—

Apprentice Pillar,
close-up view of serpents
at base. (Simon Brighton)

is a recurring theme in Western philosophical traditions of which Rosicrucianism, Hermeticism, Alchemy, and Freemasonry are a part. In Christian terms, it signifies the constant conflict between good and evil, and the divine interplay of this process through the ages.

The Veil of Veronica

Another carving that has long intrigued students of Rosslyn is that dubbed "The Veil of Veronica." Located above the south door, originally used as the women's entrance to the chapel, it was a famous medieval relic famed for its extraordinary healing qualities. The Veil of Veronica represents a rather well-known story about the lady Veronica, who is said to have compassionately wiped the face of Christ with a cloth as he was carrying his heavy cross in agony. As a reward for her kindness, legends say a miraculous image of his face remained on the cloth, known as the "The Veil of Veronica" or "Vera Icon" ("True Icon").*

The Veronica carving is now badly damaged. The actual image of the person holding the cloth is not clearly discernible,

Veil of Veronica painting.
(The Brydon Collection)

---

* This relic, portraying a head on the cloth, should not to be confused with the full-body-length image of Christ on the Shroud of Turin.

Veronica Cross, silver, 19th century, in private Edinburgh collection. (The Brydon Collection)

apparently having been chiselled away by someone unknown in the past. The head appears as though it had been decapitated. Some researchers surmise that for some reason, the identity of the figure originally depicted was deliberately erased or obscured. It is not known for certain whether the original carving represented a male or female. However, the cloth, or towel, clearly shows the head of Christ on it, all parties seem to agree on that aspect. Speculation continues. But the possibility of the deliberate alteration of this image is interesting in and of itself. Perhaps more will come to light about this enigmatic carving. But the fact that it is located above the door to what was the women's entrance may favor the interpretation of a female figure holding the cloth.

Rosslyn: A great variety of carvings

There are many other exquisite carvings in Rosslyn Chapel, covering a variety of imagery and traditions, both orthodox and esoteric. Some of the more enigmatic include an image of Moses with horns. Another is the seal of the Agnus Dei, or Lamb of God. One carving shows an angel holding a shield depicting the "engrailed cross" of the St. Clair family. Others feature musician angels with various instruments. There are depictions of themes such as the seven deadly sins and the seven virtues; the Dance of Death; astrological signs; the Gordian Knot; Melchizedek, the timeless King of Salem holding a cup; various Mason's Marks, and much more. Templar, Masonic, Rosicrucian and Christian symbolism and iconography are woven throughout Rosslyn Chapel in a fascinating tapestry of stone. Again, with these carvings, we see the constant interplay of opposites: light and dark, male and female, life and death.

On the outside of the building—on the east wall, near the southeast corner—is what appears to be a carving of a head with wings. It is too worn to be certain, but it may be a portrayal of the winged god Hermes. Some say that the Masonic Hiram Abiff is actually a corruption of the Roman Mercury, called Hermes by the Greeks. An excerpt from *Coil's Masonic Encyclopaedia* says that Hermes can be three things: a god, a philosopher, or a body of knowledge opposed to the destruction of learning. No doubt Sir William St. Clair was concerned about the destruction of learning and the burning of books at the time; and so he would want to

OPPOSITE: Lady Chapel carvings. (Simon Brighton)

Agnus Dei carving.
(Karen Ralls)

Angel holding shield of
the engrailed cross of
the St Clairs, Rosslyn
Chapel. (Karen Ralls)

Melchizedek figure
holding a cup.
(Karen Ralls)

build something that would last for posterity. A chapel made of
stone can also be viewed as a *codification* in stone of a perennial
wisdom tradition.

The Green Man

Rosslyn Chapel has more carvings of the archetypal "Green Man"
than any other medieval chapel in all of Europe. There are known
to be at least 103 carved images of the Green Man inside Rosslyn Chapel alone. This number does not include those figures on
the outside of the chapel or on the roof, ultimately said to total
around 300! A Green Man carving is usually portrayed as a head
with profuse foliage growing from its mouth—representing fertility, wisdom, growth, and nature's bounty.

The many faces of the Rosslyn Green Men appear in various guises—some are joyful, positively brimming with health
and radiant energy, while others appear decidedly skeletal, with
the rest falling somewhere in between.[12] Some believe they collectively symbolize the four seasons of nature. Interestingly, the
Green Man carvings at Rosslyn are portrayed as youthful in the

east; and, as a visitor walks around the chapel towards the north, they gradually become more aged. Its Scottish tradition, the north is associated with winter and death. Sir William was apparently acknowledging both the Celtic and early Scottish traditions of the area as well as the chapel's beautiful natural setting.[13]

Other carvings in the chapel reflect this cyclic concept as well. For example, there is an angel in the east portrayed as opening a book. As you continue walking around the chapel, you will see another angel with a closed book.

The Green Man symbol is ancient. In a medieval Christian context, it is said to be symbolic of death and resurrection. The Green Man is rooted in earlier traditions of vegetation gods who died and rose again, like Tammuz or Osiris. He is representative of the cycle of nature over time. It was not until around the sixth century that the Green Man motif finally made its way into Western Christian church carvings.

The Green Man is usually assumed to be an overwhelmingly Celtic motif. However, the Green Man is also found carved in Eastern temples.[14] Ancient images of the Green Man can still be seen in the Apo Kayan area of Borneo, where he is perceived as the Lord God of the Forest; in the chapels of Dhankar Gompa, high in the Indian Himalayas; in the temples of Kathmandu, Nepal; and in the Jain temples of Ranakpur. The Green Man is a *universal* theme, with very early roots: "Heads from the Lebanon and Iraq can be dated to the 2nd century AD, and there are early Romanesque heads in 11th century Templar churches in Jerusalem. From the 12th to the 15th centuries, heads appeared in cathedrals and churches across Europe...."[15]

And in classical antiquity, to the Romans and Greeks, the Green Man, "suggested the full flowering of education (i.e., the fruits of learning) and was, therefore, an inspirational symbol.[16] British Folklore Society scholar Jeremy Harte comments that "for all their differences in mood, these carvings give a common impression of something—someone—alive among the green buds of summer or the brown leaves of autumn. Green Men can vary from the comic to the beautiful, although often the most beautiful ones are the most sinister."[17]

Or, perhaps, as with more than a few of the Rosslyn Green Men, downright impish!

Some of the Green Man carvings are directly connected to images of musicians and musical themes, as exemplified by this

A Green Man carving in Rosslyn Chapel's ornate, stone-carved Lady Chapel. (Simon Brighton)

famous carving of two distinct Green Men carvings on either side of a musician playing the northern bagpipes.

There was a school of thought among medieval philosophers and churchmen—at Chartres for example—of those interested in exploring themes relating to the church as *Natura*. As the Green Man is clearly one of the most prolific themes in the entire interior of Rosslyn, it seems to be making a rather clear statement in acknowledgement of the spiritual aspects of the chapel in relation to nature's bounty, beauty, and blessings. The chapel is situated at the top of a hill above a beautiful river. The extensive glen with its rare plants, foliage, trees, wildlife, and birds create a stunning natural setting. No wonder Sir William St. Clair felt obliged to honor what many have dubbed the "chapel of the Greenwood," or "chapel of the Grail."

Local legends have associated this area with Sir Gawain, the Green Knight. The glen is also known to have been a site where

A hiker in Roslin Glen. (J. F. Ralls)

Roslin Glen, mysterious "face rock." (Karen Ralls)

numerous Bronze Age artifacts have been found. Roman-era finds suggest early worship of Mithras and what many believe to be runic and/or Pictish carvings.

The Inscription

In the south east corner of Rosslyn Chapel, there are inscribed the only words originally carved in Rosslyn Chapel, "*Forte est Vinu(m) Fortior est Rex Fortiores Sunt Muliers Sup(er) Om(nia) vincit veritas,*" which mean:

> Wine is Strong,
>
> the King is stronger,
>
> Women are stronger still,
>
> but above all, Truth conquers.

These words of wisdom were originally approved by Sir William St. Clair, and so one should take note of them. This particular phrase is familiar to Freemasons as it appears in certain Masonic degrees, including those of the Royal Arch, the Royal Order of Scotland, and the Ancient and Accepted Scottish Rite.

The only written inscription at Rosslyn Chapel, which states in Latin: "Wine is strong; The King is stronger; Women are stronger still, but above all, Truth conquers." (Karen Ralls)

The phrase itself comes from 1st Esdras, one of the apocryphal books of the Bible. (The Apocryphal books are those which, for one reason or another, did not make it into the orthodox canon that is called the "the Bible" today. Such decisions were made at various church councils in the first few centuries of Christianity—often for purely political as much as doctrinal reasons. Some of the apocryphal books are now recognized by respected biblical scholars as being at least as old and/or credible as a number that made it into the official orthodox canon.) First Esdras, chapter 3 discusses the time after the destruction of the first Temple in Jerusalem and the exile of the Jews to Babylon. King Darius of Persia invaded Babylon and captured it from Nebuchadnezzar, the king of Babylon and enemy of the Jews. These Jewish exiles and their descendants had been held captive in Babylon for some seventy years, after the destruction of Jerusalem in 586 BC.[18] Among the most trusted guards of King Darius was one of the exiled Jews, a man named Zerubbabel of the Royal House of David, i.e. a "Prince of Judah" who was born in exile. The king posed a question to Zerubbabel and two other guards in order to test their wisdom. He asked, "What is the strongest?" The first guard answered, "Wine." The second answered, "the King." Zerubbabel answered, "Women are the strongest, but above all things, Truth bearest the victory." (1st Esdras, chapter 3, verse 12)[19]

On hearing this, Darius decided to allow Zerubbabel to lead his people to their freedom and gave them back the temple treasures that had been seized by Nebuchadnezzar. They returned to the Holy Land to rebuild the city of Jerusalem and erect the Second Temple, "The House of the Lord." This is important, as the Book of Esdras does not give any dimensions for the Second Temple, nor does it claim it was a copy of the original design of King Solomon's Temple. It took 18 years to build the Second Temple, according to this account. These references are to be found in

"A Stone Rejected by the Builders," a sermon preached at Perth, 1732. This photo shows page 102 of a commentary on the gospel according to St. Matthew by F W Green. (The Brydon Collection)

1st Esdras, chapters 5 and 7. It is possible that Sir William St. Clair identified with Prince Zerubabbel as the master architect and builder of the chapel as the "Temple of the Lord" at the time Rosslyn was initially planned.

The vaults

Sir Walter Scott wrote in his famous poem, *The Lay of the Last Minstrel,* about twenty barons of Roslin buried in full knightly armour, beneath Rosslyn Chapel:

> … Seem'd all on fire that chapel proud,
>
> Where Roslin's chiefs uncoffin'd lie,
>
> Each Baron, for a sable shroud,
>
> Sheathed in his iron panoply …
>
> There are twenty of Roslin's barons bold
>
> Lie buried within that proud chapelle …
>
> And each St Clair was buried there
>
> With candle, with book and with knell …[20]

In 1693, John Slezer, in an account of the chapel, says of the barons: "The last lay in a vault so dry that their bodies have been found intire after Fourscore Years, and as fresh as when they were first buried. There goes a tradition, that before the death of any of the family of Roslin, this Chapel appears all in Fire."[21]

The Bishop of Caithness, Dr. Robert Forbes, in *An Account of the Chapel of Roslin* (1774) makes reference to ten barons of Roslin buried in the vaults of the chapel, but doesn't mention any treasure.[22] Critics understandably contend that if there was any treasure, it should have been cited; others point out that the treasure, whatever its nature, may have been stored elsewhere, or that there may be other vaults in or around the chapel area that were not seen by Forbes. Unless the vaults are excavated, no one can say anything for certain.

There have been countless theories about what may be hidden at Rosslyn Chapel. Its many legends reverberating through the centuries, Rosslyn has now become a modern-day "myth in the making" with an impetus all its own. Will the vaults of Rosslyn Chapel ever be excavated? Or, should they ever be excavated? Perhaps, as some believe, they are best left alone. Regarding the excavation issue, there are complex factors involved. One of which is that Scottish law includes a "Right of Sepulcher," i.e, if a full excavation were ever to be attempted, a rather lengthy Scottish legal procedure would have to be followed first, in order to secure the necessary permission to dig on church grounds. There are important existing gravestones in the burial grounds around the chapel.

Meanwhile, the focus is, and must be, on *preservation* of the building and the conservation of its features and surrounding environment.

One thing that is clear is that Rosslyn Chapel was not "built by the medieval Knights Templar Order." Why? To begin with, the complex building program at Rosslyn Chapel started in 1446. This is during the period between the dissolution of the Templar Order (1312) and the public announcement of the Freemasonic Grand Lodge of England in 1717. The Grand Lodge of Scotland officially began in 1736. Sir William St. Clair became the first Scottish Grand Master.

Freemasonry, Hiram Abiff, and the Apprentice Pillar at Rosslyn

The Masonic story of Hiram Abiff has long been noted for its parallels to the story of the murdered apprentice at Rosslyn Chapel. This tragic tale of the murder of a builder is similar, but not identical. Here, the gifted master builder of Solomon's Temple, Hiram Abiff, in a show of unshaken fidelity, refused to reveal any of his builder's secrets to the uninitiated. He was brutally murdered. He nobly sacrificed his own life rather than disclose guild secrets to the uninitiated.

One historian says that "the legend of the murdered apprentice has some superficial similarities with the murder of Hiram Abiff in Masonic lore; but a more considered approach reveals that these two stories are substantially different in detail. The legend at Rosslyn Chapel cannot be taken to be Masonic in any way …"[23] Another historian differs. He states that while the "murdered apprentice story" may be an interesting one, "there is no historical record of such an event ever taking place. It seems likely that Freemasons, having already decided that the chapel was sacred to their Craft, invented the story to fit the existence of the pillar. Scottish Rite Freemasonry, as far as its historical records are concerned, does not predate Rosslyn Chapel and the place may have been significant to the Craft since its creation. But this does not mean that the chapel was 'built' with Freemasonry in mind."[24] Finally, the tale of a gifted apprentice being murdered by a jealous master is not necessarily unique to Rosslyn. It is an allegorical theme that occurs at Rouen and other locations.

The link that many have claimed is that the Hiramic legend is supposed to have been first associated with Freemasonry in Anderson's *Constitutions* (1723). The legend that became associated with the third degree of Freemasonry was a development thought to have first appeared in Scotland in the year 1726.[25] It would appear that the story of the "murdered apprentice" at Rosslyn predates this.

Interestingly enough, the youthful-looking apprentice carving at Rosslyn that visitors see today was not originally a clean-shaven youth. Instead, he originally had a beard and moustache as confirmed by zoom lens photography. In earlier times, only a master builder or guild member at that level could sport a full beard. So it appears that this carving had been carefully chiselled off in the past to create an image of a more youthful-looking apprentice. It is anyone's guess as to why someone would go to such lengths to deliberately "demote" the Master down to the rank of a mere apprentice. Some surmise that the original carving—that of a bearded Master and not a young apprentice—would have predated the first public associations of Freemasonry with the Hiram Abiff legend in the early 18th century. One writer comments:

> The wound on the right forehead was not part of the original carving at all … It was only later, much later, indicated by the use of ochre, chalk and paint. This confirms that the legend of the murdered apprentice was a later addition to the mythology of the chapel. That means that the legend did not exist at the time the chapel was begun (1446) and only came into being more than 250 years later, that is, sometime after 1700.… The implication that parts of the chapel have been deliberately tampered with is enormous.[26]

Dr Karen Ralls, Rosslyn Chapel. (V. Hill)

Rosslyn Chapel also contains non-Christian imagery in places, as do many other medieval churches and cathedrals throughout Europe. It is interesting to note that in medieval building traditions, it is *the northeast stone* that is laid first. It is considered to be the foundation stone for the entire building. The "laying of the foundation stone" is a very important allegorical concept in the Old Testament, Freemasonry, the medieval Knights Templar, and so on.

"Son of the Widow"

In the Hiram Abiff legend, the master builder Hiram is referred to as the "son of a widow." Among the carvings in Rosslyn Chapel, the official guidebook descriptions point out the heads of the "Apprentice"; the "Master," who is said to have struck and killed him with his deadly mallet; and the "grieving Mother" of the murdered Apprentice. The Apprentice himself, like Hiram Abiff, is called a "son of a widow":

> Freemasons refer to themselves as Sons of the Widow, a term used in Masonic traditions as a title that was attributed to Hiram, the principal architect at the building of Solomon's Temple. "It is perhaps curious to note that the mother of Jesus is traditionally reported to have comported herself as a widow after the miraculous conception."[27]

AT THE TOP: Masons Marks chart of marks at Rosslyn Chapel (1446) and other Scottish locations.

BELOW: Two of the Rosslyn mason's marks enlarged

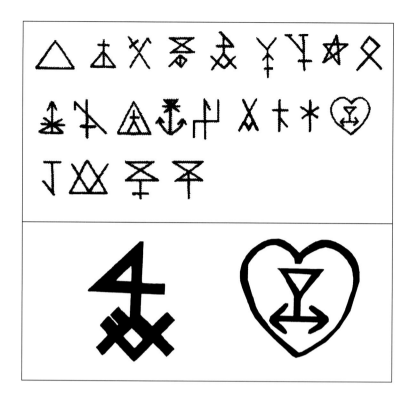

The implication is that Christ is also a "Son of the Widow." In Egyptian mythology, Horus is described in a similar fashion, and many peoples from all over the world have this motif in their mythologies. Merlin, as we recall, was described by medieval chroniclers as a "son of a widow." This epithet was often attributed to especially gifted individuals in ancient lore. J. S. M. Ward, a Masonic and esoteric author, writes about other links to the "Son of the Widow" theme:

> The title survived not only among Masons, but in the Graal legends where Perceval is called the "Son of the Widow Lady," and it would be possible to compile quite a list of "Questing Heroes," who are similarly called "Sons of the Widow."[28]

Rosslyn Castle as a medieval scriptorium

Rosslyn Castle was also a medieval scriptorium, a place where manuscripts were manufactured with great care, patience, skill, and attention. It was also one of the major Scottish centers of learning and education, part of the Collegiate system of churches.

This aspect of Rosslyn does not seem to be widely acknowledged or understood today, as most of the focus has been on the chapel itself.

THE ROSSLYN-HAY MANUSCRIPT

Five St. Clair manuscripts are in the National Library of Scotland and each one bears one or more St. Clair signatures. One of these is the Rosslyn-Hay manuscript described as follows:

> One of these is a giant compendium mostly written by James Mangnet in 1488. Commissioned by William St. Clair (for his inscription appears as that of first owner), the 1,000 hand-written pages contain significantly: GUILD LAWS, FOREST LAWS, and THE LAWIS AND CUSTUMIS OF YE SCHIPPIS. Legalities all vital to the Scottish Operative Guilds! A work also necessary for the legal guidance of their hereditary Patrons, Protectors and Arbitrators; the St. Clairs of Rosslyn.[29]

In addition to the Guild, Forest, and Shipping Laws, this manuscript, called the Rosslyn-Hay manuscript, also contains a section entitled *The Buk of the Order of Knighthede* (The Book of the Order of Knighthood). The Rosslyn-Hay manuscript is the earliest extant work in Scottish prose.[30]

The reader is informed in greater detail about the famed scriptorium at Rosslyn Castle, and about the Rosslyn-Hay manuscript:

> According to its inscription, Gilbert Hay, knight, carried out the translation and produced the three part folio on the instructions of William Sanctclare of Rosslyn. A small panel (PATRICUS LOWES ME LIGAVIT), integral to the leather binding, indicates that the binder was Patrick de Lowis, a burgher of Rosslyn who died in 1466. The heavily worked leather binding is recognised as the most important example of its kind in the British Isles.[31]

Clearly, the Rosslyn scriptorium was very important at the time. This is, however, only one of the several manuscripts now known to be associated with Rosslyn. In recent years, another medieval illuminated manuscript in the Bodleian Library at Oxford University was also found to have been made at Rosslyn Castle.

The St. Clairs and the Guilds

The St. Clairs of Rosslyn appear to have had a relationship with a number of medieval guilds in Edinburgh, and also with certain Orders of Knighthood. (32) Regarding the Rosslyn-Hay manuscript and *The Buk of the Order of Knighthede*, some have inquired:

> As hereditary judges, or "Grand Masters" administering Guild Laws, did the hereditary St. Clair mandate extend over other Orders or fraternities such as those of Knighthood? This has always remained an unanswered question.[33]

Like many unanswered questions regarding Rosslyn, experts do not always agree. It seems there will always be room for speculation.

The Rosicrucians, Rosslyn, and the year 1484

Rosslyn took forty years to build, a process which began in 1446 and was not fully finished until 1486. But two years earlier, in 1484, two illustrious people were said to have died: one, is the founder of Rosslyn Chapel, Sir William St. Clair, and the other is the mythical Christian Rosencreutz.

> The Rosicrucian traditions of medieval times adapted, spread, and grew in accordance with the interest in Hermetic subjects, all of which greatly flourished amongst the learned in the 17th and 18th centuries. The alchemical schools of Europe used the symbol of the Rosy Cross (or Rose Croix) and 'evolved a complex philosophical symbolism which incorporated elements of the old Operative Craft Guild mystery traditions.'[34]

The Rosicrucian movement first officially surfaced in 1614 in Kassel, Germany, with the publication of *Fama Fraternitatis, des Löblichen Ordens des Rosenkreutzes* (The Declaration of the Worthy Order of the Rosy Cross). The *Fama* revealed the existence of a fraternity said to have been founded by one Christian Rosencreutz. He was believed to have lived in the 14th and 15th centuries, and to have travelled extensively in the East, returning to Europe with new inspiring wisdom and knowledge. Members of the Rosicrucian movement were secretive, i.e. incognito, and were said to travel about healing the sick, and inspiring others with their special knowledge.

Upon the death of Christian Rosencreutz, in 1484, his place of burial was kept a secret. But recently, said the *Fama*, the burial vault of Christian Rosencreutz had been found by the new brotherhood of Rosicrucians. This symbolized the beginning of a New Age for humanity. Naturally, this unusual publication stimulated much discussion and debate at the time of its publication in the early 17th century.

Often simplistically thought of as a "Protestant movement"—as it advocated freedom of thought and speech—the Rosicrucian manifestos actually had fewer Catholic adversaries, as the bulk of the opposition came from other Protestants! The manifestos were certainly the talk of Europe at the time. The author of the *Fama* and other important Rosicrucian tracts is reputed to have been Johann Valentin Andreae (1586–1654), a learned and influential German Protestant pastor from Tübingen.[35]

Christian Rosencreutz, according to the *Fama,* is buried in a vault with perpetual lamps in his tomb. A mysterious book, *M,* is also buried with him. His tomb was rediscovered 120 years after his death by the Rosicrucians. When the vault was opened, it was still said to be all ablaze with the light from the ever-burning lamps.

Christopher McIntosh, an expert on the Rosicrucians, says that "in Rosicrucian legend, it is the Brotherhood which reawakens, while its founder, although ostensibly dead, remains undecayed as a symbol of his undecaying influence through his followers."[36] Another Rosicrucian text proclaims:

> At some far distant time, Rozenkreuz, wearing a white linen coat, girded crosswise with a broad red band and four red roses in his hat, made his way to a strange castle. On arrival he witnessed a Royal marriage and was invested with *"The Order of the Golden Fleece."* His

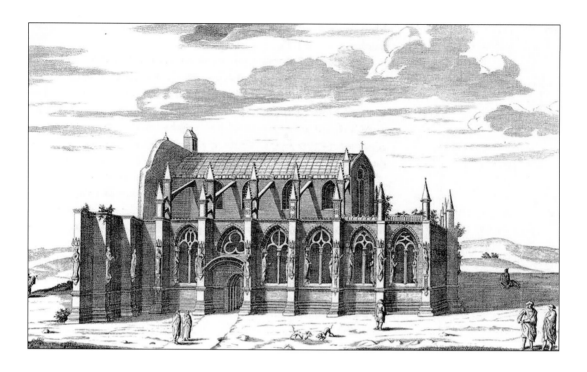

A late 17th century line drawing of Rosslyn Chapel by Capt. John Slezer, 1693

curiosity led him to a secret chamber where he found Venus asleep on a bed, and, in the Castle library, the '*King's secret books of wisdom,*' which he obtained.[37]

Capt. John Slezer in his *Theatrum Scotiae* (1693) wrote one of the earliest accounts of Rosslyn Chapel in existence today:

This Chapel lies in Midlothian, four miles from Edinburgh, and is one of the most curious Pieces of Workman-ship in Europe. The Foundation of this rare Building was laid Anno 1440 by William St. Clair, Prince of Orkney, Duke of Holdenburgh …

A Man as considerable for the public Works which he erected, as for the Lands which he possess'd, and the Honours which were conferred upon him by several of the greatest Princes of Europe. It is remarkable that in all this Work there are not two Cuts of one sort. The most curious Part of the Building is the Vault of the Quire, and that which is called the Prince's Pillar so much talk'd of. This Chapel was possess'd by a Provost, and Seven Canons Regular, who were endued with Several considerable Revenues through the Liberality of the Lairds of Roslin.

Christian Rosencreutz sits in front of the tomb in which he lay for 120 years. The date of 1604 is that of the opening of the tomb by the Rosicrucian Brothers. (From *The Mystery Traditions: Secret Symbols and Sacred Art*)

Here lies buried George Earl of Caithness, who lived about the Beginning of the Reformation, Alexander Earl of Sutherland, great Grand-Child of King Robert de Bruce, Three Earls of Orkney, and Nine Barons of Roslin.

The last lay in a Vault, so dry that their bodies have been found intire after Fourscore Years, and as fresh as when they were first buried. There goes a Tradition, that before the Death of any of the Family of Roslin, this Chapel appears all in Fire.[38]

The "Prince's Pillar" is the "Apprentice Pillar."

The Treasure of Rosslyn

Perhaps the real "treasure" of Rosslyn is not—and never was—ultimately a material one. Even if any material objects of great import are eventually found—such as, for example, the missing Holy Rood of Scotland—an important question will remain: what is the spiritual relevance of any discovery?

The hidden meaning of medieval symbolism is found in an allegorical and *visual* way. It does not rely only on printed interpretations, material objects, or intellectual extrapolations. In fact, in medieval times, only a privileged few could read or write. Yet many people could contemplate the stories and symbolism revealed in the carvings. These were often used as educational devices for teaching and learning, as they are universal.

The secret symbols point to the true spiritual nature and potential of humanity—and the quest that each of us may undergo to find their Truth. The skilled craftsmen who built these inspiring edifices, and those learned ones who sponsored and assisted them, have left us silent messages to decipher. Books can be burned, paper and wood can be destroyed. Stone tends to last far longer. Even the Inquisition could not erase such messages so easily.

The complex allegory presented by Rosslyn Chapel is: "An Arcanum, a book in stone. An unfinished labour of love that lasts forever."[39]

What can never be taken away is the true meaning and light of Rosslyn Chapel. May it continue to unfold its secrets to those who approach the Arcanum with worthy hearts.

Appendix One
Additional European Sites for Mary Magdalene

Places to Visit: a short guide to Magdalene sites in France, Belgium, Italy, London

Due to the increase of interest by modern visitors in sites related to Mary Magdalene as well as the Black Madonna, I have selected a few of the key medieval period Western European pilgrimage sites in three countries often frequently visited by travellers today—France, Belgium, and Italy—that feature Mary Magdalene, that are also Magdalene sites more easily accessible.

Of course, please note that there are many other Magdalene-related sites all over Europe; these are a few that you may wish to incorporate as part of a future holiday or spiritual journey.

Belgium

BRUSSELS—There are a number of relevant sites here, but one lovely image of St Mary Magdalene can be found at the Chapel of St Catherine; also has a Black Madonna;

HAL/HALLE—a beautiful statue of St Mary Magdalene in the Church of St Martin; also a Black Madonna.

TOURNAI—there is the Chapel of St Mary Magdalene in the Cathedral of Notre-Dame, with its stunning Black Madonna; this area was also important as the capital of the Franks.

France

CHARTRES—a large Mary Magdalene stained glass window, two Black Madonnas and much more at this cathedral;

LE PUY—painting of "The Three Marys at the Tomb of Jesus"; also has a Black Madonna (Notre Dame de Puy), a statue of Joan of Arc, and was one of the four major starting-points for pilgrims to Santiago de Compostela

MARSEILLES—a Black Virgin (Notre Dame de la Confession) in the crypt of the Abbey of St Victor; its colorful annual 2 Feb. Candlemas celebration with special green candles to commemorate the Provencal legends of the arrival of 'the Three Marys'—St Mary Magdalene, Lazarus and Martha, etc;

ORLEANS—long a key St Mary Magdalene pilgrimage site, it also has a Black Virgin (Notre Dame des Miracles) and among other things, is a site as well-known today for its historical links to Joan of Arc;

PARIS—Too many sites to list here, but, for one easier-to-visit example: in the lesser-known but beautiful Church of Saint-Merri, on the busy Rue Saint Martin on the Right Bank, there is a lovely stained glass window of St Mary Magdalene adjacent to another one of St Mary the Egyptian;

RENNES-LE-CHATEAU—with its well-known church in the stunning Languedoc, it has long been dedicated to St Marie Madeleine; this site and landscape environs has much interesting history, lore and symbolism. The church has, among much else, its famous Magdalene altar panel (painted by Fr Sauniere himself); the grounds have a lovely garden, orangery, the Tour Magdala, Villa Bethania, and much more;

Saintes-Maries-de-la-Mer at this Provencal church in the Carmargue, the place where legends say Mary Magdalene and her entourage first arrived from the Holy Land after the crucifixion; see the well-known mural of imagery featuring the Three Marys (including Mary Magdalene);

St-Maximin—a tomb and relics of St Mary Magdalene with major celebrations on July 22nd; nearby, on the hilltop, is **Sainte-Baume**, the grotto long associated in Provencal legend with earlier spiritual traditions linked to the divine Feminine, and, by medieval times, it became especially famous for its alleged association as the cave and hermitage site of Mary Magdalene in her later years;

Vezelay a shrine of St Mary Magdalene in the crypt of its towering Romanesque Basilica; this city was also a major starting point for medieval pilgrims on the road to Santiago de Compostela (Spain).

Italy

Oropa—a beautiful site in northern Italy with a striking St Mary Magdalene stained glass window and a lovely Black Madonna; it has also long been a key site important to the Savoy family;

Venice—Basilica of San Marco, which periodically displays its Precious Blood relic that is said to include unguent ointment of St Mary Magdalene; also, this church claims the head of St John the Baptist. Like any country, there are a number of other sites, but these are two that are accessible.

Appendix Two
Additional European Sites for Black Madonnas

Places to Visit: a short guide to some major Black Madonna sites

Due to the increase of interest by modern visitors about Black Madonnas, I have selected a few of the key medieval Black Madonna pilgrimage sites in Western European countries often visited today—France, Spain, Italy, etc—where the shrines have a Black Madonna as a focus and are more easily accessible to get to for travellers today.

There are many other Black Madonna sites in other areas all over the world; below are a few that you may wish to incorporate as part of a future spiritual journey or holiday to W European cities and villages.

For more information and an international Gazetteer of hundreds of Black Madonna-related sites all around the world, I recommend Jungian analyst Ean Begg's seminal book, *The Cult of the Black Virgin,* New York: Penguin, 1996 (revised edition of 1985 original).

Belgium

BRUSSELS—Chapel of St Catherine has an image of St Mary Magdalene and other saints; also, a Black Madonna

HAL/HALLE—image of St Mary Magdalene in the Church of St Martin; also a well-known Black Madonna shrine;

TOURNAI—Chapel of St Mary Magdalene in the Cathedral of Notre-Dame, a Black Madonna; Tournai was also the capital of the Franks

England

WILLESDEN (London)—The Black Virgin of Willesden can be seen at the Church Of Our Lady; a limewood statue.

WALSINGHAM—England's National Shrine of Our Lady, with both Anglican and Catholic shrines of the BVM

France

AIX-EN-PROVENCE—In the Cathedral Saint-Sauveur d'Aix, a seated Virgin hewn from stone, said to be a 1521 copy of the celebrated Vierge Noire de Notre-Dame-de-la-Seds which disappeared in the 16 century.

CHARTRES—the Mary Magdalene stained glass window; also two Black Virgins; magnificent Gothic cathedral with many important features Notre Dame du Pilier (Our Lady of the Pillar) is in the nave, early 16th c Image replacing the earlier 13th century gilt statue of pear tree wood. Notre Dame de Sous-Terre (Our Lady Under-the-Earth) in the crypt, replaced in 1856 by the present natural wood statue; the original that was destroyed during the Revolution was made of ebony.

LIMOUX—In sanctuary known since 1011, Notre-Dame de Marceille, is an 11th/12th c. black hard wood statue, the closest Black Madonna to Rennes-le-Chateau. This site also has a beautiful stained glass window of Mary Magdalene, in addition to a statue of St Vincent de Paul.

LAON—Black Madonna in side chapel in the cathedral; Laon also has an interesting Templar chapel and adjacent museum with archaeological artifacts; early Merovingian site and later, the Carolingian capital of France;

LE PUY-EN-VELAY—In Monastere Sainte Claire, Notre Dame du Puy, a cedar statue said to have been made by Jeremiah and was brought to Le Puy by St. Louis, and later unfortunately burned at the Rev. It was replaced with a copy by a local artist at the end of the 18th century of gilded wood. Small replica of original in vestry.

MARSEILLES—Black Virgin (Notre Dame de la Confession) in crypt of Abbey of St Victor; 2 Feb. Candlemas celebration to commemorate the Provencal legends of the arrival of St Mary Magdalene, Lazarus and Martha, etc, with green candles. (see also re: black St Sara.)

MEYMAC—Notre Dame de Meymac, a 12th century statue of wood with very black faces and hands, pink fingernails, red lips, white and black eyes. This Black Madonna has gold sabots and a turban, very large hands, and wears a red cloak and green dress.

ORLEANS—Black Virgin, Notre Dame des Miracles, de la Recouvrance or St Mary the Egyptian. A 16th century stone statue, replacing the ancient wooden Black Madonna that was brought to Orleans in the 5-6th century by Syrian merchants and later burned by Protestants in 1562. Orleans also has strong connections with the famed St Joan of Arc ('Maid of Orleans'), the Knights Templar and other spiritual and esoteric groups, and, since at least the 11th century, it has also been a major Mary Magdalene pilgrimage site.

PARIS—(Seine). Black Madonna, Notre-Dame de Paix, 16th century, wood, in Church of Nuns of the Sacred Heart. (35 rue de Picpus). A fascinating history; see Ean Begg's for details.

SAINTES-MARIES-DE-LA-MER—at the church, see images of the Three Marys (including St Mary Magdalene), as this is is the alleged landing spot of an early Christian entourage according to legends. The dark statue of St Sara the Egyptian, who, it is said, gave birth to the cult of the Black Virgins in the area, is also at this site and is also venerated by the gypsies. The annual gypsy pilgrimage festival is celebrated here with the statue of St Sara processed and then dipped into the sea. St-Maries is also an important stage on the road to Compostela.

Germany

ALTOTTING—Black Madonna ('Our Lady of Altotting'); also an old Roman crossroads site; Christianized by St. Rupert in 7th century.

Italy

LORETO—Ancona; the Holy House of Mary; original statue was accidentally destroyed by fire and was replaced by a new standing figure in 1921

OROPA—St Mary Magdalene stained glass window; Black Virgin (La Madonna Di Oropa), and one historically important to the House of Savoy.

VENICE—Basilica of San Marco, side chapel, a Black Virgin icon; also, the alleged head of St John the Baptist

Poland

JASNA GORA— (Jasna Gora monastery), a Black Madonna painting, and also the national shrine of Poland.

Spain

BARCELONA—View one of the finest collections of Black Virgins anywhere in the world at the Museu Nacional d'Arte de Catalunya (MNAC), the national museum of Catalan visual art. Features Romanesque, Gothic and Modern period art. Highly recommended.

GIRONA—Girona Cathedral; in the cathedral Treasury Museum, off to the left-hand side along the cathedral, there are some black madonnas in their collection as well as a number of other important artefacts and relics;

MONTSERRAT—Royal Basilica with its famous 12th century Romanesque Black Virgin (La Moreneta) at the Montserrat Monastery.

Switzerland

EINSIEDELN—at the Abbey church of the Benedictine monastery here, Our Lady of the Hermits, a major black madonna shrine, and also the national shrine of Switzerland.

Balearic Islands (Mallorca)

Cathedral of Lluc—(NW of island), and Palma Museum, both have Black Madonnas and other interesting artefacts.

Canary Islands

CANDELARIA—Tenerife is patroness of the Canaries; a major Black Madonna shrine

Malta

GOZO—Ghajnsielem Cathedral, just off Mgarr harbour, has a Black Madonna, and, in 2007, for the first time, the community here celebrate their liturgical feast of Our Lady of Loreto. The statue was purchased in Rome in 1924.

Endnotes

Chapter 1–The Knights Templar

1. Barber, Malcolm, *The New Knighthood: A History of the Order of the Temple* (Cambridge: Cambridge University Press, 1994), 44.

2 Nicolson, Helen, *The Knights Templar: A New History* (Stroud: Sutton Publishing, 2001), 12.

3 Runciman, Stephen., *The Eastern Schism: A Study of the Papacy and the Eastern Churches during the Eleventh and Twelfth Centuries* (Oxford: Oxford University Press, 1955), 105.

4 Deansley, Margaret, *A History of the Medieval Church 590–1500* (London: Routledge, 1925), 110.

5 Ralls, Karen, *The Templars and the Grail,* (Chicago: Quest Books, 2003), 38.

6 Ibid.

7 Richard, J., "Hospitals and Hospital Congregations in the Latin Kingdom during the First Period of the Frankish Conquest", in *Outremer Studies in the History of the Crusading Kingdom of Jerusalem,* Ed. By B. Kedar, H. Mayer, and R. Smail, Jerusalem: Yad Izhak Ben-Zvi Institutem, 1982, 89-100.

8 Upton-Ward, Judi, *The Rule of the Templars,* (Woodbridge, Suffolk: Boydell Press, 1992), 11.

9 Nicholson, Helen, *The Knights Templar: A Brief History* (London: Constable, 2010), 159-160.

10 Nicholson *The Knights Templar: A Brief History* (Stroud: Sutton, 2001), 131.

11 Ralls, Karen, *The Knights Templar Encyclopedia,* (Franklin Lakes, NJ: Career Press, 2007), 28.

12 Ibid., 24, 66, and 124.

13 Butler, Alan and Dafoe, Stephen, *The Templar Continuum,* (Belleville, Ont.: Templar Books, Thevou Publishing Group, 1999), 64.

14 Wasserman, James, *The Templars and the Assassins: The Militia of Heaven* (Rochester, VT.: Inner Traditions, 2001), 130–31.

15 Ibid., 64.

16 Ibid.

17 Lea, H.C., *A History of the Inquisition of the Middle Ages,* 3 vols. (1888; reprint, New York: Russell and Russell, 1955).

18 Partner, Peter, *The Murdered Magicians: the Templars and their Myth,* (Oxford: Oxford University Press, 1981), 82.

19 Burman, Edward, *Supremely Abominable Crimes: The Trial of the Knights Templar,*(London, Alison and Busby, 1994), 259.

20 Demurger, Alain, *The Last Templar: The Tragedy of Jacques de Molay, Last Grand Master of the Temple* (London: Profile Books, 2004), 195-8; Engl transl by Antonia Nevill.

21 Ralls, K., *The Knights Templar Encyclopedia,* 183-4.

22 Nicholson, H., *The Knights Templar: A New History* (2001), 149.

23 Brighton, Simon, *In Search of the Knights Templar: A Guide to the Sites in Britain,* (London: Wiedenfeld & Nicholson, 2006), 54.

24 Beamon, Sylvia, *The Royston Cave: Used by Saints or Sinners? Local Historical Influences of the Templar and Hospitaller Movements,* (Baldock: Courtney, 1992).

25 Ralls, *The Knights Templar Encyclopedia,* 184.

26 Nicholson, H., *The Knights Templar: A New History,* (2010 edition), 240.

Chapter 2–Mary Magdalene

1 Jacobus de Voragine, *The Golden Legend: Readings on the Saints,* Princeton, NJ: Princeton University Press, 1993, xiv. [Engl. transl. by Wm. Granger Ryan from the 1845 Latin Graesse edition of the 1260 Latin orig.]

2 Jansen, Katherine Ludwig, *The Making of the Magdalen*: Preaching and Popular Devotion in the Later Middle Ages, Princeton: Princeton University Press, 2000, p. 57.

3 Starbird, Margaret, *The Woman with the Alabaster Jar,* Santa Fe: Bear & Co., 1993, 60.

4 Haskins, Susan, *Mary Magdalen,* London: HarperCollins, 1993, p 222.

5 Lacordaire, Peter, *St Mary Magdalene,* Derby: Thomas Richardson, 1880, p 99.

6 Haskins, Ibid., 26.

7 Haskins, Ibid., 127.

8 Haskins, Ibid., 133.

9 Ibid.

10 Walker, Barbara, *The Woman's Dictionary of Symbols and Sacred Objects,* San Francisco: Harper & Row, 1988, p 88.

11 Ibid.

12 Chilton, Bruce, *Mary Magdalene: A Biography,* New York: Doubleday, 2005, 188.

13 Walker, Ibid., 88.

14 Ralls, Karen, *The Knights Templar Encyclopedia*, Franklin Lakes, NJ: Career Press, 2007, p. 154

15 Saxer, Victor, "Les saintes Marie Madaleine et Marie de Bethanie dans la tradition liturgique et homiletique orientale,", *RevScRel 32* [1958]: 1-37. {note: Saxer lists June 4 for the Orthodox feast day of Mary of Bethany, and June 30, July 22 and August 4 for Mary Magdalene.}

16 Brock, Ann G., *Mary Magdalene, the First Apostle,* Harvard Theological Studies 51, Cambridge, MA: Harvard University Press, 2003, 169.

17 Ralls, Ibid., 123.

18 Hutton, Ronald, *The Rise and Fall of Merry England: the ritual year 1400-1700,* Oxford: Oxford University Press, 1994, p 46.

19 Schaberg, Jane, *The Resurrection of Mary Magdalene,* London and New York: Continuum, 2004, 19.

20 Robinson, James, [Ed.], "Thunder Perfect Mind", from the revised edition, *The Nag Hammadi Library,* San Francisco: HarperCollins, 1990.

21 Qualls-Corbett, N., *The Sacred Prostitute: Eternal Aspect of the Feminine,* Studies in Jungian Psychology, Toronto: Inner City Books, 1988, 174.

22 Meyer, Marvin, *The Gospels of Mary: The Secret Tradition of Mary Magdalene the Companion of Jesus,* with E. A. de Boer. San Francisco: HarperCollins, 2004, 96.

23 Chadwick, Henry, *The Church in Ancient Society: from Galilee to Gregory the Great,* Oxford: Clarendon Press, 2001, p 28 re: the book of Sirach.

Chapter 3–The Black Madonna

1 Gabriella, V., "The Statue of Our Lady in the Holy House", *Loreto History 16,* No. 3, Loreto: 1983, 74-5 [poetic verse extract was dated 1629].

2 Lahr, Jane, *Searching for Mary Magdalene,* New York: Welcome Books, 2006, 185 [was ref # 5)

3 Warner, Marina, *Alone of All Her Sex: The Myth and Cult of the Virgin Mary,* London: Weidenfeld & Nicolson, 1985, 274

4 Shlain, Leonard, *The Alphabet versus the Goddess: The Conflict between Word and Image,* New York: Viking Penguin, 1998, 268

5 Galland, China, *Longing for Darkness: Tara and the Black Madonna,* London: Century, 1990, p 288

6 Warner, *Alone of All Her Sex,* 275

7 Boyer, Marie-France, *The Cult of the Virgin,* London: Thames & Hudson, 2000, 36

8 Markale, Jean, *Cathedral of the Black Madonna,* Rochester, VT: Inner Traditions, 2004, 174. [French orig. by Editions Pygmalion/Gerard Watelet, Paris, 1988]

9 Bull, Marcus, *The Miracles of Our Lady of Rocamadour,* Woodbridge: Boydell Press, 1999, 40. [For more information about miracles and the statue of Virgin and Child at Rocamadour, see I.H. Forsyth, *The Throne of Wisdom: Wood Sculptures of the Madonna in Romanesque France* (Princeton, 1972), p 144, p. 185 and fig. 143; and also, see D. Freedberg, *The Power of Images: Studies in the History and Theory of Response* (Chicago, 1989) p 27-8]

10 Begg, Ean and Deike., *In Search of the Holy Grail and the Precious Blood,* London: Thorsons, 1995, 73.

11 Ibid.

12 Begg, *Black Virgin,* 21

13 Gustafson, F., *The Black Madonna,* Boston: Sigo Press, 1990, 16.

14 Ibid, 180

15 Ibid., 9

16 Forsyth, I.H., *The Throne of Wisdom: Wood Sculptures of the Madonna in Romanesque France,* Princeton: Princeton University Press, *1972,* 105ff.

17 Mullen, Peter., *Shrines of Our Lady,* Piatkus, London, 1998, 69-70

18 Carr-Gomm, Philip, *Sacred Places,* London: Quercus, 2001 Ed. [2008 orig.], 101.

19 Matthews, Caitlin, *Sophia: Goddess of Wisdom, Bride of God,* Wheaton, IL: Quest 2001, 194.

20 Miller, M., *Chartres Cathedral,* Norwich: Jarrold Publishing, 2002 rev. ed. [1985 orig. ed.] 62-3

21 *The Sanctuary of Oropa*, Biella: Edizione Eco del Sanctuario di Oropa, 1963, 4-5

22 Begg, E., *Black Virgin,* 245

23 Ibid.

24 Birnbaum, Lucia C., *Black Madonnas: Feminism, religion and politics in Italy,* Lincoln, NE: ToExcel publishers, 2000, 134. [Ital. orig. 1993]

25 Ibid.

26 Durand-Lefebvre, M., *Etude sur l'origine des Vierges Noires,* Paris: 1937.

27 Begg, op cit. 10.

Chapter 4–The Grail

1 Matthews, John, *Elements of the Grail Tradition* (Shaftesbury: Element, 1990), 1.

2 Ralls, Karen, *The Templars and the Grail*, (Wheaton/Chicago, IL, Quest Books, 2003), 123

3 Wood, Juliet, "The Holy Grail: From Romance Motif to Modern Genre," *Folklore* 3 (2) (London, October 2000), 171.

4 Lively, P. and Kerven, R., *The Mythical Quest,* London: The British Library, 1996, 182.

5 Barber, Richard, *The Holy Grail: The History of a Legend,,* London: Penguin Books, 2005, 39.

6 Barber, Richard, *The Knight and Chivalry* (Woodbridge, Suffolk: Boydell & Brewer, [1970] 1995), 97.

7 Nicolson, Helen, *Love, War, and the Grail: Templars, Hospitallers and Teutonic Knights in Medieval Epic and Romance 1150–1500,* History of Warfare Series, vol. 4 (Leiden: Brill, 2001), 108.

8 Ralls, K., *The Templars and the Grail*, 137

9 Bryant, Nigel, trans., *The High Book of the Grail, A Translation of the Thirteenth-Century Romances of* Perlesvaus (Cambridge, UK: D. S. Brewer, 1978).

10 Goetinck, G., *Peredur: A Study of Welsh Tradition in the Grail Legends,* Cardiff: University of Wales Press, 1975, 1-40.

11 Ralls, K., *The Templars and the Grail*, 182

12 Ibid., 194-5

13 Carr-Gomm, Philip and Heygate, Richard, *The Book of English Magic,* London: John Murray, 2009, 153.

14 Loomis, R. S., *The Grail: From Celtic Myth to Christian Symbol,* Princeton: Princeton University Press, Mythos Paperback Series, 1991, 68.

15 Begg and Begg, *In Search of the Holy Grail,* (HarperCollins, London, 1995) xvii.

16 Ibid.

17 Ibid., xvii

18 Ibid., 206

19 Matthews, *Elements,* 52–53.

20 Nicholson, H., Ibid.

21 Silverberg, R., *The Realm of Prester John,* (Ohio University Press, Athens, OH, 1972, 8.

22 Beckingham, C.F., 'The Achievement of Prester John', *An Inaugural Lecture at the School of Oriental and African Studies (SOAS),* London, 1966, 9.

23 Knight, Gareth, *Merlin and the Grail Tradition,* Oceanside: Sun Chalice Books, 1999, 36.

24 Hutton, Ronald, *The Pagan Religions of the Ancient British Isles,* Oxford: Blackwell, 1993.

25 Jung, E., and von Franz, M-L, *The Grail Legend,* Princeton: Princeton University Press, 1970 [Engl transl, C.G. Jung Foundation (NY) of 1960 German orig.], 213

26 Proctor, H., *The Holy Grail Tapestries Designed by Edward Burne-Jones, William Morris and JH Dearle for Morris & Co.,* Birmingham: Birmingham Museums and Art Gallery, 1997, 6.

Chapter 5–The Cathars

1 Barber, Malcolm, *The Cathars: Dualist Heretics in the Languedoc in the High Middle Ages,* Longman/Pearson Education Ltd: Harlow, 2000, 1.

2 Godwin, Jocelyn, *The Golden Thread: The Ageless Wisdom of the Western Mystery Traditions,* Wheaton/Chicago, IL: Quest Books, 2007, 61.

3 de Rougemont, Denis, *Love in the Western World*, Princeton: Princeton University Press, 1983 ed. of 1940 orig., 78.

4 Lambert, Malcolm, *Medieval Heresy,* Malden, MA: Blackwell, 1992, 106.

5 Churton, Tobias, *The Gnostic Philosophy,* Lichfield, UK: Signal, 2003, 182.

6 Barber, M., *The Cathars,* 56.

7 Ibid., 173.

8 Barber, Malcolm, *"Women and Catharism",* Reading Medieval Series 3, Reading University, Graduate Centre for Medieval Studies, 1977, 50.

9 Ibid., 49.

10 Lambert, M., *The Cathars,* Oxford: Blackwell, 1998, 146.

10 Ibid., 45

12 Barber, Malcolm, "Catharism and the Occitan Nobility: the lordships of Cabaret, Minerve and Termes", *The Ideals and Practice of Medieval Knighthood 3,* [Ed.] C. Harper-Bill and R. Harvey. Woodbridge, Suffolk: Boydell Press, 1990, 12.

13 Kienzle, Beverley M., *Cistercians, Heresy and Crusade in Occitania, 1145-1229,* York: York Medieval Press, 2001, 111.

14 Kieckhefer, Richard, *European Witch Trials: Their Foundation in Learned and Popular Culture, 1300–1500* (London, 1976), 10–14, 108–12. See also R. Keickhefer, *Magic in the Middle Ages* (Cambridge: Cambridge University Press, 2000, 188.

15 Ralls, Karen, *The Knights Templar Encyclopedia,* Franklin Lakes, NJ: Career Press, 2007, 210.

16 Roach, Andrew, *The Devil's World: Heresy and Society 1100-1300,* Harlow: Pearson/Longman, 2005, 137.

17 Baigent, Michael, and Leigh, Richard, *The Inquisition,* London: Penguin, 1999, 12.

18 Ibid.

19 Martin, S., *The Cathars,* p 90.

20 Baigent, M., and Leigh, R., 13.

21 Stoyanov, Yuri, *The Hidden Tradition in Europe,* New York: Penguin, 1994, 181.

22 Hoeller, Stephen, *Gnosticism,* Wheaton/Chicago, IL: Quest Books, 2002, 152.

23 Martin, Sean, *The Cathars,* Edison, NJ: Chartwell Books, 2005, 121.

24 Markale, Jean, *Montsegur and the Mystery of the Cathars,* Rochester, VT: Inner Traditions, 2003, 48.

25 Barber, Malcolm, *The Cathars,* 158.

26 Wakefield, W.L., and Evans, A.P., *Heresies of the High Middle Ages,* New York: Columbia University Press, 1991, 41

Chapter 6–Medieval Guilds

1 Ohler, Norbert, *The Medieval Traveller,* Engl. Transl. By C. Hillier, Woodbridge: Boydell Press, 1989); [orig. German edition by Artemis Verlag, 1986, 60.

2 Ibid. 61

3 "The Origin and Rise of the Incorporated Trades of Edinburgh", from the 2012 Exhibition Catalogue, The Convenery of the Trades of Edinburgh, Ashfield, 61 Melville St., Edinburgh, 1; courtesy of Ian Robertson, Edinburgh.

4 Ibid., 3

5 Ralls, Karen, *The Knights Templar Encyclopedia,* Franklin Lakes, NJ: Career Press, 2007, 91.

6 Ralls, K, *op cit.,* 88-9

7 Coldstream, Nicola, *Medieval Craftsmen: Masons and Sculptors,* London: British Museum Press, 1991, 5

8 Hiscock, Nigel, *The Wise Master Builder: Platonic Geometry in Plans of Medieval Abbeys and Cathedrals,* Aldershot: Ashgate, 2000, 171

9 Ralls, K., *op. cit.,* 6.

10 Purvis, J.S., "The Medieval Organization of Freemasons' Lodges', 1959 lecture, *The Collected Prestonian Lectures,* [Ed. Harry Carr], *Quatuor Coronati Lodge,* no. 2076, London. 1967, 461

11 Curl, James S., *The Art & Architecture of Freemasonry,* London: B.T. Batsford, 2002, 24

12 Healey, Timothy, "St Mary's Church at Bloxham", Oxford Times, Limited Edition magazine, Oxford, 2004, 17

13 Epstein, Stephen, *Wage Labor and Guilds in Medieval Europe,* Chapel Hill: University of North Carolina, 1991, 89

14 Hall, Manly P., *Orders of the Quest, Part I., The Adepts in the Western Esoteric Tradition,* Los Angeles: Philosophical Research Society, 1949, 25

15 Ibid., 26

16 White, Eileen, *The York Mystery Plays,* Yorkshire Architectural and York Archaeological Society, York: Ebor Press, 1991 ed. (1984 orig.) , 1.

17 Barker Cryer, Rev. Neville, "Drama and Craft", *Ars quatuor coronatorum,* vol. Lxxxvii, London: 1974, 88

18 Ibid., 36

19 Simpson, Jacqueline, and Roud, Steven, *A Dictionary of English Folklore,* Oxford: Oxford University Press, 2000, 251

20 Hutton, Ronald, *The Rise and Fall of Merry England,* Oxford: Oxford University Press, 1994, 88

21 Southworth, John, *Fools and Jesters at the English Court,* (Stroud: Sutton publishing, 1998, 53

22 Holt, John C., *Robin Hood,* London: Thames & Hudson, [1982] rev. ed. 1989, 36

23 Billington, S., *A Social History of the Fool,* Sussex: Harvester Press and New York: St Martin's, 1984, 16

24 Keen, Maurice, *The Outlaws of Medieval England,* London: Routledge, [1961] rev. ed. 2000, 134

25 Hutton, Ronald, *The Rise and Fall of Merry England,* Oxford: Oxford University Press, 1994, 118

26 Simpson, J. and Roud, S., *op cit,* 223

27 Ralls, Karen and Robertson, Ian., *Quest for the Celtic Key,* Edinburgh: Luath, 2002, 350

28 Mill, A.J., *Medieval Plays in Scotland,* St Andrews University publications, No. xxiv, Wm. Blackwood & Sons Ltd., Edinburgh and London, 1927, 23-5

29 MacRitchie, David, *Scottish Gypsies Under the Stewarts,* Edinburgh, 1894, 57

30 Ibid., 58.

Chapter 7–Heretics and Heresies

1 Ralls, Karen, *The Knights Templar Encyclopedia,* Franklin Lakes, NJ: Career Press, 2007, 95

2 Deane, Jennifer K., *A History of Medieval Heresy and Inquisition,* New York: Rowman & Littlefield, 2011

3 Leff, Gordon, *Heresy in the Later Middle Ages,* Manchester: Manchester Univ Press, 1967, 267

4 Barber, Malcolm, "Lepers, Jews and Moslems: the plot to overthrow Christendom in 1321", *Reading Medieval Studies 3, Reading University, Graduate Centre for Medieval Studies, U.K., 1977, p 63.*

5 Partner, Peter, *The Murdered Magicians,* Oxford: Oxford University Press, 1981, 60

6 Ibid.

7 Ralls, K., *op cit.,* 95

8 Partner, P., *op cit,* 60

9 Ibid.

10 Lambert, Malcolm, *Medieval Heresy: Popular Movements from the Gregorian Reform to The Reformation*, Oxford: Blackwell, 1992 ed., 245

11 McCall, Andrew, *The Medieval Underworld,* New York: Dorset, 1979, 244

12 Baigent, Michael, and Leigh, Richard, *The Inquisition,* London: Penguin, 1999, 102

13 Wakefield, W.L., and Evans, A.P., *Heresies of the High Middle Ages,* New York: Columbia University Press, 1969, 267

14 Carr-Gomm, Philip, and Heygate, Richard, *The Book of English Magic,* London: John Murray, 2009, 173

15 Thomas, Keith, *Religion and the Decline of Magic,* London: Penguin, 1971, 536

16 Kieckhefer, Richard, *European Witch Trials: Their Foundation in Learned and Popular Culture 1300-1500,* London: Routledge, 1976, 191

17 Roach, Andrew, *The Devil's World: Heresy and Society 1100-1300,* Harlow: Pearson Education Ltd., 2005, 188

18 Henderson, J, *The Construction of Orthodoxy and Heresy: Neo-Confucian, Islamic, Jewish and Early Christian Patterns,* New York: SUNY, 1998, 123

19 Kienzle, Beverley M., *Cistercians, Heresy and Crusade in Occitania,* York MedievalPress, 2001, 212

20 Ibid., 218.

21 Levi, Eliphas, *The History of Magic,* (English transl of 1862 French orig. by A.E. Waite), London, 1913, 212

22 Warner, Marina, *Joan of Arc: The Image of Female Heroism,* Middlesex: Penguin Books, 1981, 130

23 Sullivan, Kathleen, *The Interrogation of Joan of Arc,* Minneapolis: Regents of the University of Minnesota, 1999, 148

24 Kieckhefer, Richard, *Magic in the Middle Ages,* Cambridge: Cambridge Univ Press, 2000, 140

25 Ralls, Karen, and Robertson, Ian, *The Quest for the Celtic Key,* Edinburgh: Luath, 2002, 216

26 Ralls, Karen, *Knights Templar Encyclopedia,* 126

27 Ibid.

Chapter 8–Troubadours

1 Keen, Maurice, *Chivalry,* New Haven: Yale Univ Press, 1984, 30 [quoting Andreas Capellanus I: vi].

2 Churton, Tobias, *The Gnostic Philosophy,* Lichfield: Signal Publishing, 2003, 159

3 Ibid., 157

4 Ibid., 192

5 Cabre, M., "Italian and Catalan troubadours", in Gaunt, Simon, [Ed.], *The Troubadours,* Cambridge: Cambridge Univ Press, 1999, 135-6.

6 Churton, T., *op cit,* 158

7 Ibid.

8 Markale, Jean, *Eleanor of Aquitaine,* Rochester, VT: Inner Traditions, 1979. [Engl transl by Jon Graham, 2007], 155.

9 Keen, M., *op. cit.,* 37

10 Hallam, Elizabeth, [Ed.], *Chronicles of the Age of Chivalry,* London: Chrysalis Books, 2000, 284

11 Ibid., 285

12 Jones, Terry, *Medieval Lives,* London: BBC Books, 2004, 48

13 Ibid.

14 Ibid., 49

15 Barber, Richard, *The Knight and Chivalry,* Woodbridge: Boydell Press, 1995 rev ed, 120

16 Foss, Maurice, *Chivalry,* London: Michael Joseph, 1995, 5

17 Markale, J., *Eleanor of Aquitaine,* 140

18 Ibid.

19 Barber, R., *The Knight and Chivalry,* 170

20 Markale, J., *Eleanor of Aquitaine,* 141

21 Keen, op cit, 162

22 Markale, Jean, *Courtly Love,* Rochester, VT: Inner Traditions, 2000, 74

23 Tuchman, Barbara, *A Distant Mirror: the Calamitous Fourteenth Century*, New York: Knopf, 1978

24 Ibid.

25 Ibid.

26 Ibid., 76

27 Ibid., 79

28 Ibid., 81

29 Andreae Capellani regii Francorum, *De amore libri tres,* ed. E. Trojel, Copenhagen, 1892. [see also Andreas Capellanus. *On Love,* [Ed.] with an English trans. by P.G. Walsh, London, 1982]

30 Ibid.

31 Saul, N., [Ed]., *Age of Chivalry,* London: Collins & Brown, 1992, 120

32 Bouchard, C. B., *Strong of Body, Brave & Noble: Chivalry & Society in Medieval France,* Ithaca, NY: Cornell Univ Press, 1998, 140

33 Markale, J., *Eleanor of Aquitaine,* 146

34 Ibid., 147

35 Churton, T., op cit., 162

36 Ibid., 164

37 Ibid., 169-70

38 Ibid., 171

39 Ibid., 173

40 Kaeuper, Richard W., and Kennedy, Elspeth., *The Book of Chivalry of Geoffroi de Charny,* Philadelphia: University of Pennsylvania, 1996, 31

41 Churton, T., op cit., 175

42 Ibid., 183

43 Ibid., 184

44 Porter, Pamela, *Courtly Love in Medieval Manuscripts,* London: British Library, 2003, 28-9

45 Ibid., 32

46 Keen, M., op cit, 38

47 Kaeuper, Richard W., *Chivalry and Violence in Medieval Europe,* Oxford: Oxford University Press, 1999, 34

48 Huizinga, John H., *The Waning of the Middle Ages, (ck p 3, pole of noble life)*

49 Barber, Richard, and Barker, Juliet, *Tournaments,* Woodbridge: Boydell Press, 1989, 1

50 Ibid., 3

51 Camille, M., op cit, 63

52 Ibid.

53 This is the famous quote composed for the important medieval troubadour gathering at Puivert in 1170 C.E., by the famous medieval French troubadour Pierre d'Auverge.

54 Gotfredsen, Lise, *The Unicorn,* London: Harvill Press, 1999, 90

55 Ibid., 91

56 Lyall, Sutherland, *The Lady and the Unicorn,* London: Parkstone Press, 2000, 129-30

57 Hodges, R. C., *Exploits, Curious Anecdotes and Sketches of the most Remarkable Scottish Gypsies,* Galashiels, 1983 reprint of 1823 orig, 24.

58 Brydon, Robert, *Rosslyn: A History of the Guilds, the Masons, and the Rosy Cross,* Rosslyn Chapel Trust, Roslin, 1994, 2.

59 Churton, T., *op cit,* 186

60 Hallam, Elizabeth, [Ed.], *The Plantagenet Encyclopedia,* New York: Random House, 1996, 197

61 Churton, T., op cit, 191

62 Ibid., 190

63 Ibid., 186

Chapter 9–Arthur, Merlin, and Glastonbury

1 Chapman, Graham, from these now immortal lines from the script of "Monty Python and the Holy Grail".

2 Doel, Geoff, Lloyd, Terry, and Doel, Fran, *Worlds of Arthur: King Arthur in History, Legend, and Culture*, Tempus: Stroud, Gloucestershire, 1998, 51

3 Doel, G., Lloyd, T., and Doel, F., *op cit.*, 52.

4 Ralls, Karen, and Robertson, Ian, *The Quest for the Celtic Key*, Edinburgh: Luath Press, 2001, 195

5 Carley, J, "Arthur in English History", *The Arthur of the English*, Ed. By W.R.J. Barron, University of Wales Press: Cardiff, 1999, 47

6 Payne, Andrew.; Corney, Mark; Cunliffe, Barry, *The Wessex Hillforts Project: Extensive Survey of Hillfort Interior in Central Southern England*, London: English Heritage, 2007, 1.

7 Littleton, C Scott, and Malcor, Linda, *From Scythia to Camelot*, Garland: New York and London, 2000, 63.

8 Hopkinson-Ball, Tim, *The Rediscovery of Glastonbury*, Stroud: The History Press, 2007

9 Whitaker, Muriel, *The Legends of King Arthur in Art*, Woodbridge: D.S. Brewer, 1990, p 310-1. [see also Chapter Six in Ralls, K, *Quest for the Celtic Key*, pgs 192-240.]

10 Brooks, C, and Bryden, I., "The Arthurian Legacy", in *The Arthur of the English,* by W.R.J. Barron, Cardiff: University of Wales Press, 1999, p 253. [see also Chapter Six in Ralls, Karen, *The Quest for the Celtic Key*, pgs 192-240.]

11 Jarman, A O H, "The Merlin Legend and the Welsh Tradition of Prophecy", *The Arthur of the Welsh*, Ed by Bromwich, R, Jarman, A O H, and Roberts B F, University of Wales Press: Cardiff, 1991

12 Carr-Gomm, Philip, and Heygate, Richard, *The Book of English Magic,* London: John Murray, 2009, 132-3

13 Ralls, K, and Robertson, I., op cit, 231

14 Ibid., 233

15 Stewart, R.J., *The Prophetic Vision of Merlin,* Loughborough: Thoth Publications, 1986; see also, Matthews, J., and Green, M., *The Grail Seekers Companion,* Loughborough: Thoth Publications, 2003]

16 Matthews, John, *Gawain: Knight of the Goddess*, London: Thorsons, 1990

17 Knight, Gareth, *Merlin and the Grail Tradition,* Cheltenham: Skylight Books, 2011 [newly expanded edition]

18 Markale, Jean, *Merlin,* Rochester, VT, Inner Traditions, 1995. (English translation by Jon Graham of 1981 French orig, entitled *Merlin L'Enchanteur*), ix.

19 Gerritsen, W P, and van Melle, A.G, *A Dictionary of Medieval Heroes*, Boydell Press: Woodbridge, Suffolk, 1998 Engl. Translation of 1993 German orig, 178.

20 Tolstoy, Nicolai, *The Quest for Merlin*, Hodder and Stoughton: Sevenoaks, Kent, 1985, 87

21 Ibid.

22 Ashcroft-Nowicki, Delores, "Merlin and the Mother Goddess", in *Merlin and Woman (*Ed. by R.J. Stewart), The Book of the Second Merlin Conference 1987*, London: Blandford, 1988, 181

23 Carley, J. *op cit.*

24 Carley, J. *op cit.*

25 Barber, Richard, *The Figure of Arthur*, Longman: London, 1972, 134.

26 Westwood, Jennifer, *Albion: A Guide to Legendary Britain*, Paladin Grafton Books: London, 1985, 24-5.

27 Mann, Nicholas, *The Isle of Avalon,* London: Green Magic, 2001, 141

28 Hutton, Ronald, *The Rise and Fall of Merry England*, Oxford and New York: Oxford University Press, 1994, p 216; citing *The Weekly Post* (26 Dec. 1654-2 Jan.1655), 4045-6.

29 Hutton, Ronald, *Stations of the Sun,* Oxford: Oxford University Press, 1996, 136. [see also: Hutton, R, *Witches, Druids, and King Arthur,* London: Hambledon Continuum, 2003.]

30 Howard-Gordon, Frances, *Glastonbury: Maker of Myths,* Glastonbury: Gothic Image, 1997, 8.

31 Ashe, Geoffrey, *The Traveller's Guide to Arthurian Britain, ,* Glastonbury: Gothic Image, 1997, 210. [for his longer description of this mythic story of Arthur's birth, see his *The Discovery of King Arthur, p 9]*

32 Bord, Janet, and Colin, *The Enchanted Land*, Thorsons/Harpercollins: London, 1995, 133.

33 White, Richard, [Ed]., *King Arthur in Legend and History.* London: Dent, 1997, 11

34 Filbee, Marjorie, *Celtic Cornwall*, Constable: London, 1996, 64

35 Hunt, Robert, *The Drolls, Traditions, and Superstitions of Old Cornwall*, 1st series, [Ed.], Llarnerch Publishers: Lampeter, 1993 reprint of 1881 orig., p. 306.

36 Hunt, op cit, 186

37 *The Arthurian Centre*, nr Camelford, Cornwall; see www arthur-online co uk

38 Ashe, G., *op cit*, 124

39 For more information, please see the National Museum of Wales (Rhagor) page on the NMW website at www museumwales. co. uk / en / rhagor

40 Bromwich, Rachel, Evans, D.S., *Culhwch and Olwen. An Edition and Study of the Oldest Arthurian Tale*, Cardiff: University of Wales Press, 1992, 64-5

41 Green, Miranda, and Howell, Robert, *A Pocket Guide to Celtic Wales*, University of Wales Press: Cardiff, 2000, 117

42 List of various south Welsh locations that relate to Arthur: From idl . newport.ac . uk/ legendsofkingarthur/locations/htm

43 Lloyd, S. and Blake, S, and Lloyd, S., *Avalon,* Shaftesbury, Dorset, 2000, 126-7 [re: north Wales Arthurian locations and related local folklore].

44 Ralls, K., and Robertson, I., *op cit,* 211

45 Ibid., 212

46 Skene, W F, *Arthur and the Britons in Wales and Scotland*, Llanerch: Lampeter, 1988 reprint of 1868 original "The Four Ancient Books of Wales", 16.

47 Moffat, Alistair, *Arthur and the Lost Kingdoms*, Weidenfeld & Nicolson: London, 1999, 221

48 Ralls, K, and Robertson, I., op cit, 214.

49 Glennie, J S, *Arthurian Localities*, Llarnerch Publishers: Lampeter, 1994 reprint of 1869 orig, 126 [re: list of Scottish-related Arthurian sites].

50 Watson, W J, *The Celtic Placenames of Scotland*, Birlinn: Edinburgh, 1993, p 208

51 Ralls, K, op cit, 227

52 Tennyson, Alfred Lord, *Idylls of the King* (1859-91), London: Penguin, 1988; [for additional commentary, see Ralls, K., and Robertson, I., *The Quest for the Celtic Key*, Edinburgh: Luath Press, 2001, p 192-240].

Chapter 10 –Rosslyn: Chapel, Castle, and Glen

1 Forbes, *R, Account of Roslin Chapel*, Edinburgh, 1774, 1.

2 Proceedings of the Society of Antiquaries, xii, Edinburgh, 1877-8, 223

3 Rosslyn, Peter St Clair Erskine, Earl of Rosslyn, *Rosslyn Chapel*, official guidebook, Rosslyn Chapel Trust, Roslin, Midlothian, 1997, 2.

4 Ibid.

5 Ibid.

6 Ralls, Karen, and Robertson, Ian, *The Quest for the Celtic Key,* Edinburgh: Luath Press, 346

7 Ibid.

8 Grant, Will, *Rosslyn: Its Chapel, Castle, and Scenic Lore,* Edinburgh, 1936, 37

9 Earl of Rosslyn, *op cit*, 27.

10 Rosslyn, Peter St Clair Erskine, Earl of; op. cit., 27

11 Kirk, T, & Thoresby, R, *Tours in Scotland 1677 and 1681,* [Ed.] P. Hume Brown, Edinburgh, 1892, 41-2

12 Ralls, Karen, *The Templars and the Grail,* Wheaton, IL: Quest Books, 2003, 183

13 Ibid.

14 Harding, M, *op. cit.,* 58

15 Harding, Mike, *A Little Book of the Green Man,* Aurum Press, London, 1998, 58.

16 Cooper, R.L.D., The Rosslyn Hoax?, Hersham, Surrey: Ian Allen Publishing Ltd., 2006, 149

17 Harte, Jeremy, *The Green Man,* Pitkin Unichrome Ltd, Andover, Hampshire, 2001, 1

18 Ralls, K., and Robertson, I., *op cit*, 362.

19 Ibid.

20 Rosslyn, Peter St Clair Erskine, Earl of; op. cit., 37

21 Slezer, John, *Theatrum Scotiae,* London, 1693, 63

22 Forbes, Robert, Dr., Bishop of Caithness, *An Account of the Chapel of Roslin 1774*

23 Cooper, R.L.D., op. cit., 143

24 Butler, Alan, and Ritchie, John, *Rosslyn Revealed,* Ropley, Hants: O Books, 2006, 15.

25 *The Year Book of the Grand Lodge of Antient Free and Accepted Masons of Scotland,* Edinburgh, 1991, 46

26 Cooper, R.L.D., *op cit.*, 146

27 MacKenzie, *K, Royal Masonic Cyclopaedia,* Aquarian, Wellingborough, 1987 edition of 1877 orig., 682.

28 Ward, J. S. M., *Who Was Hiram Abiff?,* Lewis publications, Plymouth, 1992, 232

29 Brydon, Robert, *Rosslyn: A History of the Guilds, the Masons, and the Rosy Cross*, Edinburgh: The Rosslyn Chapel Trust, 1994, 4.

30 Ibid., 5

31 Ibid.

32 Hay, Robert A, *Genealogy of the Sinclairs of Roslin,* Edinburgh, 1835, 27-8

33 Brydon, R, *op. cit.*, 18

34 Ibid.

35 Ralls, K., and Robertson, I., op. cit., 378

36 McIntosh, Christopher, *The Rosicrucians,* Wellingborough: Thorsons, 1987, rev. ed of 1980 orig, 33.

37 Brydon, R., op. cit., 18

38 Slezer, John *Theatrum Scotiae,* London, 1693, 63

39 Brydon, R., op. cit., back page.

Chapter 1–The Knights Templar

History/Academic:

Abulafia, D., *A Mediterranean Emporium: The Catalan Kingdom of Majorca,* Cambridge: Cambridge University Press, 1994

Barber, M., "Origins of the Order of the Temple", *Studia Monastica 12* (Barcelona, 1970)

_____, *The Trial of the Templars*, Cambridge: Cambridge University Press, 1978

_____, *The New Knighthood: A History of the Order of the Temple*, Cambridge: Cambridge University Press, 1994

_____, "James of Molay, the Last Grand Master of the Order of the Temple", In *Crusaders and Heretics: 12ᵗʰ – 14ᵗʰ Centuries.* Varorium Collected Studies Series. Aldershot: Ashgate, 1995 (Originally published in *Journal of Medieval History 8,* Amsterdam, 1982)

_____, and Bate, K., *Selected Sources translated and annotated.* Manchester Medieval Sources Series. Manchester and New York: Manchester University Press, 2002

Barber, M., and Bate, K., [transl's and editors]; *The Templars: Selected Sources,* Manchester: Manchester Medieval Sources Series, Manchester University Press, 2002

Bernard of Clairvaux, "In Praise of the New Knighthood", In *The Works of Bernard of Clairvaux, vol. 7, Treatises 3,* transl. By C. Greenia. Cistercian Fathers Series, vol. 19, Kalamazoo, MI: Cistercian Publications, 1977

Demurger, A., *The Last Templar: The Tragedy of Jacques de Molay, Last Grand Master of the Temple,* London: Profile Books, 2004

Forey, A., "The Emergence of the Military Order in the Twelfth Century", *Journal of Ecclesiastical History 36,* (1985): 175-95

Hamilton, B., *The Christian World of the Middle Ages,* Nottingham: BCA / Sutton Published Ltd, 2003

Nicholson, H., *A Brief History of the Knights Templar,* London: Constable & Robinson Ltd., 2010 ed. [2001 orig.]

_____, *Templars, Hospitallers and Teutonic Knights: Images of the Military Orders,* Leicester: Leicester University Press, 1993

Partner, P., *The Murdered Magicians,* Oxford: Oxford University Press, 1981

Pringle, D., "Templar Castles between Jaffa and Jerusalem". Edited by H. Nicholson, *The Military Orders: Welfare and Warfare 2* (1998): 89

Ralls, K., *The Knights Templar Encyclopedia,* Franklin Lakes, NJ: Career Press, 2007

_____ , *The Templars and the Grail,* Wheaton/Chicago, IL: Quest Books, 2003

Runciman, S., *A History of the Crusades, 3 vols.,* Harmondsworth: Penguin, 1978

Selwood, D., *Knights of the Cloister: Templars and Hospitallers in Central-Southern Occitania c.1100-1300.* Woodbridge: Boydell Press, 1999

Upton-Ward, J.M., transl. and ed., *The Rule of the Templars: the French text of the Rule of the Order of the Temple.* Woodbridge: Boydell and Brewer, 2002

Wasserman, J., *Temple of Solomon: From Ancient Israel to Secret Societies,* Rochester, VT: Inner Traditions, 2011

Related/General Interest:

Beamon, S.P., *Royston Cave - Used by Saints or Sinners?*, Watchet: Temple Publications, 2009. [2nd ed.]

Brighton, S., *In Search of the Knights Templar: A Guide to the Sites in Britain,* 2006.

Burman, E., *Supremely Abominable Crimes: The Trial of the Knights Templar,* London: Allison & Busby, 1994

Coppack, G., *The White Monks: The Cistercians in Britain 1128-1540.* Stroud: Tempus, 1998

Haagensen, E., and Lincoln, H., *The Templars' Secret Island,* London: Weidenfeld & Nicholson, 2002

Hopper, V. F., *Medieval Number Symbolism: Its Sources, Meaning, and Influences On Thought and Expression.* New York: Columbia Univ Press, 1938

Lord, E., *The Knights Templar in Britain,* Harlow: Pearson Education Ltd., 2002

Martin, Sean, *The Knights Templar,* London: Pocket Essentials, 2004

Riley-Smith, J, *Hospitallers: The History of the Order of St John,* London: Hambledon, 1999

Chapter 2–Mary Magdalene

History/Academic:

Brock, A. G., *Mary Magdalene, The First Apostle: The Struggle for Authority,* Harvard Theological Studies 51, Cambridge, MA: Harvard University Press, 2003

Chilton, B., *Mary Magdalene,* New York: Doubleday, 2005

De Boer, E., *Mary Magdalene: Beyond the Myth,* Harrisburgh, PA: Trinity Press International, 1997

Erhman, B.D., *Peter, Paul and Mary: The Followers of Jesus in History and Legend,* Oxford: Oxford University Press, 2006

Geary, P. J., *Furta Sacra: Theft of Relics in the Central Middle Ages,* Princeton: Princeton University Press, 1978

Haskins, S, *Mary Magdalene,* London: HarperCollins, 1993

Jansen, K.L., The Making of the Magdalene: Preaching and Popular Devotion *in the Later Middle Ages,* Princeton: Princeton University Press, 2000

King, K., *The Gospel of Mary of Magdala: Jesus and the First Woman Apostle,* Santa Rosa, CA: Polebridge Press, 2003

Lahr, J., *Searching for Mary Magdalene,* New York: Welcome Books, 2006

Malvern, M., *Venus in Sackcloth: The Magdalene's Origins and Metamorphoses,* Carbondale and Edwardsville: Southern Illinois University Press, 1975

Marjanen, A., *The Woman Jesus Loved: Mary Magdalene in the Nag Hammadi Library and Related Documents,* Nag Hammadi and Manichaean Studies XL, Leiden: E.J. Brill, 1996

Meyer, M., *The Gospels of Mary The Secret Tradition of Mary Magdalene, the Companion of Jesus,* San Francisco: HarperSanFrancisco, 2004

Saxer, V., *Le Culte de Marie Madeleine en Occident des origines a la fin du moyen age,* Paris: Auxerre, 1959

Schaberg, J., "How Mary Magdalene Became a Whore", *Bible Review 8.5* (1992), 30-37

Schussler Fiorenza, E., *In Memory of Her: A Feminist Theological Reconstruction of Christian Origins,* New York: Crossroad, 1985

Thompson, M.R., *Mary of Magdala,* New York: Paulist Press, 1995

Related Interest:

Baigent, M., Leigh, R., and Lincoln, H., *The Holy Blood and the Holy Grail,* London: Jonathan Cape, 1982

Bellevie, L., *The Complete Guide to Mary Magdalene,* New York: Alpha Penguin, 2005

Brown, P. R. L., *The Cult of the Saints: Its Rise and Function in Latin Christianity,* Chicago: University of Chicago Press, 1981

_____, *Relics and Social Status in the Age of Gregory of Tours,* Reading: University of Reading, 1977

Pagels, E., *Adam, Eve and the Serpent,* London: 1988

_____, *Beyond Belief: The Secret Gospel of Thomas,* New York: Random House, 2003

_____, *The Gnostic Gospels,* Harmondsworth: Penguin, 1985

Qualls-Corbett, N., *The Sacred Prostitute: Eternal Aspect of the Feminine,* Studies in Jungian Psychology, Toronto: Inner City Books, 1988. [Forward by Dr Marion Woodman].

Rossiaud, J., *Medieval Prostitution,* Oxford: Oxford University Press, 1988 [transl by Lydia G. Cochrane]

Starbird, M., *The Woman with the Alabaster Jar,* Rochester, VT: Inner Traditions, 1993

Torjesen, K.J., *When Women were Priests Women's Leadership in the Early Church And the Scandal of their Subordination and the rise of Christianity,* San Francisco: Harper and Row, 1993

Voragine, de Jacobus, *The Golden Legend: Readings on the Saints,* Vols I and II, Princeton: Princeton University Press, 1993; [transl by Wm G Ryan]

Chapter 3–The Black Madonna

History/Academic:

Begg, E, *The Cult of the Black Virgin*, Harmondsworth: Penguin [1985] rev. ed. 1996.

Birnbaum, L. C., *Black Madonnas: Feminism, religion and politics in Italy,* Lincoln, NE: ToExcel publishers, 2000, 134. [Ital. orig. 1993]

Boyer, M-F, *The Cult of the Virgin,* London: Thames & Hudson, 2000

Bull, M., *The Miracles of Our Lady of Rocamadour,* Woodbridge: Boydell Press, 1999, 40

Durand-Lefebvre, M., *Etude sur l'origine des Vierges Noires,* Paris: 1937

Gustafson, F., *The Black Madonna,* Boston: Sigo Press, 1990

Markale, J., *Cathedral of the Black Madonna,* Rochester, VT: Inner Traditions, 2004, 174. [French orig. by Editions Pygmalion/Gerard Watelet, Paris, 1988]

Moss, L.W. and Cappannari, S.C., "In Quest of the Black Virgin: She is Black Because She is Black" in *Mother Worship: Theme and Variations, [Ed] by*James J. Preston. Chapel Hill: University of North Carolina Press, 1982: pgs 53-74.

Mullen, P., *Shrines of Our Lady,* London: Piatkus, 1998

Nilson, B., *Cathedral Shrines of Medieval England,* Woodbridge, Suffolk: Boydell and Brewer Ltd., 1998

Oleszkiewicz-Paralba, Malzorata, *The Black Madonna in Latin America and Europe: Tradition and Transformation,* Albuquerque : University of New Mexico Press, 2009.

Related/General Interest:

Baring, A. and Cashford, J., *The Myth of the Goddess: Evolution of an Image*, London: Viking Penguin, 1991

Carroll, M. P, *The Cult of the Virgin Mary: Psychological Origins,* Princeton: Princeton University Press, 1986

Forsyth, I.H., *The Throne of Wisdom: Wood Sculptures of the Madonna in Romanesque France*, Princeton: Princeton University Press, *1972*

Galland, C, *Longing for Darkness: Tara and the Black Madonna,* New York: Penguin, 2007

Geraint ap Iorwerth, *Honest to Goddess,* Southampton: Crescent Books, 1998

Harding, E., *Women's Mysteries, Ancient and Modern,* London: 1971

Hieronimus, J.Zohara Meyerhoff, *Kabbalistic Teachings of the Female Prophets: The Seven Holy Women of Ancient Israel,* Rochester, VT: Inner Traditions, 2008.

Matthews, C., *Sophia: Goddess of Wisdom, Bride of God,* Wheaton, IL: Quest Books, 2001.

Patai, R., *The Hebrew Goddess,* Detroit: Wayne State University Press, 1990. third enlarged edition of 1967 orig.]

Perera, S.B., *Descent to the Goddess: A Way of Initiation for Women,* Studies in Jungian Psychology: 6), Toronto: Inner City Books, 1981.

Shlain, L., *The Alphabet versus the Goddess: The Conflict between Word and Image,* New York: Viking Penguin, 1998

Sjoo, M., and Mor, B, *The Great Cosmic Mother,* New York: HarperCollins, 1991 edition (of 1987 original).

The Sanctuary of Oropa, [guide book]; Biella: Edizione Eco del Sanctuario di Oropa, 1963

Venarde, B.L., *Women's Monasticism and Medieval Society: Nunneries in France And England, 890-1215,* Ithaca, NY: Cornell University Press, 1997

Warner, M., *Alone of All Her Sex: The Myth and Cult of the Virgin Mary,* London: Weidenfeld & Nicolson, 1985

Chapter 4–The Grail

History/Academic:

Adolf, H., *Visio Pacis: Holy City and Grail,* Harrisburg: Penn State Univ Press, 1960

Barber, R., *The Holy Grail: The History of a Legend,,* London: Penguin Books, 2005

Begg, E and D., *In Search of the Holy Grail and the Precious Blood,* London: HarperCollins, 1995

Bryant, N., *The High Book of The Grail,* A translation of the 13th-century romance of Perlesvaus, Woodbridge, Suffolk: D.S. Brewer Ltd, 1978

Chretien de Troyes, *Perceval: The Story of the Grail,* Woodbridge, Suffolk: D.S. Brewer Ltd., 1982 [Engl transl by Nigel Bryant of 13th c. orig.]

_____, *Arthurian Romances.* Transl. William W. Kibler. Harmondsworth: Penguin, 1991. [see also transl. edition by D.D.R. Owen, London, Dent, 1987].

Goering, J., *The Virgin and the Grail,* New Haven and London: Yale University Press, 2005

Goetinck, G., *Peredur: A Study of Welsh Tradition in the Grail Legends,* Cardiff: University of Wales Press, 1975

Hall, C.D., *A Complete Concordance to Wolfram von Eschenbach's Parzival.* New York: Garland, 1990.

Hutton, R., *The Pagan Religions of the Ancient British Isles,* Oxford: Blackwell, 1993

Kahane, H. and R., *The Krater and the Grail,* Urbana: Univ of Illinois Press, 1965

Loomis, R. S., *The Grail: From Celtic Myth to Christian Symbol,* Princeton: Princeton University Press, Mythos Paperback Series, 1991

McCracken, P., "Mothers in the Grail Quest: Desire, Pleasure, and Conception", *Arthuriana, vol. 8 no. 1, 1998, 35-46.*

_____, *The Romance of Adultery: Queenship and Sexual Transgression in Old French Literature,* Philadelphia: University of Pennsylvania Press, 1998

McDonald. Wm C., "Wolfram's Grail", *Arthuriana, vol 8 no 1, Spring 1998, 22-33.*

Peebles, R.J., *The Legend of Longinus in Ecclesiastical Tradition,* Baltimore: Bryn Mawr College Monographs, vol. 9, 1911

Ralls, K., *The Templars and the Grail,* Wheaton/Chicago, IL: Quest Books, 2003

Silverberg, R., *The Realm of Prester John,* Athens, OH: Ohio University Press, 1972

Nicholson, H., *Love, War and the Grail: Templars, Hospitallers and Teutonic Knights In Medieval Epic and Romance* 1150-1500, Leiden: Brill, 2000

von Eschenbach, W., *Parzival,* New York: Penguin Books, 1980 [Engl transl by A.T. Hatto]

Williams, Ifor. *Chwedl Taliesin.* Cardiff: University of Wales Press, 1960

_____, *Lectures on Early Welsh Poetry.* Dublin: D.I.A.S., 1944.

Related/General Interest:

Ashe, G., *Arthurian Britain: the Traveller's Guide,* (Glastonbury: Gothic Image Publications, 1997) 3rd revised ed.

Baigent, M., Leigh, R., and Lincoln, H., *The Holy Blood and the Holy Grail,* London: Corgi, 1984

Carr-Gomm, P., and Heygate, R., *The Book of English Magic,* London: John Murray, 2009

Godwin, M., *The Holy Grail,* London: Bloomsbury, 1994

Jung, E., and von Franz, M-L, *The Grail Legend,* Princeton: Princeton University Press, 1970 [Engl transl, C.G. Jung Foundation (NY) of 1960 German orig.]

Knight, G., *The Secret Tradition in Arthurian Legend: The Magical and Mystical Power Sources within the Mysteries of Britain,* Wellingborough UK: Aquarian Press, 1983

Lacy, N., *The New Arthurian Encyclopedia,* New York: Peter Bedrick Books, 1986

Lively, P and Kerven, R., *The Mythical Quest,* London: The British Library, 1996

Markale, J., *The Grail: The Celtic Origins of the Sacred Icon,* Rochester, VT: Inner Traditions International, 1999 [Engl transl by Jon Graham of 1982 Fr orig]

Matthews, J., and Green, M., *The Grail Seekers Companion,* Loughborough: Thoth Publications, 2003.

Proctor, H., *The Holy Grail Tapestries Designed by Edward Burne-Jones, William Morris and JH Dearle for Morris & Co.,* Birmingham: Birmingham Museums and Art Gallery, 1997

Putter, A., *Sir Gawain and the Green Knight and French Arthurian Romance*, Oxford: Clarendon Press, 1995, reprinted 1999

Ralls, K., *The Knights Templar Encyclopedia,* Franklin Lakes, NJ: Career Press, 2007

Smoley, R., *Inner Christianity,* Boston, MA: Shambhala, 2002

Strong, G., *The Sacred Stone Circles of Stanton Drew,* Cheltenham: Skylight Books, 2012

Chapter 5–Cathars

History/Academic:

Barber, M., *The Cathars: Dualist Heretics in Languedoc in the High Middle Ages,* Harlow: Pearson Education Ltd, 2000

_____, "Women and Catharism", Reading Medieval Studies 3, Reading University, Graduate Center for Medieval Studies, 1977, pgs 45-62.

_____, "Catharism and the Occitan Nobility: the lordships of Cabaret, Minerve and Termes", *The Ideals and Practice of Medieval Knighthood 3,* [Ed.] C. Harper-Bill and R. Harvey. Woodbridge, Suffolk: Boydell Press, 1990, 1-19.

Bennett, R. F., *The Early Dominicans: Studies in Thirteenth Dominican History,* Cambridge: Cambridge University Press, 1937

Brenon, A., *Le Vrai Visage du Catharisme,* Paris: Loubatieres, 1988

Churton, T., *The Gnostic Philosophy,* Lichfield, UK: Signal Publishing, 2003

Cowper, M., *Cathar Castles: Fortresses of the Albigensian Crusade 1209-1300,* Oxford: Osprey, 2006.

Duvernoy, J., *Le Catharisme,* (2 vols), Paris: Privat, 1976/9

Hamilton B., *Crusaders, Cathars and the Holy Places,* Ashgate: Variorum, 2000

Kieckhefer, R., *European Witch Trials: Their Foundation in Learned and Popular Culture, 1300–1500* (London, 1976), 10–14, 108–12

_____ , *Magic in the Middle Ages* , Cambridge: Cambridge University Press, 2000, 188

Kienzle, B.M., *Cistercians, Heresy and Crusade in Occitania, 1145-1229,* York: York Medieval Press, 2001

_____ , and Walker, P., (Ed.), *Women Preachers and Prophets through Two Millennia of Christianity,* Berkeley: University of California Press, 1998

Ladurie, E. L., *Montaillou,* London: English ed., 1980, Fr. orig. 1975.

Lambert, M., *The Cathars,* Oxford: Blackwell, 1998

Roach, A., *The Devil's World: Heresy and Society 1100-1300,* Harlow: Pearson/Longman, 2005.

_____ , *The Relationship of the Italian and Southern French Cathars, 1170-1320,* University of Oxford, 1989 (PhD thesis)

de Rougemont, *Love in the Western World,* Princeton: Princeton University Press, 1983 ed. of 1940 orig.

Roquebert, M., *L'Epopee cathars* (5 vols), Paris: Privat/Perrin, 1970-98

Runciman, S., *The Medieval Manichee,* Cambridge: Cambridge Univ Press, 1947

Stoyanov, Y., *The Other God: Dualist Religions from Antiquity to the Cathar Heresy,* New Haven, CT: Yale University Press 2000

Wakefield, W.L., *Heresy, Crusade, and Inquisition in Southern France, 1100-1250,* Allen & Unwin, 1974

Related/General Interest:

Armstrong, K., *A History of God,* New York: Mandarin, 1993

Bayley, H., *The Lost Language of Symbolism,* Totowa, NJ: Rowman & Littlefield, 1974. (1912 orig.).

Begg, I., *The Cult of the Black Virgin,* London: Penguin, 1996.

Gerber, J.S., *Jews of Spain: A History of the Sephardic Experience,* New York: Free Press, 1994

Godwin, J., *The Golden Thread: The Ageless Wisdom of the Western Mystery Traditions,* Wheaton/Chicago, IL: Quest Books, 2007

Greer, M.K., *Women of the Golden Dawn: Rebels and Priestesses,* Rochester, VT: Park Street Press, 1996

Guirdham, A., *The Great Heresy: The History and Beliefs of the Cathars,* London: Neville Spearman, 1977

Hoeller, S., *Gnosticism,* Wheaton/Chicago, IL: Quest Books, 2002

Markale, J., *Montsegur and the Mystery of the Cathars,* Rochester, VT: Inner Traditions, 2003

Martin, S., *The Cathars,* Edison, NJ: Chartwell Books, 2005

Mattingly, A., *The Cathar Way: A Walker's Guide to the Sentier Cathare,* Milnthorpe, Cumbria: Cicerone Press, 2010

Oldenbourg, Z., *Massacre at Montsegur: A History of the Albigensian Crusade,* London: Phoenix Press, 2000 ed.

O'Shea, S., *The Perfect Heresy: The Life and Death of the Cathars,* London: Profile Books, 2000

Patrick, D., [Ed.], *The Cathar View,* London: Polair Publishing, 2012.

Rahn, O., *Crusade Against the Grail: The Struggle between the Cathars, the Templars, and the Church of Rome,* Rochester, VT: Inner Traditions, 2006.

Sumption, J., *The Albigensian Crusades,* London: Faber and Faber, 1978

Weiss, R., *The Yellow Cross: The Story of the Last Cathars 1290-1329,* London: Penguin, 2001.

Fiction with Cathar-related themes:

Chaplin, P., *The Portal,* Wheaton/Chicago, IL: Quest Books, 2010

D'Aout, J., *White Lie,* a novel, amazon com

Specialist Music with Cathar-related themes:

www. aniwilliams com [harp and song at Cathar sites in France].

Chapter 6–Medieval Guilds

History/Academic:

Bolton, J.L, *The Medieval English Economy,* New York: Everyman, 1980

Cantor, N., *Inventing the Middle Ages,* New York: HarperPerennial, 1993

Chambers, E.K., *The Mediaeval Stage,* Vol. II, Oxford: Oxford University Press, [1903]; Mineola NY: Dover edition, 1996

Colestream, N., *Medieval Craftsmen: Masons and Sculptors,* London: British Museum Press, 1991

Duby, G, *The Age of the Cathedrals: Art and Society, 980-1420.* Transl. Eleanor Levieux and Barbara Thompson. Chicago: Univ of Chicago Press, 1981

Epstein, S., *Wage Labor and Guilds in Medieval Europe,* Chapel Hill: University of North Carolina, 1991

Gimpel, J., *The Medieval Machine,* New York, 1976

Harvey, J.H., *The Gothic World, 1100-1600: A Survey of Art and Architecture,* New York, 1969 ed. (1950 orig.)

Healey, T., "St Mary's Church at Bloxham", Oxford Times, Limited Edition magazine, Oxford, 2004

Hiscock, N., *The Wise Master Builder: Platonic Geometry in Plans of Medieval Abbeys and Cathedrals,* Aldershot: Ashgate, 2000

Hutton, R., *The Rise and Fall of Merry England,* Oxford: Oxford University Press, 1994

Keen, M, *The Outlaws of Medieval England,* London: Routledge, [1961] rev. ed. 2000

Knoop, D., and Jones, G.P., *The Growth of Freemasonry,* Manchester: Manchester University Press, 1947.

LeGoff, J., *Time, Work, and Culture in the Middle Ages,* Chicago: University of Chicago Press, 1980

MacRitchie, D., *Scottish Gypsies Under the Stewarts,* Edinburgh, 1894

Mill, A.J., *Medieval Plays in Scotland,* St Andrews University publications, No. xxiv, Wm. Blackwood & Sons Ltd., Edinburgh and London, 1927

Ralls, K., *The Knights Templar Encyclopedia,* Franklin Lakes, NJ: Career Press, 2007

Salzman, L.F., *Building in England Down to 1540,* Oxford: Oxford University Press, 1952

Simpson, J and Roud, S, *A Dictionary of English Folklore,* Oxford: Oxford University Press, 2000

Stevenson, D., *The Origins of Freemasonry, Scotland's Century 1590-1710,* Cambridge: Cambridge University Press, 1988.

Southworth, J., *Fools and Jesters at the English Court,* (Stroud: Sutton publishing, 1998

Spufford, P, *Power and Profit: The Medieval Merchant in Europe,* London: Thames & Hudson, 2002

Suger. *Liber de rebus in administratione sua gestis.* In Erwin Panofsky, [Ed. and transl] *Abbot Suger on the Abbey Church of St Denis and Its Art Treasures,* (2nd ed.), Gerda Panofsky-Soergel. Princeton: Princeton University Press, 1979.

Stevenson, Prof. D, *The Origins of Freemasonry,* Cambridge: Cambridge University Press, 1988

Toulmin-Smith, J., *English Guilds,* Oxford: 1870

White, E, *The York Mystery Plays,* Yorkshire Architectural and York Archaeological Society, York: Ebor Press, 1991 ed. (1984 orig.)

Young, K., *The Drama of the Medieval Church,* 2 vols., Oxford: Oxford University Press, 1933

Related/General Interest:

Barker Cryer, Rev. N., "Drama and Craft", *Ars quatuor coronatorum,* vol. Lxxxvii, London: 1974

Billington, S., *A Social History of the Fool,* Sussex: Harvester Press and New York: St Martin's, 1984

Colston, J., *The Incorporated Trades of Edinburgh,* Edinburgh, 1891

Covey-Crump., WW. [Rev]., "Medieval Master Masons and their secrets", 1931 Lecture, *The Collected "Prestonian Lectures"[Ed. Harry Carr], Quatuor Coronati Lodge,* no. 2076, London. 1967, 141-53.

Curl, J.S., *The Art & Architecture of Freemasonry,* London: B.T. Batsford, 2002.

Doel, F & G., *Robin Hood: Outlaw or Greenwood Myth,* Stroud: Tempus, 2000

Gould, R.F., *The History of Freemasonry,* vol. 1, London, 1887

Hall, M.P., *Orders of the Quest, Part I., The Adepts in the Western Esoteric Tradition,* Los Angeles: Philosophical Research Society, 1949

Holt, J.C., *Robin Hood,* London: Thames & Hudson, [1982] rev. ed. 1989

Icher, F, *The Artisans and Guilds of France,* Paris: Editions de La Martiniere, 1994; Engl. tranls., New York: Harry Abrams, 2000

Jones, T., *Medieval Lives,* London: BBC Books, 2004

McCall, A., *The Medieval Underworld,* New York: Dorset Press, 1979.

Macinlay, J., *Folklore of Scottish Lochs and Springs,* (Glasgow: Wm Hodge & Co, 1893), 282

McLeod, W., "The Old Charges", ARS Quatuor Coronatorum, *Transactions of Quatuor Coronati Lodge No. 2076, vol. 99,* Garden City Press, Hertfordshire, 1987.

Ohler, N., *The Medieval Traveller,* Engl. Transl. By C. Hillier, Woodbridge: Boydell Press, 1989); [orig. German edition by Artemis Verlag, 1986

Ousterhout, R., *Master Builders of Byzantium*, Princeton: Princeton University Press, 1999.

Purvis, J.S., "The Medieval Organization of Freemasons' Lodges', 1959 lecture, *The Collected Prestonian Lectures, [Ed. Harry Carr], Quatuor Coronati Lodge,* no. 2076, London. 1967 [pgs 453-469]

Ralls, K., *The Templars and the Grail,* Wheaton/Chicago: Quest Books, 2003.

_____, *The Knights Templar Encyclopedia,* Franklin Lakes NJ: Career Press, 2007

Ralls, K and Robertson, I., *Quest for the Celtic Key,* Edinburgh: Luath, 2002

Verdon, J., *Travel in the Middle Ages,* Notre Dame: University of Notre Dame Press, 2003, 214, [transl. By Geo. Holoch; French orig in1998]

Walford, C., Fairs, Past and Present: A Chapter in the History of Commerce, New York: Augustus Kelley, 1968.

Ward, J.S.M., *Who was Hiram Abiff?,* Plymouth: Lewis Masonic, 1992

McIntosh, C., "The Rosicrucian Legacy", in *The Rosicrucian Enlightenment Revisited,* [Ed. by Ralph White]; Hudson NY: Lindisfarne, 1999

Yates, F., *The Rosicrucian Enlightenment*, London: Routledge, 1972

Chapter 7–Heretics and Heresies

History/Academic:

Barber, M., "Lepers, Jews and Moslems: the plot to overthrow Christendom in 1321", *Reading Medieval Studies 3,* Reading University, Graduate Centre for Medieval Studies, U.K., 1977, p 63.

Berenger, J., *A History of the Habsburg Empire: 1273-1700,* New York and London: Longman, 1994 [Engl ed]

Billier, P and Hudson, A. [Eds.], *Heresy and Literacy, 1000-1530,* Cambridge: Cambridge Univ Press, 1994

Brown, H.O.J., *Heresies: Heresy and Orthodoxy in the History of the Church,* Peabody, MA: Hendrickson, 1988.

Churton, T., *The Golden Builders: Alchemists, Rosicrucians, and the first Freemasons,* Lichfield: Signal, 2002

Clark, S., *Thinking with Demons,* Oxford: Oxford University Press, 1997

Cockburn, J.S., [Ed.], *The Calendar of Assize Records: Essex Indictments: Elizabeth 1.* London: HMSO, 1978

Davies, O., *Witchcraft, Magic, and Culture 1736-1951,* Manchester: Manchester University Press, 1999

_____, *Cunning Folk.* London: Hambledon and London, 2003

Deane, J.K., *A History of Medieval Heresy and Inquisition*, New York: Rowman & Littlefield, 2011

Fichtenau, H., *Heretics and Scholars in the High Middle Ages 1000-1200*, Philadelphia: Penn State Univ Press, 1998

George, L., *The Encyclopedia of Heresies and Heretics*, London: Robson Books, 1995

Godbeer, R., *The Salem Witch Hunt: A Brief History with Documents*, Bedford/St. Martins, 2011

Gratton, J.H.G., and Charles Singer, *Anglo-Saxon Magic and Medicine*, Oxford: Oxford University Press, 1952.

Henderson, J., *The Construction of Orthodoxy and Heresy: Neo-Confucian, Islamic, Jewish and Early Christian Patterns*, New York: SUNY, 1998

Henningsen, G., "The Ladies from Outside", in *Early Modern Witchcraft*, edited by B. Ankarloo and G. Henningsen, 191-218. Oxford: Oxford University Press, 1990.

_____, "The Witches' Flying and the Spanish Inquisition", *Folklore* 120 (2009): 57-74.

Hutton, R, *Blood and Mistletoe: The History of the Druids in Britain*, New Haven: Yale University Press, 2009

_____, *The Pagan Religions of the Ancient British Isles*, Oxford: Blackwell, 1991

_____, *The Triumph of the Moon*, Oxford: Oxford University Press, 1999

_____ , *Witches, Druids, and King Arthur*, London: Hambledon Continuum, 2003

Jacobsen, T., *The Treasures of Darkness*. New Haven: Yale University Press, 1976

Kieckhefer, R., *European Witch Trials: Their Foundation in Learned and Popular Culture 1300-1500*, London: Routledge, 1976

_____, *Magic in the Middle Ages*, Cambridge: Cambridge Univ Press, 2000

Kienzle, B.M., *Cistercians, Heresy and Crusade in Occitania*, York Medieval Press, 2001

Kors, A.C., *Witchcraft in Europe, 400-1700*, (2nd ed.), Philadelphia: Univ. of Pennsylvania, 2000

Lambert, M., *Medieval Heresy: Popular Movements from the Gregorian Reform to The Reformation*, Oxford: Blackwell, 1992 ed.

Lea, H.C., *A History of the Inquisition of the Middle Ages*, 3 vols., New York, 1888

Leff, G., *Heresy in the Later Middle Ages*, Manchester: Manchester Univ. Press, 1967

Moreira, I., *Dreams, Visions ande Spiritual Authority in Merovingian Gaul*, New York: Cornell University Press, 2000

McCall, A., *The Medieval Underworld*, New York: Dorset, 1979

Moore, R.I., *The War on Heresy*, London: Profile Books, 2012

North, R., *Heathen Gods in Old English Literature*. Cambridge: Cambridge University Press, 1997.

Partner, P., *The Murdered Magicians*, Oxford: Oxford University Press, 1981

Ralls, K., *The Knights Templar Encyclopedia*, Franklin Lakes, NJ: Career Press, 2007

_____ *The Templars and the Grail*, Chicago/Wheaton, Quest Books, 2003

Roach, A., *The Devil's World: Heresy and Society 1100-1300*, Harlow: Pearson Education Ltd., 2005

Rudkin, E., Lincolnshire Folklore, Witches, and Devils, *Folklore,* Vol 45, No. 3, London, Sept 1934, 249-267

Russell, J.B., *A History of Witchcraft: Sorcerers, Heretics, & Pagans* (2nd ed.), London: Thames & Hudson, 2007

————, *Witchcraft in the Middle Ages,* New York: Cornell Univ Press, 1972 [1984].

Sanderson, S., [Ed.], Robert Kirk's *The Secret Commonwealth of Elves, Fauns, and Fairies,* Cambridge: D.S. Brewer for the Folklore Society, 1976. [based on three manuscripts: La.111.551 and Gen.308.D Edinburgh University Library and 5022 National Library of Scotland].

Stuart, J., [Ed.], *Miscellany of the Spalding Club,* 5 vols, Aberdeen: Spalding Club, 1841.

Sullivan, K., *The Interrogation of Joan of Arc,* Minneapolis: Regents of the Univ of Minnesota, 1999

Thomas, K., *Religion and the Decline of Magic,* London: Penguin, 1971

Wakefield, W.L., and Evans, A.P., *Heresies of the High Middle Ages,* New York: Columbia University Press, 1969

Whilby, E., "The Witch's Familiar and the Fairy in Early Modern England and Scotland", *Folklore* 111 (2000): 283-305.

Wood, I., *The Merovingian Kingdoms: 450-751,* London: Longman, 1994

Related/General Interest:

Aldhouse-Green, M., *Celtic Goddesses.* London: British Museum, 1995

Ambrosini, M.L., *The Secret Archives of the Vatican,* New York, 1969

Baigent, M., and Leigh, R., *The Inquisition,* London: Penguin, 1999

Briggs, K., *The Anatomy of Puck,* London: Routledge and Kegan Paul, 1959

Carr-Gomm, P., and Heygate, R., *The Book of English Magic,* London: John Murray, 2009

Conway, D., *Secret Wisdom: The Occult Universe Explored,* London: Jonathan Cape, 1987

Eliade, M., *The Forge and the Crucible,* Chicago: Univ of Chicago Press, 1978

Evans, J., *Magic Jewels of the Middle Ages and Renaissance,* Oxford: Clarendon, 1922

Greer, M., *Women of the Golden Dawn,* Rochester, VT: Park Street Press, 1996

Henry, Wm., *The Illuminator,* Hendersonville, TN: Scala Dei, 2005

Heselton, P., *Witchfather,* Loughborough: Thoth Publications, 2012

Huizinga, J., *The Waning of the Middle Ages,* Harmondsworth: Penguin, 1924

Kingsley, P., *Ancient Philosophy, Mystery and Magic: Empedocles and Pythagoean Tradition,* Oxford: Clarendon Press, 1085

Kitson, P., "Ladipary traditions in Anglo-Saxon England", *Anglo-Saxon England, 12,* (1983), 73-123.

MacCalman, I., *The Last Alchemist: Count Cagliostro, Master of Magic in the Age of Reason,* New York: HarperCollinsPerennial, 2003

Ralls, K, and Robertson, I., *The Quest for the Celtic Key,* Edinburgh: Luath, 2002

Tuchman, B., *A Distant Mirror: The Calamitous Fourteenth Century,* London: Macmillan, 1992

Warner, M., *Joan of Arc: The Image of Female Heroism,* Middlesex: Penguin Books, 1981

Yates, F., *The Occult Philosophy of the Elizabethan Age,* London: Routledge, 1979

Chapter 8–Troubadours and the Courts of Love

History/Academic:

Akehurst, F. R., and Davis, J.M., [Eds.], *A Handbook of the Troubadours,* Berkeley: University of California Press, 1995

Andreae Capellani regii Francorum, *De amore libri tres,* ed. E. Trojel, Copenhagen, 1892. [see also Andreas Capellanus. *On Love,* [Ed.] with an English trans. by P.G. Walsh, London, 1982]

Andreas Capellanus, *The Art of Courtly Love,* trans. John Jay Parry, New York: Columbia University Press, 1941. (Reprinted: New York: Norton, 1969.)

Aubrey, E., *The Music of Troubadours,* Bloomington: Indiana University Press, 1996

Barber, R., *The Knight and Chivalry,* Woodbridge: Boydell Press, 1995 rev ed

Barker, J., *The Tournament in England 1100-1400,* London: Boydell Press, 1986

Barber, R., and Barker, J., *Tournaments,* Woodbridge: Boydell Press, 1989

Boase, R., *The Origin and Meaning of Courtly Love: A Critical Study of European Scholarship,* Manchester: Manchester University Press, 1977

Bouchard, C. B., *Strong of Body, Brave & Noble: Chivalry & Society in Medieval France,* Ithaca, NY: Cornell Univ Press, 1998

Camille, M., *The Medieval Art of Love,* New York: Harry Abrams, 1998

Duby, G., *The Chivalrous Society.* Transl. by Cynthia Postan. Berkeley: University of California Press, 1977

Eco, U., *Art and Beauty in the Middle Ages,* New Haven: Yale Univ Press, 2002

Egan, M., *The Vidas of the Troubadours,* Oxford: Taylor & Francis, 1984

Foss, M., *Chivalry,* London: Michael Joseph, 1995

Gaunt, S., [Ed.], *The Troubadours,* Cambridge: Cambridge Univ Press, 1999

Gotfredsen, L, *The Unicorn,* London: Harvill Press, 1999

Goodman, J. R., *Chivalry and Exploration 1298-1630,* Woodbridge: Boydell & Brewer, 1998

Hallam, E., [Ed.], *The Plantagenet Encyclopedia,* New York: Random House, 1996

_____, [Ed.], *Chronicles of the Age of Chivalry,* London: Chrysalis Books, 2000

_____, [Ed.], *The Plantagenet Chronicles,* London: Chrysalis Books, 2002

Kaeuper, R.W., *Chivalry and Violence in Medieval Europe,* Oxford: Oxford University Press, 1999

Kaeuper, R.W., and Kennedy, E., *The Book of Chivalry of Geoffroi de Charny,* Philadelphia: University of Pennsylvania, 1996

_____, *Chivalry and Violence in Medieval Europe,* Oxford: OUP, 1999

Kelly, A., *Eleanor of Aquitaine and the Four Kings,* Cambridge, MA: Harvard University Press, 1950

Keen, M., *Chivalry,* New Haven: Yale Univ Press, 1984

Lyall, S., *The Lady and the Unicorn,* London: Parkstone Press, 2000

Markale, J., *Courtly Love,* Rochester, VT: Inner Traditions, 2000

McCracken, P., "Mothers in the Grail Quest: Desire, Pleasure, and Conception", *Arthuriana, vol. 8 no. 1, 1998, 35-46.*

_____, *The Romance of Adultery: Queenship and Sexual Transgression in Old French Literature,* Philadelphia: University of Pennsylvania Press, 1998

_____, "The Body Politic and the Adulterous Queen's Body in French Romance", *Feminist Approaches to the Body in Medieval Literature,* [Ed.] Linda Lomperis and Sarah Stanbury. Philadelphia: Univ. of Pennsylvania Press, 1993, 38-64.

Menocal, M.R, *The Arabic Role in Medieval Literary History*, Philadelphia: University of Pennsylvania Press, 2003

Paden, W.D., *The Voice of the Trobairtz: Perspectives on the Women Troubadours,* Philadelphia: Univ of Pennsylvania Press, 1989

Page, C, *Discarding Images: Reflections on Music and Culture in Medieval France,* Oxford: Oxford Univ Press, 1993

_____, *The Owl and the Nightingale: Musical Life and Ideas in France 1100-1300,* Berkeley: Univ of Calif Press, 1989

Paterson, L., [Ed.], *The World of the Troubadours: Medieval Occitan Society 1100-1300,* Cambridge: Cambridge Univ Press, 1995

Porter, P., *Courtly Love in Medieval Manuscripts,* London: British Library, 2003

Schulman, N.M., *Where Troubadours Were Bishops: The Occitania of Folc of Marseille, 1150-1231,* London: Routledge, 2001

Schultz, J.A., *Courtly Love, the Love of Courtliness, and the History of Sexuality,* Chicago: The University of Chicago Press, 2006

Southworth, J., *The English Medieval Minstrel,* Woodbridge: Boydell, 1989

_____, *Fools and Jesters at the English Court,* Stroud: Sutton Publishing, 1998

Topsfield, L.T., *Troubadours and Love,* Cambridge: Cambridge Univ Press, 1975

Vale, M., *War and Chivalry: Warfare and Aristocratic Culture in England, France, and Burgundy at the End of the Middle Ages,* Atlanta: Univ of Georgia, 1981

Wilkins, N., *Music in the Age of Chaucer,* London: Rowman & Littlefield, 1979

Related/General Interest:

Churton, T., *The Gnostic Philosophy,* Lichfield: Signal Publishing, 2003

Duby, Georges, *The Knight, the Lady, and the Priest: the Making of Modern Marriage in Medieval France*; Engl tr by Barbara Bray; New York: Pantheon Books, 1983

Duane, O.B., *Chivalry: The Origins of Wisdom,* London: Brockhampton, 1997

Elvins, M., "The Chivalry of St Francis", *Second Spring Journal,* Plater College, 2002

Hodges, R C, *Exploits, Curious Anecdotes and Sketches of the most Remarkable Scottish Gypsies,* Galashiels, 1983 reprint of 1823 orig

Jones, T., *Medieval Lives,* London: BBC Books, 2004

Lull, R., *The Book of the Ordre of Chyualry,* [trans Wm Caxton, Ed. Alfred T.P. Byles, EETS o.s. 168, London, 1926.

Markale, J., *Eleanor of Aquitaine,* Rochester, VT: Inner Traditions, 1979. [Engl Transl by Jon E. Graham, 2007]

Rowbotham, J.F., *The Troubadours and the Courts of Love,* New York: Macmillan, 1895

Saul, N., [Ed]., *Age of Chivalry,* London: Collins & Brown, 1992

Spufford, P., *Money and its use in Medieval England,* Cambridge: Cambridge University Press, 1988

Al-Sulami, Ibn al-Husayn, *The Way of Sufi Chivalry,* Rochester, VT: Inner Traditions, 1991, Engl ed.

Tuchman, B, *A Distant Mirror: the Calamitous Fourteenth Century*, New York: Knopf, 1978

Turner, R.V., *Eleanor of Aquitaine,* New Haven: Yale University Press, 2012

Chapter 9–Arthur, Merlin, and Glastonbury: Sacred Sites, Sacred Places

History/Academic:

Adolf, H., "The Esplumoir Merlin", *Speculum* XXI, 1946, 173-93.

Barber, R., *King Arthur: Hero and Legend,* Woodbridge: Boydell Press, 1992

_____, *The Figure of Arthur*, Longman: London, 1972

_____, *The Holy Grail: Imaginaton and Belief,* London: Allen Lane, 2004.

Biddle, M., *King Arthur's Round Table,* Woodbridge, Suffolk and Rochester, NY: Boydell and Brewer Ltd., 2000

Bromwich, R., *Trioedd Ynys Prydein: The Welsh Triads*, Cardiff: University of Wales Press, 1978

Bromwich, R., "Celtic Elements in Arthurian Romance: A General Survey", in Grout, P. B.; Diverres, Armel Hugh, *The Legend of Arthur in the Middle Ages*, Woodbridge: Boydell and Brewer, 1983, p. 41–55.

Bromwich, R., Evans, D.S., *Culhwch and Olwen. An Edition and Study of the Oldest Arthurian Tale*, Cardiff: University of Wales Press, 1992

Bromwich, R, Jarman, A. O. H., Roberts, B.F., *The Arthur of the Welsh*, Cardiff: University of Wales Press, 1991, p. 15–32

Brooks, C, and Bryden, I., "The Arthurian Legacy", *The Arthur of the English,* Cardiff: University of Wales Press, 1999

Carley, J., *The Arthur of the English*, Ed. By W.R.J. Barron, University of Wales Press: Cardiff, 1999

_____, "Arthur in English History", *The Arthur of the English*, Ed. By W.R.J. Barron, University of Wales Press: Cardiff, 1999

Darrah, J., *Paganism in Arthurian Romance,* Woodbridge: Boydell Press, 1994

Geoffrey of Monmonth, *The History of the Kings of Britain,* [transl. and Intro. By L. Thorpe]; London: Penguin, 1966

_____, *Vita Merlini: The Life of Merlin,* [transl. and Intro. B. Clarke], Cardiff: University of Wales Press, 1973

Green, M & Howell, R, *A Pocket Guide to Celtic Wales*, University of Wales Press: Cardiff, 2000

Hale, A., Kent, A., and Saunders, T., *Inside Merlin's Cave: A Cornish Arthurian Reader 1000-2000,* London: Francis Boutle, 2000

Hardyment, C., *Malory: The Life and Times of King Arthur's Chronicler,* London: HarperCollins, 2005

Holbrook, S.E., "Nymue, the Chief Lady of the Lake", in T.S. Fenster [Ed.] *Arthurian Women* (New York and London, 1996), 171-90; orig. published in *Speculum* 53 (1978), 761-77

Hopkinson-Ball, T., *The Rediscovery of Glastonbury,* Stroud: The History Press, 2007

Hutton, R, *Witches, Druids, and King Arthur,* London: Hambledon Continuum, 2003

_____, *Blood and Mistletoe: The History of the Druids in Britain,* New Haven: Yale University Press, 2011

_____, *The Rise and Fall of Merry England*, Oxford and New York: Oxford University Press, 1994

_____, *Stations of the Sun,* Oxford: Oxford University Press, 1996

_____, *The Druids,* London: Hambledon Continuum, 2008

Jarman, A O H, "The Merlin Legend and the Welsh Tradition of Prophecy", *The Arthur of the Welsh*, Ed by Bromwich, R, Jarman, A O H, and Roberts B F, University of Wales Press: Cardiff, 1991

_____, *The Legend of Merlin,* Cardiff: University of Wales Press, 1960

Jarman, A.O.H. [trans.], *The Gododdin,* UK: Gomer Press, 1988

Kittredge, G.L., *A Study of Gawain and the Green Knight,* Cambridge, Mass, 1916.

Lacy, N. J., *Lancelot-Grail: The Old French Arthurian Vulgate and Post-Vulgate in Translation*, New York: Garland, 1992-6, 5 vols.

_____ , *The New Arthurian Encyclopedia*, New York: Garland, 1996

Larrington, C., *King Arthur's Enchantresses: Morgan and her sisters in Arthurian Tradition,* London and New York: I.B. Tauris, 2006

Littleton, C S, & Malcor, L, *From Scythia to Camelot*, Garland: New York and London, 2000

Loomis, R.S., *Celtic Myth and Arthurian Romance,* New York: Columbia Press, 1955 ed of 1927 orig.

_____, *Arthurian Tradition and Chretien de Troyes*, New York: Columbia Press, 1949

_____, *Arthurian Literature in the Middle Ages,* Oxford: Clarendon Press, 1959

_____, *The Grail: From Celtic Myth to Christian Symbol,* Princeton: Princeton University Press, 1963

_____, *Scotland and the Arthurian Legend,* The Proceedings of the Society of Antiquaries of Scotland, 1055-6

Loomis, R.S., and Loomis, L.H., *Arthurian Legends in Medieval Art,* New York, 1975 [1938 orig.]

Lupack, A, *The Oxford Guide to Arthurian Literature and Legend.* Oxford: University Press, 2005

Mancoff, D., *The Arthurian Revival in Victorian Art,* New York and London, 1990

Minnitt, S., and Coles, S., *The Lake Villages of Somerset,* Glastonbury Antiquarian Society, Somerset Levels Project and Somerset County Council Museums Service, 1996

Moorman, C., "Myth and Medieval Literature: *Sir Gawain and the Green Knight", Medieval Studies* 18 (1956), 158-72.

Morris, J., *The Age of Arthur: A History of the British Isles from 350 to 650,* London: Phoenix Orion, 1995 [1973 orig.]

Padel, O. J., "The Nature of Arthur", *Cambrian Medieval Celtic Studies* (27): 1–31, 1994.

_____, *Arthur in Medieval Literature,* Cardiff: University of Wales, 2000

Payne, A.; Corney, M.; Cunliffe, B., *The Wessex Hillforts Project: Extensive Survey of Hillfort Interior in Central Southern England,* London: English Heritage, 2007

Rahtz, P., *Excavations on Glastonbury Tor, Somerset 1964-66;* and also, with S. Hirst, *Beckery Chapel, Glastonbury, 1967-68* (report on excavation), 1974

Rhys, Sir J., *Studies in the Arthurian Legend.* London: 1966. [1891 orig.]

_____, "The Coligny Calendar", *Proceedings of the British Academy, 1909-10,* London, p 207

Ritchie, G., *Chretien de Troyes and Scotland,* Oxford: Clarendon Press, 1952

Tabor, R., *Cadbury Castle: A hillfort and landscapes.* Stroud: The History Press, 2008

Tolstoy, N., *The Quest for Merlin,* London: Sceptre, 1988

Vita Merlini, Geoffrey of Monmouth, Ed. and transl. by J.J. Parry, Champaign-Urbana: University of Illinois Studies in Language and Literature, 1925.

White, P, *King Arthur: Man or Myth?,* Bossiney Books: Lauceston, Cornwall, 2000

Williams, J E C, and Ford, P, *The Irish Literary Tradition,* University of Wales Press: Cardiff, 1992

Ziolkowski, J., *The Nature of Prophecy in Geoffrey of Monmouth's Vita Merlini,* Ithaca, NY: Cornell University Press, 1990

Related/General Interest:

Alcock, L., *By South Cadbury, is that Camelot? Excavations at Cadbury Castle 1966-70;* London: Thames and Hudson, 1972

Ashcroft-Nowicki, D., "Merlin and the Mother Goddess", in *Merlin and Woman (*Ed. by R.J. Stewart), The Book of the Second Merlin Conference 1987, London: Blandford, 1988.

Ashe, G., "A Certain Very Ancient British Book: Traces of an Arthurian Source in Geoffrey of Monmouth's History", *Speculum* (Speculum, Vol. 56, No. 2), 1981, p 301-23.

_____, *Mythology of the British Isles,* London: Methuen, 1990

_____, *The Traveller's Guide to Arthurian Britain,* Glastonbury: Gothic Image, 1997

Barber, R., *Myths and Legends of the British Isles,* Woodbridge: Boydell Press, 1999

Baring-Gould, S., [Ed. by Edward Hardy]. *Curious Myths of the Middle Ages,* New York, 1994. (1866 orig.). [see "Melusina", "The Knight of the Swan", "Prester John", etc.]

Benham, P., *The Avalonians,* Glastonbury: Gothic Image, 1993

Broadhurst, P., and Miller, H., *The Sun and the Serpent,* Pendragon Press, 1989

Bord, J, and C, *The Enchanted Land,* Thorsons/Harpercollins: London, 1995

Carley, J.P, *Glastonbury Abbey,* Glastonbury: Gothic Image, 1996

Carr-Gomm, P, and Heygate, R., *The Book of English Magic,* London: John Murray, 2009

Cavendish, R., *King Arthur and the Grail,* London: Weidenfeld & Nicolson, 1978

Critchlow, K., *Glastonbury -- A Study in Patterns,* London: Rilko, 1969

Doel, F, & G, and Lloyd, T, *Worlds of Arthur: King Arthur in History, Legend, and Culture,* Tempus: Stroud, Gloucestershire, 1998

Filbee, M, *Celtic Cornwall,* Constable: London, 1996

Fortune, D., *Avalon of the Heart,* London: Collins, 1938 and 1986.

Glennie, J S, *Arthurian Localities,* Llarnerch Publishers: Lampeter, 1994 reprint of 1869 orig

Hardy, T, *The Famous Tragedy of the Queen of Cornwall at Tintagel in Lyonnesse: A New Version of an Old Story Arranged as a Play for Mummers, in One Act, Requiring No Theatre or Scenery,* London: Macmillan, 1923

Howard-Gordon, F., *Glastonbury: Maker of Myths,* Glastonbury: Gothic Image, 1997

Hughes, J., *Arthurian Myths and Alchemy: The Kingship of Edward IV,* Stroud: Sutton Publishing, 2002

Hunt, R, *The Drolls, Traditions, and Superstitions of Old Cornwall,* 1st series, [Ed.], Llarnerch Publishers: Lampeter, 1993 reprint of 1881 orig. {Note: his 2nd vol is a 1993 reprint of 1864 orig}.

Hunt, Wm. Holman, *Pre-Raphaelitism and the Pre-Raphaelite Brotherhood,* 2 vols., London, 1905

Knight, G., *The Secret Tradition in Arthurian Legend,* Cheltenham: Skylight Press, 2012, revised ed. of 1983 orig.

_____, [Ed.], *The Book of Melusine of Lusignan: In History, Legend & Romance,* Cheltenham: Skylight Press, 2013

_____, *Merlin and the Grail Legend,* Cheltenham: Skylight Press, 2011. (rev. ed.)

_____, *Dion Fortune and the Inner Light,* Loughborough: Thoth, 2000.

MacInnes, J, "The Arthurian Legend", *World Mythology,* Ed. By R. Willis, Piatkus: London

Maltwood, K.E., *The Enchantments of Britain,* Vancouver, 1944

_____, *Guide to Glastonbury's Temple of the Stars,* London, 1964 [1934 orig]

Mann, N., *The Isle of Avalon,* London: Green Magic, 2001

Markale, J, *Merlin,* Rochester, VT, Inner Traditions, 1995. (English translation by John Graham of 1981 French orig, entitled *Merlin L'Enchanteur*)

Matthews, C., *Arthur and the Sovereignty of Britain: King and Goddess in The Mabinogion,* London, 1989

Matthews, J., *Gawain: Knight of the Goddess*, London: Thorsons, 1990

Matthews, J., and Stewart, R.J. [Ed.], *Merlin Through the Ages: A Chronological Anthology,* London: Cassell, 1995

Matthews, J., and Green, M., *The Grail Seekers Companion,* Loughborough: Thoth Publications, 2003

Michell, J., *New Light on the Ancient Mystery of Glastonbury,* Gothic Image, 1997

_____, *The Traveller's Guide to Sacred England,* Gothic Image, 1996

Moffat, A, *Arthur and the Lost Kingdoms*, Weidenfeld & Nicolson: London, 1999

Ralls, K., and Robertson, I., *The Quest for the Celtic Key,* Edinburgh: Luath Press, 2001 [also re: the Lowland Scottish legends, place-names, and sites re: Merlin]

Scott, Sir W., *The Lay of the Last Minstrel,* Edinburgh: David Bogue, 1839

Skene, W F, *Arthur and the Britons in Wales and Scotland*, Llanerch: Lampeter, 1988 reprint of 1868 original "The Four Ancient Books of Wales".

Stewart, M., *The Crystal Cave,* New York: William Morrow, 1970. [fiction; Book One of her *The Merlin Quartet* series.]

Stewart, R.J., *The Prophetic Vision of Merlin,* Loughborough: Thoth Publications,1986

_____, *The Mystic Life of Merlin,* Loughborough: Thoth Publications, 1986

_____, *Merlin and Woman* (Ed.), *The Book of the Second Merlin Conference 1987,* London: Blandford, 1988.

Stewart, R.J. [Ed.], and Matthews, J., *Merlin Through the Ages: A Chronological Anthology,* London: Cassell, 1995

Weston, J.L., *The Legend of Sir Gawain: Studies upon its Original Scope and Significance,* The Grimm Library, no. 7. London: David Nutt, 1897

_____, *Sir Gawain at the Grail Castle,* Arthurian Romances, no. 6. London: David Nutt, 1904

_____, *The Legend of Sir Perceval: Studies upon its Origin, Development, and Position in the Arthurian Cycle,* The Grimm Library, nos. 17 and 19. London: David Nutt, 1906-9.

_____, *From Ritual to Romance,* 1920 orig; reprint Princeton: Princeton Univ Press, 1993

Westwood, J, *Albion: A Guide to Legendary Britain*, Paladin Grafton Books: London, 1985

Whitaker, M., *The Legends of King Arthur in Art,* Woodbridge: Boydell, 1990

White, R., [Ed]., *King Arthur in Legend and History.* London: Dent, 1997

Williams, C. and Lewis, C.S., *Arthurian Torso,* Oxford: Clarendon Press, 1948.

Chapter 10–Rosslyn: Chapel, Castle, and Glen

History:

Carle, F.G., [Ed.], Stevenson, W., and Meikle, V.; *The Battle of Rosslyn 1303: A Short History to Commemorate the 700th Anniversary,* Roslin Heritage Society, 2003

Crawford, B.E., *William Sinclair, Earl of Orkney, and His Family: A Study in the Politics of Survival;* in Stringer, K.J., [Ed.], *Essays on the Nobility of Medieval Scotland,* Edinburgh, 1985

_____, "Earl William Sinclair and the Building of Roslin's Collegiate Church", *Mediaeval Art and Architecture in the Diocese of St Andrews,* British Archaeological Association conference transactions, n.xiv, Leeds, 1994, 99-107

Forbes, R., Dr., Bishop of Caithness, *An Account of the Chapel of Roslin 1774* [orig. published in 1774; second ed. printed in 1778]. [Note: in 2000, the Grand Lodge of Scotland issued a new reprinting of the 1778 edition, [Ed. by Robert L.D. Cooper]

Grant, W., *Rosslyn: The Chapel, Castle and Scenic Lore,* Dysart and Rosslyn Estates, 1954

Grose, F., *The Antiquaries of Scotland,* London, 1789, vol. 11

Hay, Fr. R.A., [Ed. Maidment, James]; *Genealogie of the Sainteclaires of Rosslyn,* Edinburgh, 1835

Kerr, A., Esq., F.S.A. Scot., "The Collegiate Church or Chapel of Rosslyn, Its Builders, Architect, and Construction", Proceedings of the Society of Antiquaries of Scotland, 14 May 1877, Edinburgh: 1878, vol. xii, 218-44

_____, "Rosslyn Castle, its Buildings Past and Present", Proceedings of the Society of Antiquaries of Scotland, 10 December 1877, Edinburgh: 1878, vol. xii, 421-44

Kirk, T., and Thoresby, R., [Ed. Hume Brown], *Tours of Scotland 1677 and 1681,* Edinburgh, 1892

Lawlor, Rev. Prof. H.J., F.S.A. Scot., *Notes on the Library of the Sinclairs of Rosslyn,* Proceedings of the Society of the Antiquaries of Scotland, 1898

Pennant, T., *A Tour in Scotland,* London, 1790, vol. 11

Ralls, K., *The Templars and the Grail,* Wheaton Chicago, IL: Quest Books, 2003

_____, *The Knights Templar Encyclopedia,* Franklin Lakes, NJ, Career Press, 2007

Ross, T., "Rosslyn Chapel, a paper read at Rosslyn", *Scottish Ecclesiological Society Transactions,* 1914-5, 238-47.

Rosslyn, H., and Maggi, A., *Rosslyn: Country of Painter and Poet,* Edinburgh: National Gallery of Scotland, 2002

Rosslyn, P. St Clair Erskine, Earl of; *Rosslyn Chapel,* Rosslyn Chapel Trust, 1997

Stevenson, Prof. D., *The Origins of Freemasonry, Scotland's Century 1590-1710,* Cambridge: Cambridge University Press, 1988

Watson, J., "St Matthew's Collegiate Church, Rosslyn", *The Transactions of Edinburgh Architectural Association,* Edinburgh, vol. 9, 105-15.

Related/General Interest:

Anderson, Wm., *Green Man: An Archetype of our Oneness with the Earth,* London and San Francisco: HarperCollins, 1990

Boulton, D'Arcy J.D., *The Knights of the Crown - The Monarchical Orders of Knighthood in Later Medieval Europe 1325-1520,* Woodbridge: Boydell Press, 2000, paperback ed.

Butler, A., and Ritchie, J., *Rosslyn Revealed,* Ropley, Hants: O Books, 2006

Cameron, Sir Charles A., *Note on the Earliest Reference to the Masonic Knights Templar Degree,* Ars Quatuor Coronatorum, vol. 16, London, 1903

_____, *On the Origin and Progress of Chivalric Freemasonry in the British Isles,* Ars Quatuor Coronatorum, vol. 13, London, 1900

Clarke, J.R., *A new look at King Solomon's Temple and its connection with Masonic ritual,* Ars Quatuor Coronatum, vol. 88 (1975), London, 1976

Clerk, Sir J., *Memoirs of Sir John Clerk of Penicuik,* Edinburgh, 1893

Coil, H.W., et al, [Ed.], *Coil's Masonic Encyclopedia,* New York: Macoy, 1961

Deansley, M., *A History of the Medieval Church 590-1500,* London: Routledge, 2002, paperback ed.

Doel, F. and G., *The Green Man in Britain,* Charleston: Arcadia Publishing, 2001

Donaldson, G., *Scottish Historical Documents,* Glasgow: Neil Wilson Publishing Ltd.,1997. [orig. ed. by Scottish Academic Press Ltd. 1970]

Donaldson, I., *Midlothian Gravestones,* Midlothian District Library Service, Midlothian, Scotland, 1994

Edwards, J., *The Templars in Scotland in the Thirteenth Century,* Scottish Historical Review, Edinburgh, vol. v., 1908.

_____, *Rent-Rolls of the Knights of St John of Jerusalem in Scotland,* Edinburgh, Scottish Historical Review, vol. XIX (part 3), 1922

Gould, R F, *The History of Freemasonry,* vol. I, London, 1887

Harding, M, *A Little Book of the Green Man,* Aurum Press, London, 1998

Harte, J, *The Green Man,* Pitkin Unichrome Ltd, Andover, Hampshire, 2001

Hicks, C., *The Green Man: A Field Guide,* Fakenham: Compass Books, 2000

Knoop, D., and Jones, G.P., *The Scottish Mason and the Mason Word,* Manchester: Manchester University Press, 1939

Laughlan, Roy, MBE, JP, *The Kilwinning No. 0 Masonic Lodge in old picture postcards,* European Library, Zaltbommel/Netherlands, 1994

Raglan, Lady, "The Green Man in Church Architecture", *Folklore 50,* 1939

Ralls, K., and Robertson, I., *The Quest for the Celtic Key,* Edinburgh: Luath Press, 2002

Scott, Sir W., *The Provincial Antiquities and Picturesque Scenery of Scotland with Descriptive Illustrations by Sir Walter Scott,* London, 1826, vol. 11

Stones, A., Krochalis, J., Gerson, P., and Shaver-Crandell, *The Pilgrim's Guide to Santiago de Compostella* (2 vols.), London: Harvey-Miller Publishers, 1998

Thompson, Rev. J., *Guide to Rosslyn Chapel and Castle, Hawthornden, Etc.,* Edinburgh, 1892. [note: in June 2002, The Clan Sinclair Association USAreprinted the text of this work, which is derived from the ninth edition of Thompson's original book that was published in 1922 for the 30th anniversary of its original publication.]

Ward, J S M, *Who Was Hiram Abiff?,* Lewis Masonic publications, Plymouth, 1992

Yeoman, P., *Pilgrimage in Medieval Scotland,* Historic Scotland, Edinburgh, 1998

Photo Acknowledgments

"Wisdom begins in Wonder," as Socrates once said. And, indeed, how we have marvelled! We see a glimpse of universal wonder throughout this publication, beautifully portrayed, from the photographs in this book from a number of gifted, talented photographers and artists from around the world, for which I give many thanks. In addition to the more formal picture credits, I most gratefully acknowledge the kind offers of photographic images, paintings, time, effort, great hospitality and company that a number of generous individuals have provided. Thank you, especially, for the magical "eye" of Simon Brighton (England), whose extraordinary photos of medieval sites in the British Isles and parts of France in particular, grace these many pages and especially, too, to Ani Williams (harpist), Anneke Koremanns, Jane and Chris May, Alan Glassman, Jen Kershaw, all for photographs specifically relating to the Languedoc area of southern France in particular; to Eily Nash for lovely glimpses of Glastonbury Tor and the Chalice Well, to Eran Bauer, for sharing his local Temple Bruer knowledge and photos, The Brydon Collection (Scotland), Eric Wallace, Peter Dawkins, Dawn Gaskill, and others, for sharing your treasures with us. And finally, heartfelt thanks to Mr. Phil Rademan of Port Elizabeth, South Africa, whose photo of the only statue and memorial on earth today in memory of the mysterious medieval Grail king—the ever-elusive Prester John—is also included in this book. Like these images, may our future quests, too, take us to farther shores, beckoning us on to a higher Truth.

INDEX

A

Aaron, 81
Achambaud de St.-Amand, 10
Adam of Damerham, 201
Aga Khan, 17
Aguilar castle, 107
Alamut, 17-8
Albertus Magnus, 142
alchemical texts, 81, 90, 134
Aleppo, 17
Alexander the Great, 84
Amadour, 57
André de Montbard, 10
Andalusia, 153
Anfortas, 69
Anglesey, 202
Annwn, 74
Antioch (city), 85
Antioch chalice, 75
Aphrodite, 85
Apollo, 68
Aquinas, Thomas, 142
Arabic texts, 77
Archangel Michael, 195
Arques, 109
Artemis, 31
Ark of the Covenant, 76
Arthurian Mysteries, 185-225
Arthur, hero, chieftain, warlord, champion
Excalibur, and, 77, 81, 208, 216
historical intro, 185-191, 218-9
as Once and Future King, 191
Arthur, other associations,
Lady of the Lake, 208
Mordred, 200
Merlin, history and legends of,
unusual *birth* of, 192-4
Brittany, and, 222
cave, and, 221
Cornwall, and, 221
as druid advisor to Arthur, 192
and the Feminine, 198
"heretical" accusations, and, 194
King Rhydderch Hael of Strathclyde, 198, 223
magical abilities of, 194-5
Merlin Ambrosius, 196
Merddyn Wyllt, 196
Merlin Sylvestis, 196
Myrddin, 196
nature, and, 194-5
prophetic gifts of, 194
quest for Holy Grail, and, 192
Round Table, and, 192
Scotland, and, 223-5
"three-fold death" of Merlin, 198
Tolstoy, Nicolai, 196
tower and observatory, 194
as "wild man of the woods", 194, 196

Places and selected sites, Arthurian-related:
Brittany
Barenton fountain rock, 222
Broceliande forest, 222
Comper ("Arthur's Oak), 222
Merlin's Tomb dolmen, 222
Mont St. Michel, 222
England
Cornwall,
Bodmin Moor, 208
Dozmary Pool, 208
Merlin's Cave, 221
North Cornwall Arthurian Centre, 209
Slaughterbridge, 209
St. Michael's Mount, 195, 208
St. Nechtan's Glen, waterfalls, 221
Tintagel, 206-8, 221
"Tristan Stone", (Drustanus), Fowey, 210
Glastonbury, general, 198-206
Abbey, 198-200
Abbey fire of 1184, 201
Annwfn, and, 202-3
as Avalon, 198
Chalice Well, 80, 202-6
Dissolution of Monasteries, and, 201
early history and legends, of, 201-2
"Glastonbury Bowl" (Taunton Museum), 80
Glastonbury Thorn tree, 202, 205
Henry II, and, 200
Joseph of Arimathea, and, 201-2
King Gwyn ap Nudd, and, 188, 202-3
National Cathedral grounds, Wash D.C., 202
Pilgrimage, 205-6
springs, red and white, 204
Tor, 201-2
South Cadbury, Somerset, 189-191
Scotland,
Arfderydd (Artheret), 196
Artheret, 223
Borders area, 198, 223-5
Cat Caet Celidon wood, 218
Dunbarton, 196
Drumelzier, 198, 225
Edinburgh (Arthur's Seat), 219
"Guinevere Monument", Meigle, 221
Merlindale, 225
Merlin-related Scottish sites, 223-5
Hart Fell, 196
Stirling Castle (King's Knot), 219
Scotland, Arthurian place-names list, 220
Stobo, 196
Trapain Law, 220
Whithorn, 223
Wales,
Abergavenny, 214-5
"Arthur's Table," near Denbigh, 216
Bardsey Island, 221
Caerfallwch (Fort of Afallwch), Rhosesmor, 216
Caerleon, 213-4

Caerwys (Holywell), 216
Llangollen (Dinas Bran), 216
Maen Huail (Ruthin), 216
Moel Arthur, 216
Monmouth, 215
North Wales region, 216-7
Pen y Cloddiau (and Excalibur myth), 216
South Wales region, 214-6
Tintern, 216
Poetic and art Arthurian-related themes, 190-1
Beardsley, Aubrey, 192
Bulwer-Lytton, Edward, 191
Dryden, John, Dorset Garden Theatre, London, 191
Pre-Raphaelite paintings, 191
Purcell, Henry, 191
Tennyson, Alfred Lord, 190, 225
sources, authors and chroniclers of:
Adam of Damerham, 201
Caradoc of Llancarfon, 187
Chretien de Troyes, 188
de Boron, Robert, 192
Geoffrey of Monmouth, 187, 188, 195, 215
Giraldus Cambrensis, 187, 198-200
Nennius, 188
Ralph of Coggeshall, 201
William of Malmesbury, 187
Manuscripts, Arthurian-related:
Annales Cambriae, 212
Culhwch ac Olwen, 212
Historia Regum Britanniae, 187
History of the Britons, 188
Peredur, 212
Preiddeu Annwfn, 212
Prophetiae Merlini, 195
The Domesday Book, 202
The Mabinogion, 212
Vita Merlini, 195
Y Gododdin of Aneirin, 211-2, 218
Ashe, Geoffrey, 211
Ashcroft-Nowicki, Dolores, 198
Asia Minor, 53
Asmodeus, 114
Aurillac, 60
Authie, Peter, 137

B

Bacon, Roger, and, 141-2
bain-marie, 77
Baldwin II, 10
Bartholomew, 81
Beardsley, Aubrey, 192
Beauseant, (banner), 12
Begg, Ean, 53, 64
Beguines, 130
Benedictine Order, 67, 73, 77
Bernard of Clairvaux, 8, 15-6, 52, 83-4
Black Madonna, and, 52
geometry, and, 16
Knights Templar, and, 8, 15

nature, and, 52
relics of, (Troyes), 10
Beziers, 100-1
Bible, translation(s) of, 133
Biella (Piedmont), 64
Birnbaum, Lucia, 64
Bisol, Geoffrey, 10
Black Madonna(s), 50-66
Bernard of Clairvaux, and Black Madonna(s), 52
Blessed Virgin Mary, and, 52, 54, 57, 60
chainze (veil) of, 60
(the) "Celtic Mothers", and, 64
Chartres cathedral, 50-1, 60, 64-6
crypt, early history, 60-2, 66
Notre Dame Sous Terre (Our-Lady-under-the-Earth), 60
Notre Dame du Pilier (Our Lady of the Pillar), 60
labyrinth at, 61-2
as *omphalos,* 62
Virgo Paritura (Virgin-about-to-give-birth), 61
Puits des Saints Forts (Well of the Strong Saints), 61
Cybele, 53
crypts, and Black Madonna(s), 57, 60-2
darkness as wisdom, 53, 54
"dark night of the soul", 53
Diana of Ephesus, 53
earth, and, 53
Eleanor of Aquitaine, and, 61
fear of, and taboo(s) against, 51, 54, 58
forest, and, 59
gospel of John, and, 52
Great Mother archetype, and, 54
and healing, 50, 59
hermits and hermitage, and, 59-60
horse breeding and racing, and, 59
Horus, and Black Madonna, 52
Isis, and Black Madonna(s), 52, 56
Joan of Arc, and, 59
Joseph of Arimathea, 58
Knights Templar, and, 13, 52
Meister Eckhart, and, 52
miracles and cures of, 53
Lux Lucet In Tenebris, 53
Mary Magdalene, and, 80, 65 (window)
Narbonne area, and, 62
nature, and, 55-6, 63-65, 66
origins of, speculation(s), 57-8
Our-Lady-of-the-Brambles, 66
Our Lady of the Hermits, 59
Our Lady of the Hollies, 60
Our Lady of the Oak Tree, 65
Our-Lady-under-the-Earth, 60
pilgrimages, and Black Madonna(s), 50, 53, 57, 62, 64, 66
places associated with, (see Appendix), and also, 51, 53-55, 59-65
circumstances found in, 51, 52
hedge, grotto, tree, 52
Precious Blood reliquaries, and, 80
Provence region, and Black Madonnas, 65

prima materia, 54
ravens, and Black Madonna, 59
Queen of Heaven, and, 51
shrines, major, 50, 54-5, 57-66
Chartres, 50-1, 54, 57, 60-2
Einsiedeln, 51, 54, 59-60
and St Meinrad shrine, 59
Laon, 57
Le Puy, 51, 54
Montserrat, 50, 51, 53, 54
Orleans, 54
Oropa (Piedmont), 51, 54, 64-7
Rocamadour, 50, 51, 56-8
Henry II, and penance, 57
Narbonne and, 58
site "heretic" Cathars were sent for penance, 57
sword of Roland, and, 58
Soissons, 57
Song of Songs, and, 52
statues and visual depiction(s) of, 51, 53-4, 58-9, 66
stone carvings, Black Madonnas, 54, 61
thefts and/or alterations of, 53, 65
Waldensians, and Black Madonna(s), 64-5, 66
Wisdom, and Black Madonna(s), 52, 53, 55, 56, 66
Blessed Virgin Mary, 13, 55, 83,
Blood, as Holy relic, 82, 83
Bogomils, 91, 130
Boscastle, Cornwall, 145-6
Bruges, 80
Bull, Marcus, 57
Bulwer-Lytton, Edward, 191
Burman, Edward, 20

C

Cabaret castle, 97
Cagliari (Sardinia), 64
Candlemas, 67-8,
Canterbury Tales, 30
Caradoc of Llancarfon, 187
Carr-Gomm, Philip, 61, 192
Catalonia, 14, 76
Pyrenees frescoes of Taull (Calalonia) 76
Cathars, general, 30-31, 91- 109, 130, 133, 137
Albigensian crusade, and, 98-101, 102-9, 130, 133, 137
Arques, and, 109
Authie, Peter, Cathar preacher, 137
beliefs of, 92-3, 94
Bernard of Clairvaux, and, 92
Bogomils, 91
books and learning, 96
Cabaret castle, and, 97
Cathar cross, 109
celibacy, 91, 94
as "Church of Love", 91, 103 (memorial to), as Amor, 109
charges against, 98
consolamentum, 91
Count Raymond IV of Toulouse, 97, 104

as craftspeople, 95-6
Deodat Roche Museum, 109
as dualist heretics, 130
Esclaramonde de Foix, 94
diet, 92
dove symbolism, 103
family life, 94
fasting, 92
as fugitives, 95-6
gnostic(s), 91, 109
gospel of John, 106
guilds, and, 95-6
healing, and, 92, 94
Hildegard of Bingen (sermons against), 98
informants of Inquisition, and Cathars, 95-6
katharos, 91
Inquisition and crusades against, 98-100, 101-9
Aguilar castle, 107
Arnald-Amaury, papal legate, and, 101
Beziers, siege of, 100-1
St Mary Magdalene feast day, and, 100
Carcassonne, siege of, 102
"Five Sons of Carcassonne", 107
Castle Queribus ("last Cathar fortress"), 107
Minerve chateau, siege of, 102-3
Cathar martyrs memorial at, 103
St Mary Magdalene feast day, and, 103
Montsegur, siege of, 105-6, 109
"Field of the Burned" memorial plaque, 105
Narbonne, 101
Peyrepertuse castle, siege of, 107
posthumous burning, policy of, 100
post-Inquisition, and lingering Cathar remnants, 109
Termes, 107
Languedoc, cultured civilization of, 91-2, 97, 108
Manichaeanism, 91
Mary Magdalene, and, 100, 103
marriage and, 94
medical knowledge of, 92
meditation, and, 92, 94
merchant supporters of, 97
ministry, travelling, 94
Paulicians, 91
Peter II of Aragon, and, 104
pilgrimage (as penance), and, 95-6
preaching of Cathars, and, 94
priesthood (*Perfecti, Credentes,* and the *Believers*), 93-4
Puivert Castle, 176-9
Puivert Museum, 109
relics and mysteries of, 105-6
sacraments, rejection of, 94, 98
Rome, and, 92-3,
Simon de Montfort, and, 99, 101-2, 104
troubadours, and Cathar culture, 154, 179 (see also "Troubadours" chapter)
watermarks, 179
weavers, and, 95-6
women, and, 92, 93-4, 95-6, 109

Cathedral of St. Peter and St. Paul, Troyes; 10
Catherine of Alexandria, St., 13
Cauldron(s), 74-6
Celibacy, 29
Celtic Christians and St Maurice, 81
Celtic Mothers, The, 68
Cerridwen (cauldron of), 74
Chalice Well (Glastonbury), 80
Chapel of the Black Hand, 80
Chaplin, Patrice, 43
Charles the Bald, 60
Charles I, 127
Charles VII, 139-140
Chartres cathedral, 57, 60-2
    and Melchizedek, 80
The Chymical Wedding of Christian Rosencreutz, 85
Chinon, 13, 25,
Chrétien de Troyes, 68-70
Christ, blood of, 74, 80
Church of the Holy Sepulcher, Jerusalem, 17
Church of Love, 91, 103, 109
Cistercian Order, 16, 20, 67, 77
Clement V, pope; 8, 18,
Communion hosts, 74
Cocteau, Jean, 31
Constantine, emperor, 81
Cornucopia, 74
Cornwall, 80, 89
    Men-on-Tol quoit, 80
Council of Troyes, 8, 9
Count Raymond of Poitou, 85
Count Raymond IV of Toulouse, 97, 104
Courts of Love (see "Troubadours")
Chretien de Troyes, 188 (see also "Grail",
    "Troubadours")
Cross Bones cemetary (London), 146-7
Cybele, 31, 53

D

Dagda, The, 74
Dali, Salvador, 43
David I (Scotland), 111
de Boron, Robert, 192
Diana of Ephesus, 53
Diu Krone, 69
dove, 103
dragon (St. George, and), 114
druid, 192
Druses, 15
Dryden, John, 191
Durand-Lefebvre, Marie, 65, 70
Durandal, 58

E

Eckhart, Meister, 56
ecology and environment, 89, 109
Edward II, 18
Eleanor of Aquitaine, 57 (see also 'Courts of Love')

Eliot, T.S., 89
Einseldeln, 59-60
Elizabethan drama, 127
Emerson, Ralph Waldo, 89
Eschenbach, Wolfram von, 69-70, 77, 86-7
Esclaramonde de Foix, 94
Ethiopia, 88
Eusebius, pope, 64
Excalibur (film), 69
Excalibur (sword), 77, 81, 216

F

Fisher King, 68, 80
Flegetanis, 69-70, 86
Fool, The, general, 68, 126-8 (guilds)
Forsyth, Irene, 61
Fountain of Salvation, 69
French revolution (1789), 70

G

Galahad, Sir, 69, 72, 77-78,
Galland, China, 54
Gaul (and Grail legends), 74
Gawain, Sir, 69, 80, 86, 174-5, 237-9
Genoa, emerald cup in, 75
Geoffrey de Charney, 148
Geoffrey of Monmouth, 187, 188, 195, 215
Giraldus Cambrensis, 187, 198-200
Glastonbury, 198-206 (see also "Arthurian")
Globe Theatre (London), 147
gnostic(s), 16, 81, 91, 109
Godfroi de St. Omer, 10
The Golden Legend, 28, 30
Golgotha, 60
Gondemar, 10
Gospel of John, 106
Gothic architecture, 90
Gothic cathedrals, 90
    misericords, 90
    stained glass, 90
Graal, 74
Grail, general, 67- 90
    Byrne-Jones tapestries, and, 89
    castle, Grail, 69-70, 84, 86
    chapel of the Grail, 77, 87
    constellations and stars, and, 72, 86-7
    cubic Jerusalem and, 76, 85
    as cup, dish, cauldron, or cornucopia, 74-5, 77
    earth and land, as, 89
    Eucharist, and, 78
    Feminine, and, 84-90
    as geometry, 85-6
    hermit of, 69-70
    Isis, and, 52, 56, 90
    Joseph of Arimathea, and, 69-70, 74, 75, 78-9
    Kingship and sovereignty, and, 92
    labyrinth, and, 85
    with 'light', luminous qualities, 69, 76

Mandylion, and, 87
Mary Magdalene, and Grail, 78, 82 (see also "Mary Magdalene")
Melusine, and, 85
Merovingians, and, 78-9, 80
Mysteries, Higher, and, 90
pentagram and, 85
Platonic solids, and, 86
poets, and, 93
Precious Blood, and, 78-9, 80
Prester John, and, 84-5
Pyrennes frescoes, and, 76
rose, 85 (see also 'Mary Magdalene')
Rosslyn Chapel, "Grail(s)", speculations about, 76, 226, 252
sacred sites, and, 92-3
severed head, and, 87
Shroud of Turin, and, 87
sovereignty, 88
as spear, sword, or lance, 68, 80-2
as a stone, 75, 76, 80, 82
forms and varieties of, 74-6, 84-6,
Veil of Veronica, and, 91
Venus and, 85
vesica piscis, 85
vine as, 78
Wasteland, 80, 89
water and forms of the Grail, 77, 85
well, 77
womb as, 78
Grail romances, 67-75
Great Mother archetype, 58
Green Man, Rosslyn carvings of, 237-9
    ancient origins of, 238
    cycle of seasons, and, 237-8
    as "chapel of the greenwood", 226
    in Classical antiquity, 238
    as a living energy in nature, 238
Guilds, general, 110-128
    Abbots Bromley Horn Dance, 125-6
    builder(s) and medieval concept of "architect", 112
    legends of gifted builders, 114
    Cathars, and, 95-6
    Chamber of Commerce, and, 110
    Chartres, and oldest reference to guild, 115
    Compagnonnages (France), 113
    craft guild(s), 110, 111 (varieties of), 117 (training),
    definition of, 110
    distribution network(s) of, 111
    fairs, and guilds, 47, 125
    "The Fool" and medieval guilds, 126-8
    guildhall(s), 110
    Knights Templar, and, 15-6
    Mary Magdalene, St., and guilds, 119-120,
    mason brothers, Templar Rule 325, and, 112
    masons marks, and, 116
    merchant guilds, 110
    mutual aid fellowship, and, 110, 128
    oral tradition(s) and guilds, 116
    parish guilds, Western European, 110, 118 120
        miracle plays and pageants, 118

medieval English drama(s), 118-9, 121-3
    gradual decline of, 120
ports and guilds, 110-1
Rosslyn Chapel, and guilds, 228-9, 247-252
    craftsmen, skilled, and, 252
    Book of the Order of Knighthood, 247
    Forest laws and guilds, 247
    Hay, Sir Gilbert, and guilds, 247
    Robin Hood and Little John, guild plays, 123-5, 181-2
    Roslin Glen, 123-5, 181-2, 252
    Rosslyn-Hay manuscript and guilds, 247-8
    shipping laws and guilds, 247
    St. Clair family, and guilds, 248
Scottish guilds, general, 111
    stonemason(s), and guilds, 112
        Master masons, and, 114
    structure of medieval guild(s), 112
        Apprentice, 112
        Journeyman, 112, 113 ('tour de France'),
        Master, 112-3,
    symbolism, and, 116-7
    towns, and growth of guilds, 114
Guilhelm de Gellone, 97
Guillaume de Tyre, 9
Guiot de Provins, 70
Guiraud Riquier of Narbonne (1254–92), 156, 182-3

H

Hans Fiesko, 128
Henry II, 61
    and Black Madonna shrine, 61
Heresy and heretics, general, 129- 149
    Albigensian crusades, and, 98-101, 102-9, 130, 133
    Authie, Peter (Cathar preacher), 137
    Bacon, Roger, and, 141-2
    Beguines, 130
    Black Madonna(s), fear of and 'taboo(s)', 51, 54, 58, 62
    definition of "heresy", medieval, 129
    Cathars, accused as heretics, 57, 98-100, 101-9, 130, 130, 133-5, 137
    Charges against medieval heretics, general, 131-6
        relating to magical artifacts, beliefs, or practices, 133-6
    Cross Bones cemetary (London), 146-7
    Dominican order, and, 133
    dualist heretics, 130
    Fourth Lateran Council, 130
    heresy of the Free Spirit, 130
    Hussites, 130
    Inquisition, the, 130-136
        legal process of, 131-4
        "relapsed heretics", policy of, 148
        torture, use of, 131-6
    Inquisitional committees in region(s), 130
    issues about heresy, (within church itself), 129-130
    Jews, accused of, 130
    Joan of Arc, and, 138-141
        charges and trial, 138-140

controvery over remains of, 140-1
Notre Dame cathedral, and, 141
visions, and, 140
Knights Templar, charges and trial(s), 15-20, 24-5,
131-3, 137, 148-9
"not proven" verdict, 19
use of torture and, 131-3
lepers, accused of, 130
Lollards (England), 133
Mary Magdalene, 78, 79, 80, 82
"orthodoxy", and, 129-130
public gullibility, and charges, 133
Scot, Michael, 142-5
Scottish trial(s), and, 134
Southwark cathedral, and, 147
trial(s) of medieval heretics, 131-6
troubadour(s) as "heretical", 182-4
Waldensians, 130, 133-5
witchcraft, general, 133-136, 144-6
accusations in Joan of Arc trial, 140
Bideford witches (Devon), 145
legend of "Witch of Fauldshope" and Michael
Scot, 144
Museum of Witchcraft, Boscastle, Cornwall, 145-6
Trial(s), and, 133-136
women, and heresy, 129, 133-136, 140
female clergy and charges against, 135-6
Hermann I of Thuringia, 72
Hildegard of Bingen, 98
Hiram Abiff, 114
horn of plenty, 74
Hospitallers (see "Knights Hospitaller")
House of Savoy, 64
Hugh de Payns, 9
Hughes I, Count of Champagne, 9
Hussites, 130
Hutton, Professor Ronald, 47, 123, 205

I

India, (Prester John, and), 88
Innocent II, pope, 16-7
Innocent III, pope, 99, 130
Inquisition, 16, 20, 95-6, 98-100, 101-9, 130-1,
Isis, 56, 85
Black Madonna(s), and, 52, 56
Grail, and, 85

J

Joan of Arc, 138- 141
Jacob de Voragine, 28
Jacques de Molay, 20, 137, 148-9
James II of Aragon, 18
Jerusalem, 77, 78
Joan of Arc, 138-141
John of Luxembourg, 138
Joseph of Arimathea, 69-70, 74, 75, 78-9
Joseph d'Arimathie, 69
jousting (see 'tournament')

K

Kabbalistic schools of learning,
Troyes (school of Rabbi Rashi), 10
Lunel, 97
Narbonne, 97
katharos, 91
Kempe, Will (Elizabethan clown), 176
Kieckhefer, Prof Richard, 98
King, Karen, 27
Knight, Gareth, 85
Knights Hospitaller, 15, 20, 44-5, 85,
Mary Magdalene, and, 28, 44-5 (relic)
Knights Templar, (general) 8-25, 77, 78, 83, 137,
148-9
Aleppo, and, 17
Antioch, and, 17
Architecture of, 15-6
St. Bernard, and, 15
castles, 16
Church of the Holy Sepulchre, 16
circular nave, 16
octagon, 16
Templar churches, 16
Temple of Solomon, 16
Archives (general historical overview), 14-5
Acre, 14
and Knights Hospitaller, 14
Cyprus, 14
local/regional, 11-13
Jerusalem, 15
Turks, and; 15
Arrests of, 17-19
baphomet, 18
charges, 18-9
"not proven" verdict, 19
Assets (see "Knights Templar, Wealth of")
Atlit (Castle Pilgrim), 16
Druses, and, 15
Geoffrey de Charney, treasurer and Preceptor of
Normandy, 148
Geoffroi de Paris, chronicler, 148-9
geometry, 15
graves, Templar, 24
guilds, and, 15-6
Hasan-i-Sabbah, 17
In Praise of the New Knighthood 8
Ismailis, Nizari ("Assassins"), and Templars, 16-7
Jacques de Molay, last Grand Master, 20, 137, 148-9
martyrs, 16
mason brothers, and, 15-6
mathematics, 16
Milites Templi Salomonis, or Knights of the Temple
of Solomon, 9
Organization of Order, 11-13
bailies, 12
chaplain, 12
clerk, 12
Commander, 12
diplomat, 13

Draper, 12
Female saints (feast days), 13
Grand Master(s), general, 12
   Jacques de Molay, 20, 137, 148
   William of Chartres, 17
Interfaith/diplomacy, 16
Judges, 14
Marshal, 12
Novices, 13
Pilgrimage operations, 14
Reception into, 13
Rule, 12-13
Seneschal, 12
Sergeant(s), 12
Warrior training, 16
Places, Templar-related, (see *Appendix);* and 20-23
   Cyprus, 22
   England, 21
   France, 22
   Italy, 22
   Middle East (Acre), 23
   Poland, 22
   Portugal (Tomar), 22
   Scotland, 21-2
   Slovenia, 22
   Spain, 22
   The Knights Templar Encyclopedia, 20
relics, general, 19, 24-5, 83
   list of, 24-5
Saracens (and Knights Templar), 15
suppression of Order, 15-6, 20,
   role of Philip IV, King of France, 8, 18, 148-9
   Ad providam Christi Vicari, (papal bull), 19
   survival(s) after suppression, 20
Symbols, major, Knights Templar, 23-5
   Abraxas, gnostic seal, 24-5
   Agnus Dei (Lamb of God), 23
   calvary step-cross, 25
   eight-sided cross, 24
   geometric grid patterns, 24
   hand, with heart, 24
   official seal, 23
   red cross, 23
   star(s), 24
   other(s), 24-5
Trial(s) of, 19-20, 137, 148-9
   Jacques de Molay, Grand Master, 19, 20, 137,
     148-9
   Geoffrey de Charney, 19, 137, 148-9
   Vox in excelso, (papal bull)*,* 19
Wealth of, 13-15
   agriculture, 14
   animal husbandry, 14
   branch of royal government, 14
   gold, 13
   land, 14
   letter of credit, 13
   mills, 14
   money, 13
   pilgrimage operations, 14

   produce, 14
   property, 14, 20
   safe deposit box, 13
   security code cipher, 13
   shipping enterprises, 14
   treasuries, 14
   wine trade, 14
   wool, 14
  Women, 12-13
   sisters *(soror), 13*
   associates *(donata), 13*
Konrad, bishop of Constance, 59
Kyot, (of Provence), 70-1

L

Lady of the Lake, 77, 208
Languedoc region,
  and Cathars, 97
  and Knights Templar, 13
lapsit exillas, 86-7
Last Supper, The, 78, 79
Lateran Council of 1123, 29
  of 1215, 130
Latin texts, 77
The Lay of the Last Minstrel, 144
Lea, Charles, 19
Le Conte du Graal, 68
Le Morte d'Arthur, 69-71
le Puy, 60
Longinus, 78, 80, 81
Louis IX (France), 85
Louis XI (France), 61
Lucifer, 86
Lucius Artorius Castus, 190
Lugh, 84
Lusignan (France), 85

M

Majorca, 153
Malory, Sir Thomas, 74
Mandylion, 91
Manichaeanism, 91, 130
Marco Polo, 16-7
Markale, Jean, 57
Mary Magdalene, (general), 26-49, 82-4,
  alabaster jar, and, 36, 44-5
  anointing oil(s), 44
  Bethany, and, 32
  Black Madonna site Magdalene window, 65
  Cathars, and, 31, 33
  chrism, 44
  Coptic manuscript fragment, 29
  Easter, 40, 45
  fairs, in honor of, 47
  feast day(s) of, (Western), 40, 46
   (Eastern Orthodox), 45-7
    red egg story, 47
   regarding siege against Cathars, 100, 103

Golden Legend, 28, 31-2
gnostic(s), 31-32, 48
Grail, and Mary Magdalene, 80 (see also 'Grail' chapter)
guilds, and, 30, 47, 119-120
Harvard Divinity School, 27
Knights Hospitaller, and, 28, 44-5
Knights Templar, and, 13
as "light-bringer", (Illuminatrix), 30-1
Mary of Bethany, 45
Meyer, Prof Marvin, 48
myrrh, 44
    myrrophores, 45
as mystic, 31
Nag Hammadi Library, 49
pageants, in honor of, 47
as partner, 27
perfume(s), 44-5
pilgrimage, and, 30, 33-43
    Abbey of St Maximin, 35
    Abbey of St. Victor, 39-40
    Girona, 43
    Marseilles area, 34, 38-40
        Church of St. Lazarus, 40
        Limoux, 41
        Rennes-le-Chateau, 41-2, 47
        Saintes-Marie-de-la-Mer, 33-4
        Santa Maria-de-Ratis, 34
    Spain, 43
    St-Baume grotto, 36, 47
    Vezelay, 37-40, 80, 83-4,
Plays, in honor of, 47
as preacher, 31
priestesses, 44
Provence, and, 33-4
Relics, in Western tradition(s), 37-8, 40-1, 45
    in Eastern Orthodox tradition(s), 46
rose, and the Grail, 85
as saint, 29-30
spikenard, 45
Thunder, Perfect Mind, 48
Waldensians, and, 30
as wealthy patron, 33
Wisdom (Sophia) and, 48-49
    as exile, 47
Mary of Guise, Queen Regent of Scotland, 76
Mary, Queen of Scots, 76, 127
Matthews, John and Caitlin, 198,
Melchizedek, 76
Melrose Abbey (Scotland), 143
Melusine, 85
Men-on-Tol quoit (Cornwall), 76
Merlin, 192-223
mermaid, 85
Merovingians, 70-1, 78, 97
Meymac, 61
Militi Templi Salomis, 9
Minerve chateau, 102-3, 109
mirror, scrying, 88
misericord(s), 168
Monferrato, 67

Montsegur, 33, 105-6, 109
Munsalvaesche (Mount of Salvation), 75
Musician carving(s) in cathedrals, 161-4

N

Nanteos cup, 75
Narbonne, 97, 101
Nennius, 188
Nicodemus, 78
Nicola Ambruzzi La Jardiniere, 127

O

Occitania, 150, 153,
Old French (texts), 72
Old Irish sagas, 74
Old Man of the Mountain, 17
Omphalos, 67
Order of Christ, 20
Order of Montesa, 20
Ovid, 167 (see also "Troubadours")

P

Paracelsus, 59
Partner, Peter, 132
Parzival, 69-72, 81-2, 91
    sword of, 69-72, 81
Paulicians, 91, 130
Payen de Montdidier, 10
Perceval, 68-70, 77
Perlesvaus, 72, 73
Pierre de Castelnau, papal legate, 99
Peter II of Aragon, 104
Peyrepertuse castle, 107
Philip II of Spain, 127
Philip IV, King of France, 8, 18, 148-9
Philosopher's stone, 87
Phineas, 81
Phoenix, 87, 109
Pius XII, pope, 67
pilgrimage,
    to Jerusalem, 10-11
    as "penance", 95-6
Port Elizabeth (So. Africa), 85
Prats-de-Mollo, 70
Precious Blood (see Blood, as Holy relic)
Pre-Raphaelite paintings, 191
Prester John, myths of, 84-5
    kingdom of, 84-5
    Port Elizabeth, South Africa memorial of, 85
    scrying mirror of, 85
Provins (Champagne), 75
Puivert,
    Castle, 176-9 (see also "Cathars")
    museum, 109, 176-9
    troubadours, and, 176-9
Punch and Judy, 127
Purcell, Henry, 191

Q

Quercorb museum, 177
Queribus ("last Cathar fortress"), 107
Queste del Saint Graal, 72

R

Ralls, Dr Karen, Rosslyn Chapel, and, 245
Rashi, Rabbi (see also Solomon ben Isaac), 10
Relics (see individual chapter headings, i.e, "Grail",
  etc.)
Robert de Boron, 73-5
Rome, 92-3
rose, 85
Rosicrucians, 231, 233, 234, 248-9
  Fama, and, 248-9
Rossal, 10
Rosslyn Chapel (general) 80, 226-252
  A Genealogie of the Saintclaires of Rosslyn, 228
  Agnus Dei ("Lamb of God"), 234
  Alchemical symbolism and philosophy, 233
  An Account of the Chapel of Roslin (1774), 242
  angel carving(s), and, 234, 238
  apocryphal book of First Esdras (Ch 3), 241
  Apprentice pillar, 226, 231-3
    Master Mason and "murdered apprentice" legend,
      231-2
    "Prince's Pillar", 251
    serpents at base, 232
  altar(s), general,
  as "idolatrous" in Reformation, 230
  as arcanum in stone, 230, 252
  Bower, Walter, 228
  building process, and, 228-9, 248
  The Buk of the Order of Knighthede (The Book of the
    Order of Knighthood), 247
  carvings, great variety of, 234
  "chapel in the woods", 226
  Clerk, Sir John, (Penicuik), and renovation of
    chapel, 230
  Collegiate Chapel of St. Matthew (official name),
    226, 230
  College Hill, site of, 226
  crown jewels, (Scottish), and, 226
  crypt of, 76
  Dance of Death symbolism, 234
  "engrailed cross", St Clair family, 234
  excavation, speculation(s), 76, 242-3
  First Esdras, chapter three, 241
  Forbes, Dr Robert, Bishop of Caithness, 242
  Freemasonry and Rosslyn Chapel (general),31, 232,
    233, 234, 240, 241-2, 245-6,
    Anderson's *Constitutions* (1723), 244
    Grand Lodge of England (1717), 243
    Grand Lodge of Scotland (1736), 243
    Masonic degrees, and, 240-2
      Ancient and Accepted Scottish Rite, 240
      Royal Arch, 240
      Royal House of David, 241
      Royal Order of Scotland, 240

mason's marks, Rosslyn, 246
  northeast stone, 245
  Sir William St. Clair as first Scottish Grand
    Master, 243
  "son of the Widow", 245-6
Gawain, Sir, 174-5, 237-9
Gordion Knot carving, 234
"Grail(s)", speculations about, 76, 226, 252
Green Man, Rosslyn carvings of, 237-9
  ancient origins of, 238
  cycle of seasons, and, 237-8
  as "chapel of the greenwood", 226
  in Classical antiquity, 238
  as a living energy in nature, 238
guild(s) and (Rosslyn) building works, 228-9, 247-
  252
  craftsmen, skilled, and, 252
  Book of the Order of Knighthood, 247
  Forest laws and guilds, 247
  Hay, Sir Gilbert, and guilds, 247
  Rosslyn-Hay manuscript and guilds, 247-8
  shipping laws and guilds, 247
  St. Clair family, and guilds, 248
guild plays, Robin Hood and Little John, 123-5,
  181-2
Hay, Sir Gilbert, 229
Hay, Fr Richard Augustine, 228
heart stone carvings, 76
Hermeticism, 233
Hiram Abiff, 232, 234, 243-4
Holy Rood of Scotland, 226
Inscription, in, 240
King Darius of Persia, 241
Kirk, Thomas, 17th c account of, 232
Knights Templar
  (Agnus Dei) symbolism, 234
  Rosslyn Chapel not built by medieval Templar
    Order, 243
Mary of Guise, Queen Regent of Scotland, letter
  of, 76
meaning of symbolism, as wisdom, 252
Melchizedek figure with cup, 23
"murdered apprentice" carving legend, 231, 244
musician carving(s) in, 238-9
  Chartres cathedral, 239
National Library of Scotland, manuscript(s), 247
North Esk river, 226
Reformation, devastating effect on chapel, 229-230
"Right of Sepulcher", 243
Rosicrucians, 231, 233, 234, 248-9
  Fama, and, 248-9
Roslin glen, general, 226, 238-9
  early history and, 240
  and guild plays, 123-5, 181-2
Rosslyn Castle, 246-7 (as medieval scriptorium)
Rosslyn-Hay manuscript, 247-8
Shroud of Turin and Veil of Veronica, 233
Slezer, Capt. John, and Theatrum Scotiae (1693),
  250
St. Clair, James, and 18th c. restoration of windows,
  230

St Clair knights in effigy (crypt), 80, 242 (vaults and)
St. Clair, Sir William, the third and last St. Clair Prince of Orkney (founder), 226-8
St. Clair of Rosslyn, Lord William, (re: 1546), 80, 223
Temple of Solomon (Jerusalem), 226, 230, 232, 243-4
  Second Temple of Solomon, 241
The Old Rosslyn Inn, 228
The Lay of the Last Minstrel, 242
"treasure" also as allegorical, 252
troubadours, minstrels, and gypsies, 181-2
vaults, and, 242
Veil of Veronica, 233
  decapitated carving, damage to head, 234
vera icon, ("true icon"), 233
visitors to chapel, previous centuries, 226-7, 228 (Inn)
  Boswell, James, 226
  Burns, Robert, 226
  Johnson, Samuel, 226
  Queen Victoria, 226
  Scott, Sir Walter, 226, 242
  Turner, J.W., 226
  Wordsworth, William and Dorothy, 226
wine, Rosslyn inscription, and, 241
women, and Rosslyn Chapel,
  regarding sole written carving, 240, 241
  women's entrance to chapel, (earlier times), 233-4
Rule of the Order of the Temple (Knights Templar), 9,
Rumi, 56

S

Safed, 24
Saints
  St. Amadour, 60
  St. Anne, 65
  St. Augustine, 202
  St. Bernard of Clairvaux, 8, 83-4,
  St. Bethaire, 64
  St. Brigid, 205
  St. Collen, 202
  St. David, 202
  St. Eberhard, 59
  St. Eusebius, 69
  St. George, 114
  St. Helena, 85
  St. Joachim, 65
  St. Kentigern, 223
  St. Lazarus, 34
  St. Luke, 60, 64
  St. Mary Magdalene, 27-51
  St. Maurice, 81-2
  St. Maximin, 34
  St. Meinrad, 59-60
  St. Michael, 65
  St. Ninian, 223
  St. Patrick, 205
  St. Sara (the Egyptian), 34, 65

  St. Sidoine, 38
  St. Veronica, 57
  St. Victor, 65
Sardinia, 64
Scot, Michael, 142-5
  Aikwood Tower, and, 144
  Bocaccio, and, 145
  Dante assigned to eighth circle of Hell, 145
  Eildon Hill, legend of, 144
  diplomacy and papal service, 143
  magical knowledge and skills of, 143
  at court of Frederick II of Sicily, 143
Scott, Sir Walter, 144
Scottish trial(s), heresy, 134
Septamania, 97
Shakespeare, 147
Shroud of Turin, 83, 91, 233
Sicily, 153 143
Simon de Montfort, 99, 101-2, 104
Sion (Switzerland), 69-70
Sir Gawain and the Green Knight, 174-5
Solomon ben Isaac ('Rabbi Rashi'), 10
Solomon, king, 77
Spear of Destiny, 84-6
Soulac, 60
South Africa, 85
Spain, 14, 91
Stewart, R.J., 198
Strachan, Dr. Gordon, 225
Switzerland, 59-60, 85 (see also 'Einseldeln')
  Lake Neuchâtel, 70
  Sion, 70-1

T

Tancred, 17
tantra, 83-4, 164
Tempelherren, 71
Templeisen, 69, 79, 82
Temple of Solomon, 114, 226, 230, 232, 243-4
  Second Temple of Solomon, 241
Tennyson, Alfred Lord, 89
Termes castle, 107
The Golden Legend, 30
Toledo, 70
Tournament(s),
Trencavel, house of, 97
Trevrizent (hermit), 70, 71, 86
Trier (Germany), 134
Tristan, 81
  sword of, 86
Troubadour(s), 75, 150-184
  Andreas Capellanus, 150, *164-7*
  Cathars, and, 154, 179
  cathedrals, and, 178-181
    musician carving(s) in, 161-4
  Chretien de Troyes, 152, 156,
  chivalry and troubadour culture, 150, 173
  chivalric code and knighthood, 173
  courtesy, 150, 173
    "courtesy book(s)" of, 162

Courts of Love, and, 151-3, 161-4, 167-8
Dante, 150
De Amore ("On Love"), 164-8
  Andreas Capellanus and, 150, 164-7
decline of troubadour culture, 171-4
definition of, 150
Duke William IX of Aquitaine, 151
Eleanor of Aquitaine, and, 151, 152-3, 167
Eschenbach, Wolfram von, 157 *(Parzival)*
final end of medieval troubadour culture, 182-4
  death of "last troubadour", and, 182
  Inquisition, and, 182-4
  Toulouse, 182-4
Fin' Amors, ('Fine Love'), 161-4
  courtly love, and, 151-3, 161-4,
  jealousy, and, 163
Guilhèm de Peitieus, earliest troubadour work, and,
  151
joy, and troubadour culture, 183-4
la dompna, the Lady, and, 182-3 (see also "Fin'
  Amors")
Marie, Countess of Champagne, 152, 165, 168
music and the troubadours,
  Catalan and Italian troubadour culture, 155
  competitions of bards and poets (Brittany), 156
  historical troubadours, records of, 154
  major genres of (*canso, sirventes* and *tensos),*
    150
  minnesangers (Germany), 150, 156
  styles of troubadour songs, 150
    trobar leu (light), 150
    trobar ric (rich), 150
    trobar clus (closed), 150
  survivals of troubadour music, 153
  trobairitz (female troubadours), 150, 160-1
  troubadours (southern France), 150
  trouveres (northern France), 150
  trovadorismo (Portugal), 150
  vidas 154
Occitania, and troubadour(s), 150, 153
Performers, troubadour(s),
  Bernart de Ventadorn, 154
  England, 157-9
  Guiraud Riquier of Narbonne (1254–92), 156,
    182-3 (as "last troubadour")
  jongleurs as distinct from professional *troubadours,*
    151-156
  Pierre d'Auvergne, 177
  Raimon de Miraval, 156, 169-171, 184
  secular entertainers and minstrels, 157-9
Poitiers, 156
Puivert museum, troubadours, and, 109, 176-9
Roman de la Rose, 171-172
Rosslyn Chapel (Scotland), and,

The Lay of the Last Minstrel, (Sir Walter Scott), 242
  musician bagpiper flanked by two Green Man
    carvings, 181
  troubadours, minstrels, strolling players, and
    gypsies, 181-2
  Roslin glen pageants, music, and plays (May-June),
    181-2
  symbolism, varieties of troubadour-related, 179-181
    animals and birds, 178-9
    foolscap, 179
    heraldic, and, 179
    lion, 178-9
    mermaid, 178
    swan(s),
    tapestries, and, 178-9
    unicorn, 178-9
tournaments, 175-6
women, and troubadours, (general), 150, 160-1
  trobairitz, (female troubadours), 150
Troyes, 10
True Cross, 85
Tuatha de Danaan, 74
Tubal Cain, 114
Twrch Trwyth, 215

V

Valencia Chalice (Spain), 75
Veronica, veil of, (general), 60, 91, 233 (and Rosslyn)
Venus, 85
Vezelay, 38, 84,

W

Waldensians, 28, 64, 130
Warmund of Picquigny, Patriarch of Jerusalem, 9
Welsh (cauldron), 79
Whitsun, 70-1
Wiercinski, Andrzej, Prof., 54
William of Malmesbury, 187
William of Villaret, (see also "Knights Hospitallers"),
  45
William St. Clair of Rosslyn, Lord, (re: year 1546), 80
witchcraft trial(s), 133-136 (see also "Heresy and
  Heretics")
  accusations of (Joan of Arc trial), 140
  Museum of Witchcraft, Boscastle, Cornwall, 145-6
Wolfram (see 'Eschenbach, Wolfram von')
Wycliffe, John, 133

Z

Zaccheus, 57
Zerubabbel, 241